AMERICAN EXPANSIONISM

The Critical Issues

Edited by

MARILYN BLATT YOUNG

University of Michigan

LITTLE, BROWN AND COMPANY BOSTON

LIBRARY OF CONGRESS CATALOG CARD NO. 72-12237

FIRST PRINTING

Published simultaneously in Canada
by Little, Brown & Company (Canada) Limited

PRINTED IN THE UNITED STATES OF AMERICA

AMERICAN EXPANSIONISM

The Critical Issues

CRITICAL ISSUES IN AMERICAN HISTORY SERIES

Barton J. Bernstein, *General Editor*

Robert F. Berkhofer, Jr., *The American Revolution*
Gordon S. Wood, *The Confederation and the Constitution*
Sheldon Hackney, *Populism*
Marilyn Blatt Young, *American Expansionism*
David M. Kennedy, *Progressivism*
Joan Hoff Wilson, *The Twenties*
Otis L. Graham, Jr., *The New Deal*
* Barton J. Bernstein, *The Origins of the Cold War*

* Not yet published. Additional titles to be announced.

CONTENTS

INTRODUCTION vii

CAUSES OF THE WAR

Why the United States Went to War with Spain in 1898 1
PHILIP S. FONER

American Business and the Spanish-American War 20
JULIUS W. PRATT

That "Splendid Little War" in Historical Perspective 42
WALTER LAFEBER

CHINA: THE MISSING LINK

The Influence of Strategy upon History: The Acquisition of the Philippines 53
JOHN A. S. GRENVILLE AND GEORGE BERKELEY YOUNG

Insular Imperialism and the Open Door: The China Market and the Spanish-American War 71
THOMAS MCCORMICK

American Expansion, 1870–1900: The Far East 83
MARILYN BLATT YOUNG

METHODS OF EMPIRE: FORMAL AND INFORMAL

Our Mylai of 1900: Americans in the Philippine Insurrection 103
STUART C. MILLER

The Philippine Peace 117
FINLEY PETER DUNNE

The United States in Cuba, 1898–1902 120
DAVID F. HEALY

IMPERIALISM

The Vicious Circle of American Imperialism 129
WILLIAM APPLEMAN WILLIAMS

American Imperialism: Some Tentative Explanation 138
ERNEST R. MAY

Notes 159

Suggestions for Further Reading 179

INTRODUCTION

> I have lived inside the monster and know its insides — and my weapon is only the slingshot of David.
> José Martí

This book of readings explores a central question which opened the twentieth century in America and may close it — why imperialism? Is imperialism the error bred in the bone of capitalism; is it necessary, an original sin whose single redemption is revolution? Put bluntly without metaphor, is imperialism the inevitable result of modern capitalism, as V. I. Lenin argued? Or is it some kind of recurrent sickness, caught by an elite or even a whole people, curable by poultice or purge without radical surgery? Can imperialism be eliminated, as J. A. Hobson asserted, and capitalism still maintained? Or was it, as many liberal American historians claim, a brief infection, a foreign bug, from which the country recovered completely and with the boon of future immunity? We are all children of what Carl Oglesby has called the ice age of imperialism. If we are to survive, we must help each other find answers to these questions.

Thirty-six years ago, Joseph Barnes introduced a book of essays, *Empire in the East* (New York: Doubleday, Doran, 1934), with the same question: "For a modern industrial state, is empire an integral expression of its national life? Is the imperial tendency rooted too deep in the economy and institutions of the United States to be considered apart from them?" (p. vii). Perhaps, had scholars addressed themselves to this question with the same unrelenting zeal they applied to such topics as counterinsurgency, Kremlinology, Pekinology, and the like, we might today be closer to an answer. For it is clear now that we have failed to understand either our "enemies" or ourselves. We pay for these failures in blood, at home and abroad. Worse, we make others pay for them.

The particular significance of the 1890s in this effort to get at the origins of American globalism is evident in the concentration of attention that period has received in recent scholarship. Much about the nineties reminds us of recent years. In the passionate oratory and self-serving apologia of its politicians and generals we hear the echoes of all that has plagued us in the past decade of reckless slaughter. The attempts by some liberal scholars to tame this period are no longer convincing. The suppression of the Philippine insurgency, soothed by time and independence; warfare between capital and labor, buried in the apparent success of bread-and-butter unionism; nativism and racism, deemed soluble by legislation — all the safely battened hatches of tranquilizing historical interpretation are coming off. The nineties have broken loose and we recognize them as most profoundly *our* history.

The wider the net we cast to catch the truth of the past, the greater the chance we have of understanding. The selections in this reader meet no single ideological or political test. They are intended to indicate the varying, sometimes colliding vectors of interpretation, and, where possible, shape a direct debate, sometimes where none was originally intended. In addition, by including two pieces which discuss directly the reality of America's rule over its formal and informal empire, it may be possible to begin seeing the problem of American imperialism as more than just an issue in historiography. For whatever we finally decide about American motives, we must still deal with the results of American actions.

The current quasi debate about the nature of nineteenth-century American foreign policy is mired in definitional confusion and evasion. The sides are unclear and shifting. On the one hand, there are historians such as William A. Williams, Walter LaFeber, and Thomas McCormick, who see the Spanish-American War, its origins and consequences, as a coherent bid for "informal empire" by the realistic representatives of hard-pressed but ultimately confident capitalists. In this interpretation, annexationism is minimized, the general urge for noncolonial expansion is stressed, and the primacy — though not necessarily the determining force — of economic causes and motives is underlined. McKinley, in this view, is generally seen not as an incompetent bungler, nor as a reluctant warrior, but as a calm and certain leader who knew what he wanted and why.

On the other hand, historians such as Richard Hofstadter, Ernest May, and Julius Pratt define their subject narrowly as annexationism, separate the issues of origin and consequence, and generally avoid taking a stand on which was *most* basic in a whole bag of basic causes. Here McKinley appears as the victim of mass national hysteria. His competence lay in holding off the war as long as he did, his failure in eventually giving way. Imperialist thinkers — Brooks and Henry Adams, Captain A. T. Mahan, and others — are discussed at great length, whereas the economics of the situation assumes clearly subordinate importance and receives only occasional attention.

Perhaps the most significant difference between these two groups lies in whether they see the 1890s as the beginning or the end of expansionism; whether they believe that "the policy expressed the basic strategy and tactics of America's secular and imperial expansion in the twentieth century," in William A. Williams's words, or "the last phase of territorial expansion," in Julius Pratt's phrase; whether they place the war and its aftermath at the very center of American history, the fruit of "deep roots," as Williams argues, or on the periphery, the malignant flower of a mutant seed. And this difference, in turn, may rest on a much broader difference in philosophy of history, one not likely to be resolved by recourse to archives, however opulent.

We have, in a sense, been through it all before in somewhat different form. When Charles A. Beard in 1934 wrote *The Idea of National Interest* (reprinted in Chicago: Quadrangle Books, 1966), he was, like Williams, bent on producing a radical critique of a foreign policy that had led to a disastrous war and a monstrous peace: World War I and the Versailles treaty. He saw in the period of the nineties the first phase of a "commercial expansion" that would dominate and shape the future. It was neither accidental, nor mysterious, nor imported from abroad. As American as their opponents, the expansionists built on a view of national possibilities as old as the country itself. Beard isolated two strands in American expansion — agrarian and commercial. Both were intimately related to internal politics and economics, both were territorial, both embodied a total conception of the nature of the country. For the agrarians, whom Beard traced back to Jefferson and associated with the Democratic party, America was to be a continental nation, homogeneous in culture and race, economically self-sufficient, and defended by a small military arm. "It was essentially isolationist in outlook and opposed to territorial adventures which brought the United States into economic rivalry with the imperialist powers of Europe . . ." (p. 87). Territorial expansion for agricultural use was advocated, but nothing more. The commercial expansionists, however, took commerce (and later investment) as the touchstone of foreign policy. Cosmopolitan, wanting new territory for market use, this group "eagerly assumed what it characterized as 'international responsibilities,' creating a strategic situation which called for a huge naval establishment" (p. 87). For the agrarians, the "center of gravity of state reason" lay in the "heart of the continental domain"; for their opponents it rested in the "periphery of the trade empire" (p. 88).

Nor was the triumph of commercial expansionism a sudden event, fortuitous and unexpected. On the contrary, it was the product of a

> Federalist-Whig-Republican succession [which] sought to change the structure of the internal economy by affording protection to manufacturing, and openly espoused the vigorous promotion of commercial expan-

> sion by lending aid to shipping, the construction and use of an effective navy, the acquisition of naval bases and points of trade support, . . . the use of force in distant places as well as nearer home in aid of private enterprise, and a frank recognition of the system later known as "dollar diplomacy" [p. 166].

Presenting American history in this way, Beard would seem to have believed that the country might have gone either way, that the triumph of the commercial interests was not a *necessary* or inevitable one. He presents us with the fact that the definition of national interest held by the commercial expansionists was made to prevail over the nation as a whole, but he fails to explain how this was accomplished.

Given the enormous shift in historical opinion since the 1930s, it is easy to forget that Beard was not then writing as an iconoclast. Indeed, it was Julius Pratt who felt he was going against the weight of received opinion when in 1936 he published *Expansionists of 1898* (reprinted in Chicago: Quadrangle Books, 1964). His noneconomic approach would, he wrote, "controvert . . . current fashions in historical interpretation." By defining imperialism exclusively as territorial and economic, Pratt concluded that "American business in general, at the opening of 1898, was either indifferent to imperialism, or definitely opposed" (p. 257). In the course of demonstrating these conclusions, however, Pratt incorporated significant information about the business world which could be, and has been, interpreted in quite different ways. The obsession of virtually *all* businessmen with foreign markets, for example, and the fascinating shift in business opinion that occurred in the spring of 1898 as a result of events in China, is brilliantly described by Pratt. He argues that the strength of free-trade sentiment expressed in business journals is proof of their anti-imperialism. However that may be, he notes the dramatic change that occurred with the threat of the partition of China. In just a few weeks the "pacifist, anti-imperialist" free-trade *Journal of Commerce* was converted to support for the isthmian canal, the acquisition of Hawaii, and naval increases — all of which it had previously opposed, "justifying its change on each point by the needs of the hour in the Far East" (see especially pp. 259–266).

What is significant is the way Pratt has been used by historians since 1936. For if he was vigorous in asserting that businessmen were, in the territorial sense, anti-imperialistic in January of 1898, he was equally emphatic that by February of that year, a decided change in opinion had taken place. Moreover, he concluded that after the battle of Manila Bay in May of 1898 ". . . American business became definitely imperialistic — that is, if a wish to retain the Philippines is evidence of an imperialistic attitude"

(p. 273). Yet these themes in Pratt were not explored further by most historians. Instead, concentrating on Pratt's conclusions about attitudes in late 1897 and the first month of 1898, most subsequent historians neglected his evidence about the later shift in business opinion.

Of course, most historians pay at least lip service to the multiplicity of causes. Such and such an event, we are told, was the result of economic, social, and political forces. Yet having made obeisance to diversity, the usual course is to focus almost entirely on either the economic or the social or the political force, leaving the reader with the reasonable impression that the author regards the one he spends most time on as most important. The effect of Pratt's work has been that historians treat the economic as of decidedly secondary importance and concentrate on the social and political causes of the war and its aftermath. Thus Richard Hofstadter, in his widely reprinted essay on "Cuba, the Philippines, and Manifest Destiny" (included in his book, *The Paranoid Style in American Politics* [New York: Alfred A. Knopf, 1966]), mentions in passing the "maturation and bureaucratization of American business," the "development of trusts on a scale sufficient to stir anxiety that the old order of competitive opportunities was approaching an eclipse," and the severe labor crises of the nineties. But he analyzes them all in terms of how they made middle-class people *feel,* not in terms of how they changed the structure of the society and its necessities. Having described the jingoism that grew out of the tremendous anxiety of the period, Hofstadter posits a "psychic crisis" – a profound discontent, a mixture of fear and anger – that could only be resolved by war, a war lusted for by "the people," though resisted by conservative business groups (p. 149).

"The primary significance of this war in the psychic economy of the 1890's" Hofstadter argues, "was that it served as an outlet for expressing aggressive impulses while presenting itself, quite truthfully, as an idealistic and humanitarian crusade" (p. 161). One can challenge Hofstadter's basic social-psychological model of mass displaced aggression. One might accept the use of the theory in this case and still be puzzled by the particular shape of that idealism and humanitarianism. Why did it extend so easily to the conquest and annexation of Puerto Rico or to an insistence on retaining a determining voice in the eventual structure of a "free" Cuba? Why did the pattern of America's acquisitions fall so handily into preexistent concerns for China markets? As Charles Beard says in another context, "If such things are 'accidents,' what are the deliberate determinations of policy?" (*Idea of National Interest,* p. 84).

Hofstadter, Pratt, and the host of historians who have drawn on their analyses, disagree with their opponents mainly in the definition of empire. If advocacy of free trade is held to be prima facie incompatible with imperialism, then clearly only those with a specific and avowedly aggressive expansionist policy, such as Henry Cabot Lodge or Theodore Roosevelt, can be called imperialist. If, on the other hand, one looks at actual relations between a strong and a weak nation, the picture is more complicated. "When an advanced industrial nation plays, or tries to play, a controlling and one-sided role in the development of a weaker economy," William A. Williams argues in *The Tragedy of American Diplomacy* (rev. ed.; New York: Delta, 1962), "then the policy of the more powerful country can with accuracy and candor only be described as imperial" (p. 47). The more powerful nation can define the terms of trade and through its economic power even shape the pattern of economic development in the weaker nation in such a way as to benefit the industrial nation. Put simply, free trade can be the mechanism of creating an empire.

We are faced further with this problem of territory. If we define imperialism territorially, the acquisitive phase of America's imperialist career seems, at first glance, brief and by the standard of other empires quite modest. If we include military bases (which do after all occupy territory), the picture changes. Add to bases outright protectorates, disguised protectorates, satellite or client governments, and heavily dependent allies, and the tide of the Stars and Stripes runs very strongly indeed as the twentieth century progresses. If we include preponderant economic influence, there would seem to be very few countries (apart from the socialist nations) outside the American empire.

On the issue of humanitarianism as well it would be wise to take a skeptical view. It is logically possible to act out of overtly humanitarian concerns and still to exploit other people. Exploitation need not be intentional. Indeed, according to Williams, it is often an unrecognized result of American economic expansion. No doubt there were some among the perpetrators of America's Philippine policy who believed what they said about bringing freedom to the Filipinos. That they so believed is irrelevant unless we can understand how they arrived at such a pathological definition of freedom. We must know how Americans in a "psychic crisis" happened to "choose" war and conquest as the preferred method of resolution. In this matter, novelists such as Joseph Conrad would seem to have much to teach us as historians. Charles Gould, knight errant of material interests in *Nostromo* (New York: New American Library, 1960), justifies his attachment to an inherited concession in the fictional Central American state of Costaguana this way:

> What is wanted here is law, good faith, order, security. Anyone can declaim about these things, but I pin my faith to material interests. Only let the material interests once get a firm footing, and they are bound to

> impose the conditions on which alone they can continue to exist. That's how your money-making is justified here in the face of lawlessness and disorder. It is justified because the security which it demands must be shared with an oppressed people. A better justice will come afterwards. That's your ray of hope [p. 80].

To which, several hundred pages later, the cynical Dr. Monygham answers:

> No! . . . There is no peace and no rest in the development of material interests. They have their law, and their justice. But it is founded on expediency, and is inhuman; it is without rectitude, without the continuity and the force that can be found only in a moral principle [p. 406].

The "ray of hope" Gould held out to Costaguanans (and his own conscience) was as much a part of Gould's life as the actual riches he hoped to extract from the country. So too the nineteenth-century American elite found Duty and Interest comfortably interdependent and they managed, in the way of all successful elites, to transmute their class interests into a national ideology. But there *is* neither peace nor rest in "material interests," and the contradiction that faced Gould in Costaguana faced McKinley and his successors.

Rarely does one find a simplistic one-to-one relationship between the specific economic needs of particular individuals or corporations and the policies of the government. The State is not merely a reflection of the desires and interests of its ruling class, even if one assumes this class to be cohesive, self-conscious, and overwhelmingly powerful (and in America this is less than certain). Rather the State mediates, in complex and often contradictory ways, between the powerful interests *it* observes in the world and at home, acting sometimes as reflexive chairman of the board, at others as an intrusive managing director.

It would be astonishing to find the government ruling *against* major corporate interests except by accident or in merely trivial ways. But the ability of the government rationally and consistently to rule *for* those interests is not perfect. It would be inconceivable for McKinley to have conscientiously set out to work *against* American economic expansion. But how much was he able, or willing, to do *for* it? Who set what kind of limits? Even if we grant that the great debate over annexation of the Philippines was essentially an argument over alternative strategies toward the same goal — economic expansion through overseas markets — the debate remains. We can dismiss it as uninteresting or meaningless only at the risk of distorting history. For it was clearly a monumental debate at the time and people took seriously the positions they argued and the consequences they predicted.

It may be that the senatorial opponents of the current administration's foreign policy differ only on the tactics of the matter, that all are committed to some form of the American empire. Yet I think we would miss both the reality of contemporary politics and the possibility for change if we simply dismiss their differences. Tactics matter. They mattered to the Filipinos crushed by American troops in 1900 as they matter to Vietnamese, Cambodians, and Laotians today.

My own view is that President McKinley, Secretary of State John Hay, Far Eastern expert William Rockhill, and the rest were realists responding rationally and concretely to specific international and domestic crises. But an important part of the world they thought they saw was patently unreal. The American economy was not in a state of glut that could only be alleviated by oriental markets. The open door notes did not establish America as a balancer of powers in the Far East, nor did they save China from anything, least of all from the European powers. Yet the myth was domestically important – to offset the "unpleasantness" in the Philippines, to reassure a country shaken to its roots by the depression of 1893, to assert American nationalism – and for this reason, consciously or unconsciously, it was assiduously maintained.

The present offers a useful parallel. In a brilliant article on "American Imperialism and the Peace Movement" (in *Studies on the Left,* vol. 6, no. 6 [1966]), Robert Wolfe has noted the "disproportion between the actual pattern of American foreign investment and the global scale and uniform character of American foreign policy." Wolfe argues that the United States, while seeking to "defend real interests, . . . seeks to do so on the basis of a mythological view of the world. . . ." Operating mythologically, it is impossible for the administration to distinguish between real and unreal threats. But the importance of the myth is domestic: "The mythology of anti-Communism not only justifies military spending and domestic reaction; it also provides the necessary confirmation for its own distorted perceptions. In this sense one might almost argue that the real goal of American imperialism today is not so much to preserve the capitalist holdings abroad as it is to preserve and give substance to the myth upon which capitalism at home now rests" (pp. 30, 35, 36). Nineteenth-century imperialism, like its modern manifestation, served domestic needs – not merely psychological, as Hofstadter would argue, but economic as well. To serve such needs, the *fulfillment* of the promises of the China market was less important than the pursuit of its riches.

By focusing on transient ideological, political, or social factors as Hofstadter, Pratt, and May do, structural problems are evaded. For them, imperialism is understood as a phase passed through and abandoned. And yet this insistence on strictly minimalist definitions of imperialism seems to me to be the result of ideological evasion, not scholarly precision. The effort to drain meaning from the conception and to restrict its application derives, in my view, from a refusal to look America full in the face. Imperialism is, in one serviceable definition:

> . . . the extension of sovereignty or control, whether direct or indirect, political or economic, by one government or society over another together with the ideas justifying or opposing this process. Imperialism is essentially about power both as end and means . . . Underlying all forms of imperialism is the belief — at times unshakeable — of the imperial agent or nation in an inherent right, based on moral superiority as well as material might, to impose its pre-eminent values and techniques on the "inferior" indigenous nation or society. [George H. Nadel and Perry Curtis, *Imperialism and Colonialism* (New York: Macmillan, 1964), p. 1.]

It is difficult, indeed impossible, to deny the applicability of the term, so defined, to American foreign policy of at least the years since about 1890.

To some extent, William A. Williams, despite the vital ways in which he has insisted on a proper remembrance of things past, also avoids the systemic issue. His analysis, articulated in the *Tragedy of American Diplomacy,* places economic issues in the context of a total *Weltanschauung:*

> To an extensive degree . . . American leaders of the 1890's entertained a *Weltanschauung* that organized data around economic criteria. They explained difficulties, and likewise advanced solutions and alternatives, by reference to economic phenomena. This did not make them economically motivated in the pocketbook sense, but it did lead them to believe that their objectives in the political and social realms could only be attained through economic means. . . . Wanting democracy and social peace, they argued that economic depression threatened those objectives, and concluded that overseas economic expansion provided a primary means of ending that danger [p. 30].

While insisting on the thematic continuity of that ideology and its effects, Williams does not in fact see imperialism as the result of inevitable structural developments, but rather reaches a conclusion quite similar to Hobson's — that capitalism can be purged of imperialism. As one critic, G. Stedman Jones, notes in his essay, "The American Empire," (*New Left Review,* no. 60 [March–April, 1970]), "Williams seems to envisage the possibility of a modified American capitalism shorn of its unnecessary imperialist outworks, and asks whether the ruling class of corporation capitalism has 'the nerve to abandon the frontier as Utopia' and 'to turn its back on expansion as the open door of escape' " (p. 62). This notion that we need only grit our teeth and face the world without our ancient frontier-blinkers is encouraging, but is it really satisfactory?

Perhaps the central diagnostic question — Is imperialism a misguided policy or a necessity? — can never be answered through historical research or analysis but only through experience. As we press for change, we will be able to note the nature of the forces that resist our efforts. But history can assist us in reexamining our past in order to understand the earlier sources of American imperialism. We must be able to demythologize both past and present. In one degree or another, and despite their disagreements, the selections that follow all contribute to that effort.

CAUSES OF THE WAR

Why the United States Went to War with Spain in 1898

PHILIP S. FONER

Philip Foner, now a professor of American history at Bryn Mawr, is an outstanding Marxist historian whose work covers a remarkable range of subjects, from his two-volume history of the labor movement through his four-volume consideration of the life and writings of Frederick Douglass. Foner's multi-volume history of Cuban-American relations is probably the most complete treatment of the subject.

His examination of the causes of the Spanish-American War, reprinted in its entirety below, is unique in many respects. It combines the best review of the published and unpublished material on that event with a straightforward Leninist interpretation of the nature of American imperialism. Moreover, by citing dissident groups, such as the socialists, usually ignored by historians, Foner challenges the common opinion that all *Americans lusted for war. For Foner imperialism is, simply, the result of monopoly capital's insatiable, inevitable drive for markets. In his conception, other factors — political, social, psychological, and humanitarian — only reinforce basic economic impulses. Given this unbreakable equation, which lies at the heart of a Leninist approach, one need only ferret out the economic roots in order to demonstrate the imperialist nature of any particular action. The risky corollary, that the absence of such roots clears the policy of imperialist odium, would not seem to bother Foner, perhaps because of an a priori conviction that no action is without economic gestation.*

Foner's demonstration of business interests in market expansion is impressive. What remains problematic is how far businessmen were ready to go in advocating wars of conquest to attain those markets. It should come as no surprise that capitalists defined the largest possible area of expansion and control as desirable. But what determined how much or how little they were ready to settle for? Moreover, direct *support for the war would seem, from Foner's own evidence, to have come rather late in the day.*

In the *New York Times Book Review* of January 29, 1961, Frank Friedel, the author of *Splendid Little War,* a pictorial history of the Spanish-American War, wrote: "Today, when Fidel Castro and his claque are screaming epithets at the United States and charging that the Spanish-American War was fought only for imperialistic reasons, it is heartening to be reminded of the fundamentally humanitarian motives that took America into the war." The reminding was done by Ernest R. May's *Imperial Democracy: The Emergence of America as a Great Power,* which Friedel was reviewing. But Friedel did not quote from May the following sentences which subvert his thesis: "An imperialist movement had come into being and was not to be demolished. . . . Its leaders had discerned that public opinion could be captured for an imperialist cause, if only that cause could be clothed in the rhetoric of piety. They were stubborn, willful men. . . ." [1] *

As Professor Friedel must know, the thesis that the Spanish-American War was an imperialist war, fought for imperialist reasons, did not originate with Fidel Castro. Long before Castro and the Revolutionary Army ousted the dictator Fulgencio Batista and later set up the first socialist government in the Western hemisphere, this thesis was already advanced. Keir Hardie, the British labor and socialist leader, wrote shortly after the Spanish-American War began: "Personally all my sympathies are with the Cubans — that they are entitled to self-government is not to be denied — but I cannot believe in the purity of the American motive. . . . The American man in the street is doubtless honest and sincere in his zeal for Cuban freedom, but he is simply shouting — without knowing it, of course — at the prompting of others." The "others," he made it clear, were the trusts and Wall Street financiers who were intent on extending American economic dominance over Cuba, Latin America, and the Far East. Hardie concluded: "Desiring as I do to see Cuba freed, I frankly declare that I have not the slightest sympathy with this American-made war, nor do I believe in the motives which inspire it." [2]

In France, too, the United States' profession of humanitarian mo-

Reprinted by permission from *Science & Society,* XXXII, No. 1 (Winter, 1968), pp. 39–65.

* [See pp. 159–162 for notes to this article. — Ed.]

tives as a basis for intervention was ridiculed. Socialists and non-socialists alike emphasized that humanitarian motives were merely a disguise for commercial desires — the major cause being the desire for commercial conquest of all the Caribbean Islands and Latin America. Paul Louis, the socialist, declared that the United States, a great capitalist power, was simply following the example of France, England, Germany, and Italy in its desire for expansion.[3]

In the United States, of course, there were many who questioned that the war was caused by the humanitarian desire to obtain Cuban freedom, and none more effectively than *The People,* official organ of the Socialist Labor Party, edited by Daniel DeLeon. *The People* challenged the sincerity of the capitalists' pretended sympathy for the struggling Cubans by pointing to the multitude of oppressions and injustices at home. In America, too, "the 'Reconcentradoes' [*sic*] are seen all around . . . famishing figures of all ages and all sexes, premature corpses, bearing either the marks of slow and gradual starvation, or the marks of sudden death by bullet and bayonet, or mutilation by factory machine." [4] Cuban freedom was only a ruse to justify war.

War, *The People* argued, was necessary as a result of economic conditions in the United States where "good times" had failed to materialize and external conflict was always a good way of diverting attention from social evils at home. War was necessary "to protect American commercial interests in Cuba." War was necessary because American capitalism was finding it necessary to "spread out and fight for markets," and capitalism had to expand in order to survive. "The capitalist class needs markets. It needs them because it has on hand more goods than the people can buy." Not only would the war provide markets in Cuba for American capitalism, but it would open the vast new markets of the Far East. "To make any attempt to capture part of that new market for the capitalists of this country requires a larger naval force and army than we now have. We will need ships to take territory, and men to hold the territory when taken. To attempt to do that in time of peace has failed; let us therefore raise trouble with some back-numbered country — Spain, for instance, and during the excitement get what we want. Presto, it is done." [5]

On October 26, 1907, the Socialist weekly *Appeal to Reason,* published in Girard, Kansas, carried an answer to a question sent in by a reader, inquiring what were the causes "which brought about the war with Spain." The answer read in part:

> Cuba was the prize for which the Spanish-American war was fought. The island was rich in natural resources, the development of which would yield profits to the capital invested as well as supply a market for

> the growing surplus of American manufacture. . . . The capital of the United States was under the necessity of finding new fields in which to operate. Visions of Havana franchises and fertile sugar plantations rose before the profit-hungry ruling class of this country. . . .

The adherents of the theory that the war was caused solely by humanitarian factors dismissed these socialist interpretations as reflecting "the Marxist Machiavellian analysis of history." But they could not so easily dismiss the analysis presented by Frederick Emory, chief of the Bureau of Foreign Commerce of the Department of Commerce, who wrote in *World's Work* of January, 1902:

> Underlying the popular sentiment, which might have evaporated in time, which forced the United States to take up arms against Spanish rule in Cuba, were our economic relations with the West Indies and the South American republics. So strong was this commercial instinct that had there been no emotional cause, such as the alleged enormities of Spanish rule or the destruction of the *Maine,* we would have doubtless taken steps in the end to abate with a strong hand what seemed to be an economic nuisance. . . . The Spanish-American War was but an incident of a general movement of expansion which had its roots in the changed environment of an industrial capacity far beyond our domestic powers of consumption. It was seen to be necessary for us not only to find foreign purchasers for our goods, but to provide the means of making access to foreign markets easy, economical and safe.

Commenting editorially on this analysis, the New York *Tribune* concluded: "The war in which we intervened was pre-eminently an economical war, provoked by commercial, financial and industrial forces." [6]

This interpretation of the forces that produced American intervention in Cuba was endorsed in the same year, 1902, by the noted British economist J. A. Hobson in his book, *Imperialism: A Study*: "It was this sudden demand for foreign markets for manufacturers and for investments which was avowedly responsible for the adoption of Imperialism as a political policy and practice by the Republican Party to which the great industrial and financial chiefs belonged, and which belonged to them. . . ." Hobson warned his readers not to be deceived by such slogans as "humanitarianism," "manifest destiny," and "mission of civilization," raised by politicians and propagandists. They were merely the spokesmen for the monopolists. "It was Messrs. Rockefeller, Pierpont Morgan, and their associates who needed Imperialism and who fastened it upon the shoulders of the great Republic of the West. They needed Imperialism because they desired to use the public resources of the country to find profitable employment for their capital which otherwise would be superfluous." Hobson concluded that the Spanish-American War was an imperialist war, and that "American Imperialism was the natural product of the economic pressure of a sudden advance of capitalism which could not find occupation at home and needed foreign markets, for goods and investments."

In his classic work, *Imperialism: The Highest Stage of Capitalism,* written in 1917, V. I. Lenin paid tribute to Hobson's analysis as "an excellent and comprehensive description of the principal economic and political characteristics of imperialism." Although Lenin differed with Hobson on basic issues,[7] he agreed with the British economist in characterizing the Spanish-American War as an imperialist war, fought by the United States for imperialist reasons.[8]

During the 1920s and early 1930s, several American historians also characterized the Spanish-American War as an imperialist war, although their description of imperialism was closer to Hobson than to Lenin. Harold U. Faulkner stated in 1924 that the cause for the war with Spain was to be found in the fact that by 1898 the United States was "sufficiently advanced for financial imperialism," and that the war was fought for markets and fields for investments.[9] Professor Harry Elmer Barnes wrote in 1930 "that the passing of the frontier in 1890 produced the necessity of discovering a field for expansion and investment elsewhere than within the boundaries of the United States. The dispute with Spain over Cuba provided but a welcome pretext and provided a moral issue which allowed the formal and systematic initiation of a process which had long been in preparation." [10] Likewise, Charles A. Beard, in his study *The Idea of National Interest,* published in 1934, wrote: "Within a few years the movement for territorial expansion, conforming to the commercial type, was renewed in the Caribbean direction, with the Cuban Revolution of 1895 as the occasion for action." Beard acknowledged that American concern about Cuba came under the heading of "the national interest," but that "supplementary interests were plainly economic." [11]

The 1930s also saw the publication of several historical works which challenged the interpretation of the Spanish-American War as having been caused by United States imperialism in need of markets, sources of cheap raw materials, and new fields for investment. Writing in 1930, Louis Hacker suggested that the war resulted from an attempt by the Republican Party "to take men's minds off vexing domestic concerns." [12] Several historians designated the "yellow press" as the primary cause of the war. Marcus M. Wilkinson in 1932 concluded that the press drove McKinley, Congress, and the people into war. He declared that the war marked a triumph of the sensational press which, led by the New York *Journal* and *World,* "left the American public reeling from a bombardment of half-truths, misstatements of facts, rumors, and faked dispatches," and that the McKinley administration, "sensing the popular tide . . . and egged on by a 'jingo' Congress, proposed war." [13] Two years later, Joseph E. Wisan singled out one sensational newspaper publisher, William Randolph Hearst, and accorded him first place in promoting the war. He concluded that the fighting would not have started "had not the appearance of Hearst in New York journalism precipitated a bitter battle for newspaper circulation." [14] This school of interpretation received an additional adherent in 1940, George W. Auxier, Jr., who published a study of the Midwestern press in which he noted that while sensationalism was not particularly well represented in the area, the newspapers caused the war.[15]

But so far as the vast majority of American historians was concerned, the decisive blow to the interpretation of the Spanish-American War as an imperialist war was delivered by the appearance in 1934 of Julius W. Pratt's "American Business and the Spanish-American War," and in 1936 of his work, *Expansionists of 1898: The Acquisition of Hawaii and the Spanish Islands.* After a study of financial and commercial journals, Pratt stated that the vast majority of business and financial interests of the country until the last moment "strongly opposed action that would lead to war with Spain," and the few who did support it did so solely "on humanitarian grounds." While he does not exonerate the entire American business community of any responsibility for the Spanish crisis, this is clearly implied in his thesis that American business did not favor, but rather actively opposed, the Spanish-American War, and in his statement that "business interests in the United States were generally opposed to expansion or indifferent to it until after May 1, 1898." Not the business community, Pratt argued, but strategically placed intellectuals (with non-economic motives) were responsible for American imperialism.[16] But once the war started, and once the expansionists had begun to press for the retention of the Philippines, the attitude of the business community changed. Then the arguments of the expansionists about the commercial possibilities in the new Pacific acquisition brought a significant number of businessmen over to the expansionist side.[17]

Now American historians, taking their cue from Wilkinson, Wisan, and especially from Pratt, began to construct the thesis that the Spanish-American War was the result of mass hysteria produced by the propaganda of the "yellow press," aided and abetted by the Cuban *Junta;* the "self-assertive egoism and altruistic idealism" of the American people, apart from business leaders, who wanted war and got it after a "popular clamor for war"; the rise of Social Darwinism with its insistence that a struggle for existence "among the nations and peoples would result in the survival of the fittest," e.g., the United States and white Anglo-Saxons; the result of the influence of "a little group of young Republicans" who sought "National power for its own sake." The latter – the "original imperialists" – were motivated (according to this theory) solely by the "political possibilities of imperialism," and they forced a weak and indecisive President McKinley, who displayed "no interest in international politics" and had "no policy of imperialism on which to stand or fall" to lead the country into war.[18]

In the rush to present the new picture of the causes of the Spanish-American War, economic factors were cast aside. Charles A. Beard joined the group of American historians who emphasized that emotional and psychological factors were largely responsible for the war. In 1939, he advanced the theory that the war was sold to the country by politicians who were frightened by the "specter of Bryanism," and were seeking to divert the attention of the people from the grave problems that lay beneath the revolt of the farmers expressed in the populist movement. His earlier emphasis on territorial expansion and economic interests that stood to gain from the war was now abandoned.[19] Twenty-seven years after he had first stressed the prominence of economic causes for the war, Harold U. Faulkner stated in 1951 that "the point of view taken by certain economic historians that the United States went to war with Spain primarily for economic reasons seems not warranted by the evidence." [20] In *Politics, Reform and Expansion, 1890–1910,* published in 1959, Professor Faulkner found that the business interests in 1898 were worried about the possibility of war, and were definitely on the side of peace.[21] Also influenced by Pratt, Foster R. Dulles rewrote his earlier works on American imperialism to lay added emphasis upon psychological and political factors while virtually eliminating previous allusions to economic causes for the conflict between the United States and Spain.[22]

The non-economic interpretation of the causes of the war was reflected in nearly all historical works dealing with this period. Matthew Josephson emphasized that opposed to the "war party" was a group strong for peace, the "Big Business faction." [23] Arthur M. Schlesinger wrote that there can be no question that McKinley was for peace and that his desire "was ardently backed by Big Business and Wall Street." [24] Thomas A. Bailey stated that during the hectic months before the actual intervention, "perhaps the most important single restraint on the jingoistic spirit was big business. Except for a relatively small group . . . the financial and commercial interests of the United States were almost solidly opposed to war." [25] Samuel Flagg Bemis called the charge that American business desired intervention "a legend once eagerly accepted in academic circles." But now it was clear that rather than desiring intervention, "business interests in the United States were to the last opposed to any war with Spain." [26] Nor, states A. Whitney Griswold, did commercial groups interested in the Far East desire a war, and he goes on to say that "it is safe to say that the handful of Americans engaged in commerce with the Far East at first saw no connection between *Cuba Libre* and the open door in China. Neither did the American people as a whole." [27]

If economic forces did appear as a factor in the agitation for the war, they appeared in a strangely inverted way. "The threat to peace came from a new quarter," writes W. E. Leuchtenberg, "from the South and the West, the strongholds of Democracy and Free Silver." The Bryanites had hoped that the war would put a strain on the currency so that the opponents of free silver would collapse. Since they saw that Wall Street opposed the war, they claimed that the Administration's "peace policy" was the product of a bankers' conspiracy to deny free silver to the American people and independence to the people of Cuba. This theory, Leuchtenberg concedes, can be questioned, but there can be no doubt that, in the main, the business interests of the country opposed the war.

> McKinley came to power as the "advance agent of prosperity" and business interests were almost unanimous in opposing any agitation of the Cuban Question that might lead to war. Contrary to the assumption of Leninist historians, it was Wall Street which, first and last, resisted a war which was to bring America its overseas empire.[28]

Richard Hofstadter summed up the position of the dominant school of American historians when he wrote that "since Julius W. Pratt published his *Expansionists of 1898* . . . it has been obvious that any interpretation of America's entry upon the path of imperialism in the nineties in terms of rational economic motives would not fit the facts and that the historian who approaches the event with preconceptions no more supple than those, say, of Lenin's *Imperialism,* would be helpless." While uncritically accepting Pratt's thesis, Hofstadter, in accounting for the Spanish-American War, advances what he calls "The Psychic Thesis." He concedes that a number of factors, in varying degrees of intensity, were responsible for the war, including economic factors. But he argues that war finally came because at the moment these war-producing factors came to a head, the country was undergoing what he calls a "psychic crisis." The depression which followed the Panic of 1893 frustrated the American people, Hofstadter argues, and they responded to their frustrations with aggression in all directions. Imperialism followed naturally from the psychic — not basically economic — necessities of the moment. For their own selfish purposes, the "manufacturers of inevitability," the "yellow press" and the imperialist "junto" around Theodore Roosevelt and Henry Cabot Lodge, were thereby able to pervert the sympathies of the American people for the suffering Cubans into a palatable argument for a war and an empire against the basic interests and traditions of the American people. Pointing to McKinley's war message to Congress, Hofstadter notes that the Spanish had actually capitulated and that war was unnecessary. "Evidently," he writes, "McKinley had concluded that what was wanted in the United States was not so much the freedom of Cuba as a *war* for the freedom of Cuba." [29]

The first critical analysis of the Pratt thesis was made by Arthur Barcan in his unpublished Master's thesis presented to the graduate faculty of Columbia University in 1940, entitled "American Imperialism and the Spanish American War." Beginning by noting that big business controlled the government of the United States under McKinley, Barcan observed that it was inconceivable "that the administration's decision to enter a war was supposedly unfavorable to big business." He then proceeded to a detailed analysis of business, financial, and industrial journals for the period 1895 to 1898, a number of them ignored by Pratt, and concluded that he was convinced from this study that the Spanish-American War was "no more the freak – a non-imperialist venture in an imperialist setting, a war opposed by businessmen in a country controlled by them – but it now becomes a more plausible account of how the United States was forced into war to satisfy her new imperialist appetities, aided and abetted by business men who were in it to gain directly or indirectly from the war." He found nothing in his research to justify the conclusion of "mass business opposition to war" in commercial, business, and financial journals, or the concept that "the United States did not find its imperialist urge until the war was under way, as if a country can, within the space of one month, develop the necessary resources and needs that produce imperialism." He showed in his study that the rapid economic growth of the United States had developed an increasing need for markets for surplus goods and capital. By 1898, these expanding American capitalists found themselves in discouraging, and even precarious straits. In Cuba, the Revolution had for three years disrupted economic activity, destroyed valuable capital investments, and held back further exploitation of the island's great resources, while Spain had proven herself impotent to restore order, a condition highly necessary for continued imperialist activity in the "Pearl of the Antilles." In Hawaii, Americans had already assumed control, but their desire and need for annexation to the United States was balked by persistent efforts of domestic beet and cane sugar growers, aided by anti-imperialist elements in the country. In China, American capitalists found profitable fields for trade and capital increasingly menaced by the monopolistic encroachments of European imperialisms. American capitalists, Barcan discovered from his research,

> now turned covetous glances in the direction of the Philippines, which were sufficiently close to the Asiatic mainland to serve as an excellent base for American navy and ships, thus bolstering the American position in

> China. It was the need to acquire the Philippines, and the inability to annex Hawaii except under extreme conditions as a "war measure" that bolstered and gave impetus to the war drive in March and April, 1898, supposedly concerned merely with the desire to free the Cubans from the Spanish "yoke.". . . Nor is it mere accident that the first important step in the fight to drive Spain out of Cuba was Admiral Dewey's victory in Manila Bay.

Barcan concluded his study with the statement that while the war cannot be explained only in terms of economic factors, "the business imperialist interests were dominant." [30]

Since Barcan wrote his study — in many ways a limited analysis of the whole problem because of a failure to examine many available sources which would have further buttressed his conclusion — the Pratt thesis has come under increasing criticism. In 1953, in an unpublished doctoral dissertation at the University of Pittsburgh, Ralph Dewar Bald, Jr. proved that the journals of the leading industries and businesses in the United States repeatedly emphasized, beginning with 1885, "that the country was faced with the necessity of securing overseas markets for industrial surpluses." These journals published and endorsed the call by Mahan, Roosevelt, Lodge, and other imperialist-minded intellectuals and politicians, demanding overseas expansion, and giving special attention to the value of annexing Cuba as a source for trade and investment of capital. Rather than remaining indifferent to imperialism, as Pratt had asserted, the organs of the business community in the early 1890s "contributed importantly to the creation of an atmosphere of opinion favorable to expansion." [31] Since Pratt relied heavily on a few trade journals in reaching his conclusions, Bald's more intensive study of these periodicals showed that the Pratt thesis was in need of revision.

A more direct critical analysis of the Pratt thesis appeared in 1958 in Nancy Lenore O'Connor's article, "The Spanish American War: A Re-evaluation of Its Causes," published in *Science & Society*. Miss O'Connor emphasized that "economic considerations had much more to do with the coming of the [Spanish-American] War than has generally been acknowledged by American historians." Challenging Pratt, she notes that his conclusion is based on inadequate evidence, since he relied mainly on "eastern and coastal opinion." Then too, Pratt underestimated the role played by American bankers, merchants, manufacturers, steamship owners, and agents engaged in the export and import trade to Cuba who favored intervention. Miss O'Connor finds, moreover, that even in the East there was "a strong split in business opinion" over the question of war with Spain, with a substantial group calling for military intervention. She challenges Pratt's contention that "American business had been either opposed or indifferent to the expansion philosophy which had arisen since 1890," citing specific examples where "industrial and commercial interests demanded new bases of operation." She concludes:

> Thus, on the eve of the conflict with Spain, business interests accepted war as a necessary extension of the American Policy. To assume that the foment of mass ideology, *real politik,* and lust for power can explain away the operation of economic factors which led the business community to support different forms of expansion in accord with their own best interests is convenient, but misleading. . . . Given the milieu of the expansionist philosophy of the eighteen-nineties, the notion that American business opposed the Spanish-American War is subject to considerable revision.[32]

Another challenge to Pratt's thesis was presented by Martin J. Sklar in *Science & Society* a year later in an article entitled, "The N.A.M. and Foreign Markets on the Eve of the Spanish-American War." Analyzing the proceedings of the National Association of Manufacturers, founded in 1895, Sklar points out that

> . . . for more than two years, at least, prior to the Spanish-American War, a significant body of U.S. industrialists was convinced of the necessity of expanding their trade into foreign markets. The continued depression following the Panic of 1893 had demonstrated to them that the domestic market had finally passed the stage of indefinite elasticity capable of accommodating the growing productive capacity of the nation's industrial plant; [33] that the crisis required for its solution "the conquest of foreign markets" in order to "make room for the further expansion of our industries," not to mention the mere restoration of current production to full capacity; that unless something were done in this direction *post haste,* not only economic but social and political disaster for the capitalist way of life as they so fondly knew it might result.

Although Sklar does not discuss the attitude of this large and influential body of U.S. businessmen toward the Cuba crisis, he effectively demolishes Pratt's thesis that the American business community was either opposed or indifferent to the expansionist ideology of the 1890s. He proves that, on the contrary the leading businessmen were among the foremost advocates of this philosophy, and pointed repeatedly to Latin America and Asia as promising "the most glittering market opportunities for U.S. manufactures" — markets needed to "absorb glutted commodities, renew demand, and permit profitable expansion of productive capacity as an investment outlet for accumulated capital." Moreover, it was becoming clear to U.S. industrialists just prior to the Spanish-American War that in order to obtain "their 'share' of world markets," they had to throw themselves into the struggle for these markets, "and do so without further delay, before the world had been too hopelessly divided by the other industrial nations without U.S. participation. . . ."[34] Sklar demonstrates that for at least two years prior to the war, the U.S. industrialists embarked upon an aggressive struggle against the business interests of other industrial nations in competition for the markets of the world, and spheres of influence and control. This they did with the full cooperation and support of the business-minded McKinley administration. The implication thus is clear that United States industrial and financial capital viewed war with Spain as part of the aggressive drive to gain a dominant place in the markets of the world.[35]

Over a half-century before Sklar presented this thesis, the National Executive Committee of the Socialist Labor Party pointed to the proceedings of the N.A.M. convention in late December, 1897, as throwing "valuable light . . . upon the purpose of the Spanish-American War." It described the event as "a Congress of the owners of the United States to decide what their Government should do about expansion." It quoted Warren Miller, chairman of the convention, as telling the delegates: "Wars to-day are for commerce. The killing of a missionary furnishes the excuse for opening up of a market." Charles Emory Smith, Postmaster General in McKinley's cabinet, and a leading Republican spokesman for big business, told the delegates: "The economic problem of the world to-day is the distribution of the surplus. . . . Under this stress the nations of Europe are struggling for empire and trade. . . . We have come to the point in our national development where we must decide. . . . Why should we not obtain our legitimate share of the great stake? . . . The United States must not be counted out in determining the fate even of the coast of Asia." Less than four months later, the Socialist Labor Party pointed out, war was declared against Spain, and the first step taken was to seize its Pacific possessions. The current of events had been started, "under capitalist guidance," by the businessmen and their representatives in Washington. It was "to issue forth like a Gulf Stream, and operate 'way around on the other side of the world on the shores of China. . . ."[36]

Pratt's thesis has also been criticized by Professor William Appleman Williams. He contends that in 1938 many businessmen were convinced that recovery from the recession had been due to overseas economic expansion and thus became advocates of an "active foreign policy." Like Sklar, he cites the president of the N.A.M. as having asserted that "many of our manufactures have outgrown or are outgrowing their home markets, and the expansion of foreign trade is the only promise of relief." And like Miss O'Connor, he criticizes Pratt for underestimating the role of American businessmen whose interests in Cuba were being threatened with destruction by the continued fighting. The Cuban situation had to be stabilized in order to protect these interests, and American investors, looking for new areas for investing capital, did not welcome the prospect of continued strife in Cuba. Moreover, the need to "pacify the island" was supported by businessmen who agreed with McKinley that continued war in Cuba "injuriously affects the normal functions of [American] business, and tends to delay the condition of prosperity to which this country is entitled." Then again, Williams stresses, many businessmen in the United States feared the victory of the radical revolutionaries — "the troublesome adventurers and non-responsible class" — whose attitude toward American interests in Cuba was considered unreliable. By 1898, many businessmen favored American intervention in order to secure the ascendency of conservative elements (many of them Spaniards) in a Cuba free from Spain. Finally, Williams stresses "the clear and increasing interest in acquiring the Philippines as a base for winning a predominant share in the markets of China," an interest shared by many businessmen and not only by "Theodore Roosevelt and his imperialist cronies. . . ." Williams then concludes that American business, though preferring not to go to war as long as it could attain its objectives peacefully, had no objection to war "as the court of last resort." President McKinley "did not go to war simply because the businessmen ordered him to do so; but neither did he lead the nation to war against their economic wishes, as is so often asserted." [37]

Writing in 1960 and again in 1963, Thomas McCormick demonstrated the tremendous interest on the part of American businessmen and the McKinley administration in "the penetration, and, ultimately, the domination of the fabled China market," and clearly showed the link between the Cuban crisis and expansion in the Far East.[38] During this same period, Walter LaFeber's research in materials related to American foreign policy confirmed the findings of other critics of Pratt's thesis. He proves in his study, *The New Empire: An Interpretation of American Expansion, 1860–1898,* published in 1963, that the American business community considered foreign markets, especially those of Latin America and Asia, a solution to the domestic depression of 1893 (although he notes that even after 1873 there were signs of excess capacity in major segments of the American economy). Translating this viewpoint into action, businessmen after 1893 not only began systematically opening Latin American markets, but prodded the State Department to assist them in formulating Latin American policies. By 1897–98, they were beginning to move in the same way toward Asian markets and calling upon the McKinley administration to act diplomatically in behalf of their interests in the Far East.

American business, in short, was not a passive onlooker while Roosevelt, Mahan, Lodge, and the other "young imperialists" shouted for American expansion abroad, but was the initiator of the expansionist policy, and urged government officials to adopt the necessary strategy to advance the interests of a business community urgently seeking new markets. Many businessmen, LaFeber points out, supported intervention against Spain not only because it would open the Cuban market for further U.S. economic penetration, but also because they had their eyes on Spain's possessions in the Far East. "It is possible to suggest," he writes with specific reference to Pratt's thesis, ". . . that by the middle of March important businessmen and spokesmen for the business community were advocating war. It is also possible to suggest that at the same time a shift seems to be occurring in the general business community regarding its over-all views on the desirability of war." In short, businessmen and leading politicians thought alike on the need for foreign markets and acquisitions of colonies, and the foreign policy of the U.S. government flowed from this state of affairs.[39]

My own research confirms recent conclusions that the thesis advanced by Julius W. Pratt and accepted uncritically by so many historians is not tenable. For one thing, there is ample evidence that businessmen were just as concerned about foreign markets and exports as the only feasible way of overcoming the industrial glut at home as were the imperialist-minded politicians and intellectuals. The Caribbean area and Latin America were frequently mentioned in trade journals and meetings of manufacturers as a field for American investment and trade expansion, but expansion in the Pacific was also increasingly being mentioned and linked with the others. On November 5, 1897, Francis B. Loomis, a leading spokesman for American business, wrote in a "confidential" letter to William R. Day, Assistant Secretary of State:

> *Above all,* let me say in conclusion I would send a commercial attaché to the Orient to operate in China and Japan. It is in that direction the great markets of the immediate future will be found. I happen to know that England sees this with distinctness and is acting promptly on her foresight. This administration can make a powerful and lasting impression upon the imagination and the welfare of the whole business world in the United States, and a richly deserved prestige for originality and progressiveness by taking up and exploiting the idea of trade in the Orient. . . .
>
> If you have not done so, let me suggest to you to read the article by Cpt. Mahan in the October number of Harper's Monthly. It is a strategic "Study of the Caribbean sea," and the writer is the foremost of authorities on that subject.[40]

Captain Mahan's article emphasized the need for naval bases, particularly in the strategically important Caribbean area and in Hawaii, as a major step toward expansion of American economic activity in Latin America and Asia. The prophet and apostle of sea power argued that the U.S. must begin to look outward. Deploring the country's self-imposed isolation in the matter of markets and the decline of its shipping, Mahan asserted that the growing production of the country would necessitate new markets, and this, in turn, would require facilities for their protection – a powerful navy dominated by an aggressive spirit, a healthy merchant marine, and secure bases and coaling stations from which they could operate. Strategically, the Caribbean area was crucial; Mahan considered control of the Isthmus of Panama by the United States vital. Such control was in turn contingent upon control of its approaches and of the bases that dominated them. Nothing less than American supremacy in the Caribbean would suffice. With the Caribbean and Hawaii, the United States could dominate Latin American commerce and move aggressively into the markets of the Far East. Mahan saw a clear relationship between the Caribbean and the vast market of China – via Cuba and Puerto Rico, the Isthmus, Hawaii, the coaling and cable station system in the Ladrones and Samoa, the Philippines to the Asian mainland. Appraising the value of all the Caribbean islands, Mahan directed American attention to Cuba as offering the best position for the United States in that area.[41]

As Loomis' letter to Day indicates, Mahan's outlook was shared by leading business interests. On February 3, 1898, the New York State Chamber of Commerce sent a memorial to President McKinley urging the government to pay careful attention to the opportunities for the expansion of trade with China and the danger that this might be affected by "the changes now going on in the relation of the European powers with the Empire of China." In other words, the American businessmen faced the threat of being cut out of that potentially great market. The memorial was referred to Secretary of State John Sherman, who replied as follows to A. E. Orr, President of the Chamber of Commerce:

> This government having been the first to bring about the opening of the ports of China to foreign commerce, and the commercial relations of the United States with the Chinese Empire having been of large and growing importance during the forty years since its treaties with that Empire went into effect, this Department necessarily feels a deep interest in conserving and expanding the volume of trade with that country. I have pleasure, therefore, in assuring the Chamber of Commerce of the State of New York that this subject is being given the most careful consideration.[42]

The letters and memorials quoted above are only a few examples of many that could be cited to demonstrate that the important business interests were deeply concerned with the need for foreign markets before the outbreak of the Spanish-American War, and were concerned, too, at the danger of pre-emption of these markets by European interests. In this connection, John J. McCook's report of a meeting with the heads of the Standard Oil Company, America's leading trust, in the fall of 1896, is significant. McCook wrote that the Standard Oil people were extremely interested in "Manifest Destiny in Asia," and added: "Mr. [Henry M.] Flagler thought that the increase of Russian influence in China after the railway [being constructed by Russia] was completed would be hurtful to them as Russia would of course use all its power to have their petroleum, which has become a large article of commerce with them, used in China and in all countries coming under their influence." [43]

Not long after the start of the Spanish-American War, Henry Cabot Lodge, in a letter to Theodore Roosevelt, expressed the conviction that the McKinley administration had committed itself to the "large policy we both desire." [44] By this Lodge meant using intervention in Cuba as the stepping stone for expansion in the Far East through the acquisition of Spain's Pacific possessions. Many American businessmen were fully committed to the "large policy" long before May 1, 1898. They prodded the government and the government responded. On October 14, 1900, the *Daily People* reminded the American people that "in 1895, the American capitalists organized the American Manufacturers Association, later the American Asiatic Association, etc., to reach into foreign trade." Later, with the cooperation of the McKinley administration, "they proceeded with the further formation of Trusts at a terrific rate, in order better to encounter the world's markets.[45] By 1898 they were ready, and determined to aid in forcing open the Chinese market, the last considerable unexploited market in the world. Hence occupation of the Philippines as a base at the doorway of China." It continued:

> Hence the Spanish-American War, whereby while fighting Spain in the Antilles, the color of plausibility could be given to the seizure of the Philippines as belonging to the same power. Observe that Manila, so absolutely disconnected from the Cuban question that it lies almost directly straight through the earth from us and Cuba, 8000 miles beneath our feet, was where the first battle was fought! Cuba was simply the fulcrum of the lever used by the capitalists in prying the "Open Door" of China.

The *Daily People* ignored the fact that there were American businessmen who had direct economic interests in Cuba, and, as we have seen, had for three years prior to the war been repeatedly calling attention to the losses they were sustaining because of the government's refusal to intervene. Most of them were elated by the steps taken by McKinley for intervention, and they urged prompt and efficient measures to restore peace in the island, which would mean the restoration of a most valuable field for investment and trade. To what degree were they joined by other business interests? My own research demonstrates that while much business sentiment, especially in the East, opposed war with Spain in the early months of 1898, primarily because "it would endanger our currency stability, interrupt our trade and threaten our coasts and commerce," [46] numerous business spokesmen began to emphasize that uncertainty, generated by the Cuban Revolution, was holding back business recovery. By mid-March many began to feel that even war was better than continued suspense, and that war would not seriously affect American business, for after the first shock, "things would whirl as usual." [47] Senator Proctor's speech had a marked effect upon the business community. The *Wall Street Journal* declared: "Senator Proctor's speech converted a great many people in Wall Street who had heretofore taken the ground that the United States had no business to interfere in a revolution on Spanish soil." For one thing, the men in Wall Street and other business areas had been skeptical of sensational reports in the "yellow press" about terrible conditions in Cuba, and Proctor, who had a reputation for being a moderate, convinced them that these reports were not exaggerated. Then again, Proctor did much to allay conservative fears that if Spanish domination was removed, "the people of Cuba would be revolutionary." The fact that the white population of Cuba was growing more rapidly than the decreasing Negro population, the fact that many educated and intelligent people lived on the island, and "the large influx of American immigration and money," Proctor assured conservatives, "would all be strong factors for stable institutions." [48]

With the stock market moving from one level to another, there was an increasing cry from the business community for an immediate solution. Such business giants as John Jacob Astor, William Rockefeller, Stuyvesant Fish, Thomas Fortune Ryan, and John Gates declared themselves for a more belligerent policy toward Spain, and J. Pierpont Morgan joined the group in late March, 1898, when he declared that nothing more could be obtained by arbitration.[49] At the same time, a leading New York journalist sent a telegram to a friend of McKinley which was passed on to the President: "Big corporations here now believe we will have war. Believe all would welcome it as relief to suspense. . . ." [50] On the declaration of war, *American Banker noted,* "call loan rates which had averaged about 2 percent in February rose sharply during March and touched 5 percent at the opening of hostilities." [51] The approach of war, in other words, had had a highly stimulating effect on American capital!

With the support of a substantial section of, if not the entire, business community, McKinley moved to war. Thus it is clear that Pratt's conclusion that most big businessmen opposed the declaration of war in 1898 requires a thorough re-evaluation. Likewise in need of re-evaluation is the concept in many historical works that the President moved hesitantly and fearfully under the impact of a popular clamor too great for him to withstand.[52] As Ernest R. May puts this thesis, "mass hysteria" compelled President McKinley to lead his country "unwillingly toward a war that he did not want for a cause in which he did not believe." [53] A corollary to this thesis is that McKinley moved to war without being aware of, to say nothing of being influenced by, the requirements of expansion to meet the needs of American business for foreign markets. McKinley, like most American leaders, May argues, was "at most only incidentally concerned about real or imagined interests abroad." [54]

McKinley moved resolutely to war, following a course mapped out months before, and in so doing contemptuously ignored the overwhelming popular and Congressional demand for recognition of the independence of the Cuban Republic. In fact, he was so indifferent to popular clamor that he steadfastly refused to yield to almost universal popular demand to recognize Cuban belligerency, much less Cuban independence.

A study of what McKinley did and said reveals that the demands of the business community and of the political and intellectual expansionists met a very favorable response from the President.[55] McKinley delivered the keynote address at the organizational meeting of the National Association of Manufacturers in 1895, and he pointed out to these leading industrialists, organized to push trade overseas, that industry as a whole "cannot be kept in motion without markets." Foreign markets were essential "for our surplus products." As President, McKinley gave the featured address at the 1897 meeting of the Philadelphia Commercial Museum, also organized to push overseas economic expansion. "No worthier cause [than] the expansion of trade," he declared, ". . . can engage our energies at this hour." [56]

Like all advocates of the "large policy," McKinley called for a big navy and an increase in the American merchant marine. Like them, too, he advocated the immediate annexation of the Hawaiian Islands, recommending it as soon as he assumed office on the grounds of inevitable destiny. When the treaty was first submitted to the Senate, he referred to annexation as the "inevitable consequence" of history and the following year, he observed that annexation was "manifest destiny." McKinley worked to implement other parts of the expansionist program. Upon becoming President, he moved toward the ownership and construction of an Isthmian canal. He also tried to purchase Cuba, and he would have annexed the island or placed it under a protectorate if the Spanish had been willing to sell. As John D. Offner writes in his study of McKinley's foreign policy: "McKinley's naval ideas and his interest in acquiring Hawaii, Cuba, and an American canal appear to form a well-rounded plan of expansion and development of American power . . . [and] his acts indicate that he was aware of the currents of expansionism behind a more comprehensive foreign policy."[57]

These "currents of expansionism" played a crucial part in the decision to go to war. McKinley was aware of the relationship between military action against Spain over Cuba and the establishment of an American base of operation in the Philippines from which to venture into the lucrative Far Eastern markets. He talked about this connection with Theodore Roosevelt and others as early as September, 1897, and he was involved in the plans which readied the entire Pacific campaign for immediate action even before the war was officially declared. Timothy G. McDonald puts it well in his article, "McKinley and the War with Spain":

> McKinley had his eyes on the Philippines as well as Cuba and wished to wage war on both fronts if war came. . . . Exactly when McKinley began to take an interest in the Philippines is uncertain. We do know, however, that strategic discussions involving those islands were underway not later than September 21, 1897. Quite possibly, Spain's Far Eastern possessions occupied the thoughts of Washington strategists from the moment McKinley's diplomatic offensive commenced. . . . In September of 1897, McKinley and his advisors were discussing both operations, but only the attack on the Philippines was carried out. Further, virtually everyone concerned knew the importance of the Philippines and there was general knowledge within and without the government that Americans had better hasten the coming of their Asian base, given the development of China.
>
> American business leaders, increasingly concerned with world markets, heard disquieting reports in the fall of 1897. European nations, it appeared were plotting to restrict the potentially vast Far Eastern markets for American staples. Washington shared this concern — on December 24, 1897, European efforts to dismember the Chinese Empire provided the principal topic at a Cabinet meeting in the White House. One of the participants told reporters that the President intended to keep a watchful eye upon the situation in order that full protection be given to the interests of the United States in China. Again, toward the end of January in 1898, McKinley assured American businessmen, in a speech before the National Association of Manufacturers in New York City, that America must reoccupy the fields temporarily lost to her and go on to peaceful conquests of new and greater fields of trade and commerce. American naval power, based in the Philippines, would be able to protect present and future American interests in East Asia. Keeping these factors in mind, it would appear that the decision to attack the Philippines was crucial. As a matter of fact, McKinley planned the American conquest of the Philippines almost before the echoes of gunfire at Manila Bay had ceased. . . .

> To put the matter briefly, eliminating Spain from both Cuba and the Philippines were equal objectives. . . .[58]

To put it again briefly: the Cuban policy of the United States culminating in the use of force against Spain had its root in the rise of monopoly capitalism and its drive for markets. There were political, social and psychological roots, too, and no analysis of the road to war can ignore humanitarian sentiments, the role of the press, the sinking of the *Maine*, the influence of the ideologists of expansionism. But these reinforced economic factors. The predominance of economic factors in the sequence of events which led to the outbreak of conflict between the United States and Spain has been sufficiently demonstrated in recent historiography to warrant the conclusion that the Spanish-American War was indeed an imperialist war.

American Business and the Spanish-American War

JULIUS W. PRATT

Julius Pratt, one of the senior historians of American foreign policy, is the author of many monographs and a popular text; he is also the originator of an influential thesis about the role of American businessmen in the coming of the Spanish-American War that has been used and abused ever since its original publication in 1934. Given the centrality of the "Pratt thesis" to almost all sides in the debate about the sources of American imperialism, it would be well to read its initial statement with care. There are two major points to ponder: (1) How essential to Pratt's approach is his preoccupation with colonial *aspirations? (2) Does he draw the fullest possible conclusions from his own evidence on the shift in business opinion as a result of events in China? Mapped against the chronology of McKinley's diplomatic activity, might not this change in business opinion have influenced the president in ways unexplored by Pratt?*

The student who seeks from the standard historians an explanation of why the United States embarked upon the war with Spain and the resulting career of territorial expansion and imperialism can hardly fail to meet with two contradictory opinions. James Ford Rhodes, whose close relations with Mark Hanna enabled him to speak with much authority of the attitude of American business men, has stated in no uncertain terms that "the financial and business interests of the country were opposed to the war." [1] * According to this thesis, the war resulted from a combination of humanitarian sympathy for Cuba and popular excitement skillfully engineered by the sensational press, and the annexations which followed were accepted as unsought responsibilities thrust upon the nation by the exigencies of the war. On the other hand, Professor H. U. Faulkner, in his excellent *American Economic History,* contends that the expansion of American industrial and financial power had created a readiness for "financial imperialism," which "provided the great cause for the war." [2] These two opinions seem irreconcilable. How could the war be caused primarily by the desire of American industry and finance for imperial expansion, and at the same time be opposed by "the financial and business interests of the country"?

Two separate but related questions here call for examination. First, can we accept Rhodes's generalization that American business was opposed to a course which would lead to war with Spain? Second, did American business and finance display an interest in acquiring colonies either before war was declared or in the months between the declaration and the peace treaty? Evidence bearing upon these two questions has been sought in a large number of financial and trade periodicals which supposedly spoke the minds of their clientele, in proceedings of chambers of commerce and boards of trade, and in the *Miscellaneous Files* in the department of state, containing letters and petitions from business men and organizations.[3] While conclusions drawn from such data are subject to the dangers which beset all studies of public opinion, there seems, on each question, a sufficient preponderance of evidence to warrant a fairly confident answer.

That business sentiment, especially in the east, was strongly anti-war at the close of 1897 and in the opening months of 1898, is hardly open to doubt. Wall Street stocks turned downward whenever the day's news seemed to presage war and climbed again with information favorable to peace.[4] Bulls and bears on the market were those who anticipated, respectively, a peaceable and a warlike solution of the Cuban question.[5] The

Reprinted by permission from the *Hispanic American Historical Review,* XIV, No. 2 (1934), pp. 163–201.
* [See pp. 162–168 for notes to this article. – Ed.]

"jingo," in congress or the press, was an object of intense dislike to the editors of business and financial journals,[6] who sought to counteract his influence by anti-war editorials in their columns.[7] Boards of trade and chamber of commerce added their pleas for the maintenance of peace to those of the business newspapers and magazines.[8] So marked, indeed, was the anti-war solidarity of the financial interests and their spokesmen that the jingoes fell to charging Wall Street with want of patriotism. Wall Street, declared the Sacramento *Evening Bee* (March 11, 1898), was "the colossal and aggregate Benedict Arnold of the Union, and the syndicated Judas Iscariot of humanity." Senator Thurston, of Nebraska, charged that opposition to war was found only among the "money-changers," bringing from the editor of *The American Banker* the reply that "there is not an intelligent, self-respecting and civilized American citizen anywhere who would not prefer to have the existing crisis culminate in peaceful negotiations." [9]

This anti-war attitude on the part of several leading financial journals continued up to the very beginning of hostilities. The New York *Journal of Commerce and Commercial Bulletin* declared on February 28 that the only possible excuses for war would be (1) a finding by the naval board investigating the *Maine* disaster that the ship had been destroyed by an official act of the Spanish Government; or (2) a refusal by Spain to make reparations if the board should hold that that country had failed to exercise due diligence in safeguarding the vessel. Either of these events it held to be almost inconceivable. The *Commercial and Financial Chronicle* expressed the belief on March 12 that the opposition of the financial interests would yet prevent war; and on April 2 the same journal branded as "monstrous" the proposition to settle the Cuban and *Maine* questions by war while the slightest chance remained for a peaceful solution. And on April 16, after the House of Representatives had passed the Cuban resolutions, the Boston *Journal of Commerce* declared: "Sober second thought had but little to do with the deliberations. . . . The members were carried off their feet by the war fever that had been so persistently worked up since the Maine explosion. . . ." [10]

The reasons for this attitude on the part of business are not far to seek. Since the panic of 1893 American business had been in the doldrums. Tendencies toward industrial revival had been checked, first by the Venezuela war scare in December, 1895, and again by the free silver menace in 1896.[11] But in 1897 began a real revival, and before the end of the year signs of prosperity appeared on all sides. The *New York Commercial* conducted a survey of business conditions in a wide variety of trades and industries, from which it concluded that, "After three years of waiting and of false starts, the groundswell of demand has at last begun to rise with a steadiness which leaves little doubt that an era of prosperity has appeared." January, 1898, said the same article, is "a supreme moment in the period of transition from depression to comparative prosperity." [12] This note of optimism one meets at every turn, even in such a careful and conservative sheet as the *Commercial and Financial Chronicle.* As early as July, 1897, this paper remarked: "We appear to be on the eve of a revival in business"; and in December, after remarking upon the healthy condition of the railroads and the iron industry, it concluded: "In brief, no one can study the industrial condition of today in America without a feeling of elation. . . ." [13] The *Wall Street Journal* found only two "blue spots" in the entire country: Boston, which suffered from the depressed demand for cotton goods, and New York, where senseless rate cutting by certain railroads caused uneasiness. "Throughout the west, southwest and on the Pacific coast business has never been better, nor the people more hopeful." [14] A potent cause for optimism was found in the striking expansion of the American export trade. A volume of exports far in excess of those of any recent year, a favorable balance of trade of $286,000,000, and an especially notable increase in exports of manufactures of iron, steel, and copper, convinced practically every business expert that the United States was on the point of capturing the markets of the world. "There is no question," said one journal, "that the world, generally, is looking more and more to the United States as the source of its supply for very many of the staple commodities of life." [15] Especially elated were spokesmen of the iron and steel industry. Cheaper materials and improved methods were enabling the American producer to undersell his British competitor in Europe and in the British possessions,[16] and Andrew Carnegie was talking of a great shipbuilding yard near New York to take advantage of these low costs.[17] The *Iron Age,* in an editorial on "The Future of Business," foretold the abolition of the business cycle by means of a better planned economy, consolidation of railroads and industries, reductions of margins of profit, higher wages and lower prices to consumers – in other words a "new deal" resembling that attempted in 1933.[18]

To this fair prospect of a great business revival the threat of war was like a specter at the feast. A foreign complication, thought the *Commercial and Financial Chronicle,* in October, 1897, would quickly mar "the trade prosperity which all are enjoying." Six months later (April 2, 1898), after a discussion of the effect of war rumors on the stock exchange, it declared: ". . . Every influence has been, and even now is, tending strongly towards a term of decided prosperity, and that the Cuban disturbance, and it alone, has arrested the movement and checked enterprise." [19] The *Banker and Tradesman* saw in the Cuban complication the threat of "a material setback to the prosperous conditions which had just set in after five years of panic and depression." The same journal summarized a calculation made by the Boston *Transcript* showing that in February, 1898, the wave of prosperity had carried the average price of twenty-five leading stocks to within 5½ points of the high for the preceding ten years and 30 points above the low of 1896, and that the Cuban trouble had, in a little over two months, caused a loss of over ten points, or more than one-third of the recent gain.[20] "War would impede the march of prosperity and put the country back many years," said the *New Jersey Trade Review*.[21] The *Railway Age* was of the opinion that the country was coming out of a depression and needed peace to complete its recovery. "From a commercial and mercenary standpoint," it remarked, "it seems peculiarly bitter that this war should have come when the country had already suffered so much and so needed rest and peace." [22]

The idea that war could bring any substantial benefits to business was generally scouted. It would endanger our currency stability, interrupt our trade, and threaten our coasts and our commerce, thought the *Commercial and Financial Chronicle*. It would "incalculably increase the loss to business interests," said the *Banker's Magazine;* while the *United States Investor* held that war was "never beneficial from a material standpoint, that is, in the long run." [23] The *Railroad Gazette* predicted that war would result in "interruption of business enterprise of every kind, stopping new projects and diminution of the output of existing businesses and contraction of trade everywhere." Railroads would lose more than they would gain. Even arms manufacturers were not all agreed that war would be profitable.[24] Journals speaking for the iron and steel industry also argued that war would injure business. It "would injure the iron and steel makers ten times as much as they would be benefited by the prevailing spurt in the manufacture of small arms, projectiles and steel plates for war ships," in the opinion of one of these.[25] The *American Wool and Cotton Reporter* of New York and the *Northwestern Miller* of Minneapolis agreed that war was never materially beneficial in the long run, while trade journals in Atlanta, Chattanooga, and Portland, Oregon, saw as fruit of the approaching conflict only destruction, debt, and depressed industry.[26]

Many conservative interests feared war for the specific reason that it might derange the currency and even revive the free-silver agitation, which had seemed happily dead. The subsidence of that agitation and the prospect of currency reform were among the hopeful factors at the close of 1897.[27] It had been not uncommonly charged that the "jingoes" were animated in part by the expectation that war would lead to inflation in paper or silver. The New York *Journal of Commerce*, in an editorial on "The Breeding Grounds of Jingoism," had called attention to the fact that the jingoes were generally silverites, including in their number "the financiers who desire to force bankruptcy on the country as a means of breaking down the gold standard," and had quoted with approval an editorial from another paper charging that Senator Morgan's championship of the Cuban insurgents was part of "his wild scheming in the interest of the silver standard." [28] The *Commercial and Financial Chronicle* endorsed this view, declaring that many of the Cuban agitators "are only interested in the establishment of a free-silver standard, a plan which they think war would advance." [29] Similar views were expressed by the *American Banker* of New York, the *United States Investor* of Boston, and the *Rand-McNally Bankers' Monthly* of Chicago. The last-named quoted from a speech of Secretary of the Treasury Gage, delivered in Chicago in February, 1898, in which he had declared that "it would be scarcely possible for this nation to engage in war in its present condition . . . without a suspension of specie payments and a resort to further issues of Government notes." A war of any duration, in the opinion of the *United States Investor,* would certainly derange the currency and reduce business to a gambling basis.[30]

Something of a freak among New York financial journals was the *Financial Record,* which, in November, 1897, denounced "the cowardice of our Administration in refusing the phenomenally brave Cubans the commonest rights of belligerency" as "a disgrace to the United States," and argued that war with Spain, far from depressing securities or injuring business, "would vastly increase the net earning power of every security sold on our market today." [31] The mystery of this jingo attitude is explained when we discover that this journal had been a warm advocate of the free coinage of silver, thus becoming clearly the exception that proves the rule.

Business opinion in the west, especially in the Mississippi Valley, appears to have been less opposed to war and less apprehensive of its results than that of the Atlantic coast. The Kansas City Board of Trade, at the beginning of 1897, had urged recognition of Cuban independence.[32] The Cincinnati Chamber of Commerce, at a meeting on March 29, 1898, adopted "amidst much enthusiasm" resolutions condemning Spain for cruelties to the Cubans and the destruction of the *Maine* and calling for a "firm and vigorous policy which will have for its purpose – peacefully if we can, but with force if we must – the redress of past wrongs, and the complete and unqualified independence of Cuba." [33] The Chicago *Economist* denied that war would seriously hurt business or endanger the gold standard and asserted that the liberation of Cuba, by peace or war, would mean another star of glory for the United States and would produce "results of the highest value to mankind." [34] *The Rand-McNally Bankers' Monthly,* of the same city, while opposing war, called attention to the fact that while the war scare had demoralized the stock market, "general business activity apparently received an impetus." [35] Similarly the *Age of Steel* (St. Louis), while much preferring peace, "when not secured at the price of national honor," comforted its readers with the thought that although foreign trade might suffer, home trade and industries would be stimulated by war.[36] A St. Louis bank president, Mr. Lackland, believed that war would "cause a boom in many lines of business in this country . . . and give employment to a large number of persons who are now out of work." [37] The Chattanooga *Tradesman* stated on March 1, 1898, that a "small prospect" of war had already stimulated the iron trade in certain lines and had benefited the railroads by hurrying forward shipments of grain and other commodities in anticipation of war prices.[38] The *Mining and Scientific Press,* of San Francisco, while holding that, in general, war "lets loose havoc and waste, and entails destructive expense," conceded that "to nearly everything related to the mining industry the war will be a stimulus." [39]

Even in New York, business men saw some rays of light piercing the war clouds. Stock market operators, according to the *Wall Street Journal,* just after the *Maine* explosion, "did not look for any great break in the market, because actual war with Spain would be a very small affair compared with the Venezuela complication with Great Britain." Their expectation was for a drop in stocks at the beginning of hostilities, followed by a resumption of the recent advance. In fact, the first shock might well be followed by a boom.[40] "The nation looks for peace," declared *Dun's Review,* March 5, "but knows that its sources of prosperity are quite beyond the reach of any attack that is possible." *Bradstreet's* contrasted the jumpiness of Wall Street over war news with "the calm way in which general business interests have regarded the current foreign complications"; and *Dun's Review* of March 12 stated that no industry or branch of business showed any restriction, while some had been rapidly gaining, that railroads were increasing their profits while speculators sold their stocks, and that there was a growing demand for the products of all the great industries.[41]

Despite such expressions as these, there seems little reason to question the belief that an overwhelming preponderance of the vocal business interests of the country strongly desired peace. By the middle of March, however, many organs of business opinion were admitting that a war with Spain might bring no serious disaster, and there was a growing conviction that such a war was inevitable. In the senate on March 17, Senator Redfield Proctor of Vermont described, from his own observation, the terrible sufferings of the Cuban "reconcentrados." Proctor was no sensationalist, and his speech carried great weight. The *Wall Street Journal* described its effect among the denizens of the Street. "Senator Proctor's speech," it said, "converted a great many people in Wall Street, who have heretofore taken the ground that the United States had no business to interfere in a revolution on Spanish soil. These men had been among the most prominent in deploring the whole Cuban matter, but there was no question about the accuracy of Senator Proctor's statements and as many of them expressed it, they made the blood boil." [42] The *American Banker,* hitherto a firm opponent of intervention, remarked on March 23 that Proctor's speech showed an intolerable state of things, in view of which it could not understand "how any one with a grain of human sympathy within him can dispute the propriety of a policy of intervention, so only that this outraged people might be set free!" It still hoped, however, for a peaceful solution, declaring that the United States ought to urge the Cubans to accept the Spanish offer of autonomy.[43] That this growing conviction that something must be done about Cuba was by no means equivalent to a desire for war, was clearly revealed a few days later. Rumors circulated to the effect that Spain was willing to sell Cuba and that J. P. Morgan's return from a trip abroad was connected with plans to finance the purchase. "There is much satisfaction expressed in Wall Street," said the *Wall Street Journal,* "at the prospects of having Cuba free, because it is believed that this will take one of the most disturbing factors out of the situation. . . . Even if $200,000,000 is the indemnity demanded it is a sum which the United States could well afford to pay to get rid of the trouble." Even $250,000,000, it was thought, would be insignificant in comparison with the probable cost of a war.[44]

It remains to examine the attitude of certain American business men and corporations having an immediate stake in Cuba, or otherwise liable to be directly affected by American intervention. Much American capital, as is well known, was invested in the Cuban sugar industry. Upon this industry the civil war fell with peculiarly devastating effect, not only cutting off profits on capital so invested, but also crippling a valuable carrying trade between Cuba and the United States. Naturally enough, some firms suffering under these conditions desired to see the United States intervene to end the war, though such intervention might lead to war between the United States and Spain. In May, 1897, a memorial on the subject bearing over three hundred signatures was presented to John Sherman, Secretary of State. The signers described themselves as "citizens of the United States, doing business as bankers, merchants, manufacturers, steamship owners and agents in the cities of Boston, New York, Philadelphia, Baltimore, Savannah, Charleston, Jacksonville, New Orleans, and other places, and also other citizens of the United States, who have been for many years engaged in the export and import trade with the Island of Cuba." They called attention to the serious losses to which their businesses had been subjected by the hostilities in Cuba and expressed the hope that, in order to prevent further loss, to reestablish American commerce, and also to secure "the blessings of peace for one and a half millions of residents of the

Island of Cuba now enduring unspeakable distress and suffering," the United States Government might take steps to bring about an honorable reconciliation between the parties to the conflict.[45]

Another memorial, signed by many of the same subscribers, was presented to President McKinley on February 9, 1898, by a committee of New York business men. It asserted that the Cuban war, which had now continued for three entire years, had caused an average loss of $100,000,000 a year, or a total loss of $300,000,000 in the import and export trade between Cuba and the United States, to which were to be added

> heavy sums irretrievably lost by the destruction of American properties, or properties supported by American capital in the Island itself, such as sugar factories, railways, tobacco plantations, mines and other industrial enterprises; the loss of the United States in trade and capital by means of this war being probably far greater and more serious than that of all the other parties concerned, not excepting Spain herself.

The sugar crop of 1897–1898, continued the memorial, appeared for the most part like its two predecessors, and unless peace could be established before May or June of the current year, the crop of 1898–1899, with all the business dependent upon it, would likewise be lost, since the rainy season of summer and fall would be required "to prepare for next winter's crop, by repairing damaged fields, machinery, lines of railways, &c." In view of the importance to the United States of the Cuban trade and of American participation "in the ownership or management of Cuban sugar factories, railways and other enterprises," the petitioners hoped that the president would deem the situation "of sufficient importance as to warrant prompt and efficient measures by our Government, with the sole object of restoring peace . . . and with it restoring to us a most valuable commercial field." [46]

How much weight such pressure from special interests had with the administration there is no way of knowing. But it is to be noted that the pressure from parties directly interested was not all on one side. Mr. E. F. Atkins, an American citizen who divided his time between Boston and his sugar plantation of Soledad near Cienfuegos, Cuba, which he had developed at a cost of $1,400,000, had been able, through protection received from the Spanish Government and through a corps of guards organized and paid by himself, to continue operations throughout the period of the insurrection. He was frequently in Washington, where he had influential friends, during both the Cleveland and McKinley administrations and worked consistently against the adoption of any measures likely to provoke war.[47] Unlike some of the sugar plantations, American-owned iron mines in Cuba continued to do active business despite the insurrection. Three American iron and manganese enterprises in the single province of Santiago claimed to have an investment of some $6,000,000 of purely American capital, a large proportion of which was in property which could easily be destroyed. "We are fully advised as to our status in case of war," wrote the representative of one company to the assistant secretary of state, "and that this property might be subject to confiscation or destruction by the Spanish Government." War between Spain and the United States, wrote the president of another company, "will very likely mean the destruction of our valuable plant and in any event untold loss to our Company and its American stockholders." [48] An American cork company with large interests in Spain; a New York merchant with trade in the Mediterranean and Black Sea; a Mobile firm which had chartered a Spanish ship to carry a cargo of timber — these are samples of American business interests which saw in war the threat of direct damage to themselves.[49] They are hardly offset by the high hopes of an enterprising gentleman of Norfolk, "representing a party of capitalists who are enthusiastic supporters of the Government," who applied to the state department for a letter of marque "to enable us to lawfully capture Spanish merchant vessels and torpedo boats," adding: "We have secured option on a fine steam vessel and on receipt of proper documents will put to sea forth with." [50]

It seems safe to conclude, from the evidence available, that the only important business interests (other than the business of sensational journalism) which clamored for intervention in Cuba were certain of those directly or indirectly concerned in the Cuban sugar industry; that opposed to intervention were the influence of other parties (including at least one prominent sugar planter) whose business would suffer direct injury from war and also the overwhelming preponderance of general business opinion. After the middle of March, 1888, some conservative forces came to think intervention inevitable on humanitarian grounds, but many of the most influential business journals opposed it to the end.[51]

We can now turn to the question whether American business was imperialistic; whether, in other words, business opinion favored schemes for acquiring foreign territory to supply it with markets, fields for capital investment, or commercial and naval stations in distant parts of the world. American business men were not unaware of the struggle for colonies then raging among European nations. Did they feel that the United States ought to participate in that struggle?

We have seen above that the rising tide of prosperity was intimately connected with the increase in American exports, particularly of manufactured articles. That the future welfare of American industry was dependent upon the command of foreign markets was an opinion so common as to appear almost universal. The New York *Journal of Commerce* pointed out, early in 1897, that the nation's industrial plant had been developed far beyond the needs of domestic consumption. In the wire nail industry there was said to be machinery to make four times as many nails as the American markets could consume. Rail mills, locomotive shops, and glass factories were in a similar situation. "Nature has thus destined this country for the industrial supremacy of the world," said the same paper later in the year.[52] When the National Association of Manufacturers met in New York for its annual convention in January, 1898, "the discussion of ways and means for extending this country's trade, and more particularly its export business, was, in fact, almost the single theme of the speakers," according to *Bradstreet's,* which added the comment: "Nothing is more significant of the changed attitude toward this country's foreign trade, manifested by the American manufacturer today as compared with a few years ago, than the almost single devotion which he pays to the subject of possible export-trade extension." [53]

But if business men believed, prior to the opening of the war with Spain, that foreign markets were to be secured through the acquisition of colonies, they were strangely silent about it. It cannot be said that the idea had not been brought to their attention. For almost a decade intellectual and political leaders such as Mahan, Albert Shaw, Murat Halstead, and Senators Lodge, Frye, and Morgan had been urging upon the country the need of an imperialistic program in the interest of its industrial and commercial development.[54] The business world had, to all appearances, remained apathetic or frankly opposed to such a policy, which it regarded as simply one manifestation of dangerous jingoism. A large section of business opinion had, indeed, favored plans for the building of a Nicaraguan canal with governmental assistance,[55] and some spokesmen for business had favored annexation of the Hawaiian islands.[56] But beyond these relatively modest projects, few business men, apparently, wished to go.[57] Two of the most important commercial journals, the New York *Journal of Commerce* and the *Commercial and Financial Chronicle* had stoutly opposed both the canal scheme and Hawaiian annexation.[58] The former satirized the arguments of the proponents of both schemes. "We must certainly build the canal to defend the islands, and it is quite clear that we must acquire the islands . . . in order to defend the canal." The canal was not only unnecessary, but unless fortified at each end and patrolled by two fleets, it would be a positive misfortune. Such protection — "the price of jingoism" — might

> easily cost us $25,000,000 a year, besides the lump sum that will be required for the original investment, and there is absolutely no excuse what-

> ever in our commercial or our political interests for a single step in this long procession of expenses and of complications with foreign powers.[59]

As for Hawaii and Cuba, neither was fit for self-government as a state — and the American constitution provided no machinery for governing dependencies. The Hawaiian Islands would have no military value unless the United States was to build a great navy and take an aggressive attitude in the Pacific.[60] The *Commercial and Financial Chronicle* saw in colonies only useless outposts which must be protected at great expense, and the St. Louis *Age of Steel* warned lest the expansion of the export trade might "lead to territorial greed, as in the case of older nations, the price of which in armaments and militarism offsets the gain made by the spindle and the forge." [61]

Colonies were not only certain to bear a fruit of danger and expense; they were valueless from the commercial point of view. Did not the colonies of Great Britain afford us one of the most valuable of our export markets? [62] Did we not trade as advantageously with Guiana, a British colony, as with independent Venezuela? "Most of our ideas of the the commercial value of conquests, the commercial uses of navies and the commercial advantages of political control," said the *Journal of Commerce,* dated back to times when colonial policies were designed to monopolize colonial trade for the mother country.[63] The *Commercial and Financial Chronicle* believed that the current European enthusiasm for colonies was based on false premises; for although trade often followed the flag, "the trade is not always with the home markets of the colonizer. England and the United States are quite as apt to slip in with their wares under the very Custom-House pennant of the French or German dependency." [64] Outright opposition, such as this, to the idea of colonial expansion is not common in the business periodicals examined; much more common is complete silence on the subject. Positive and negative evidence together seem to warrant the conclusion that American business in general, at the opening of 1898, was either indifferent to imperialism or definitely opposed.[65]

Confidence in the continued expansion of the export trade was based upon faith in the working of *laissez-faire* in a world given over largely to a system of free trade. American industry had reached a point where it could meet the world on more than even terms in both the price and the quality of its products. Given a fair chance, these products would make their own way. Government could aid them, not by acquiring colonial markets but by removing or lowering the barriers that restricted imports of raw materials and exchange commodities. To one who has in mind the subsequent tariff history of the United States, it is surprising to discover the amount of free-trade sentiment which found expression in these months of

1897–1898. The preoccupation of congress with the raising of duties in the Dingley Act was disturbing to those interested in the export trade, "It is pitiful," said the *Journal of Commerce,*

> to see the national legislature bending its whole force to readjusting the trammels of a system which can only obstruct, and closing its eyes to the manifest, though unconscious, struggling of industry for a freedom that will enable it to compete successfully in any market of the world.[66]

The futility of expecting to increase exports while at the same time barring out imports was stressed by more than one writer for business journals,[67] and a change toward free trade in American policy was freely predicted. "We are gradually losing our fear of the bugaboo of cheap foreign labor," said the *Iron Age,* "and are slowly realizing that we hold the key of the position, since there are no indications that European manufacturers will ever displace us in the van of progress." The *American Machinist* declared that the recent growth in the export trade showed that in many lines the tariff was a dead letter, that goods which could be sold under the nose of the foreign producer no longer needed protection in the home market, and that the machinery interests would in all probability bring pressure to bear on Congress "toward action which will equalize these matters." [68] The Chattanooga *Tradesman* was convinced that the great development in the export of manufactures was certain to have upon tariff policy an effect "both broad and radical," and the president of the Baltimore Chamber of Commerce, speaking on the same theme to that body in December, 1897, predicted that "the day is not so far distant when free trade, in some measure, at least, will become part of our political faith." [69]

In a free-trade world, colonies would be of no importance. But if countries to which American producers looked for their markets should adopt restrictive policies, then a change in the American attitude might easily occur. Two events in the late fall of 1897 gave warning that the world at large might not continue hospitable to American products. The first was an address by Count Goluchowski, Austro-Hungarian Foreign Minister, to the Austro-Hungarian Delegations, in which he complained of the "destructive competition with transoceanic countries" and warned that the peoples of Europe "must fight shoulder to shoulder against the common danger, and must arm themselves for the struggle with all the means at their disposal." The twentieth century, he declared, would be "a period marked by a struggle for existence in the politico-commercial sphere," and "the European nations must close their ranks in order successfully to defend their existence." [70]

In the United States, the Austrian's pronouncement was generally interpreted as aimed principally at this country. It caused widespread comment but little serious alarm. Many papers doubted the possibility of any European cooperation to exclude American products, pointing out that a stoppage of trade would injure Europe more than the United States, since we provided Europe with necessities in return for commodities most of which were either luxuries or articles that we could produce ourselves.[71] Even if Europe should exclude our products, thought the New York *Commercial,* we should find an outlet in those other markets now cherished by Europe. This opinion was shared by the Philadelphia *Ledger,* which believed that, though concerted action in Europe might cripple our markets there, our trade with South America and the Far East could not "be directly disturbed through any European alliance." But the New York *Journal of Commerce,* in a thoughtful editorial, took a more serious view of the speech. In their determined quest for markets, it said, the industrial nations of Europe were following two courses: acquisition of colonies and the enactment of discriminatory tariffs. Hitherto each country had worked alone, but now there were signs of the rise of alliances or combinations in tariff policy. Since Austria-Hungary had a trade of but $10,000,000 a year with the United States, the idea put forward by Count Goluchowski must have been initiated elsewhere, and the paper suggested that a probable source was Russia, which had reason to seek to restrict the markets for American staples in both Europe and Asia.[72]

The suspicion voiced by the *Journal of Commerce* that behind the Austrian's speech might lie concealed a threat to the American market in the Far East seemed partially confirmed within a few days, with the coming of news of European aggressions in China. Under the color of retaliation for the death of two German missionaries, a German force, on November 14, expelled the Chinese garrison at Tsingtau, at the mouth of Kiaochow Bay, seized the forts and occupied the port. Eight days later the German Government presented its formal demands, which included a naval station on Kiaochow Bay and the grant of the sole right to build railways and open coal mines in Shantung. By early January, 1898, China had yielded all, and a convention to that effect was signed March 6. Meanwhile, within a week after the occupation of Tsingtau, Russian warships arrived at Port Arthur, and by May, 1898, China had agreed to the cession to Russia for twenty-five years of Port Arthur, Dalny, and other territory in the Liaotung peninsula. Compensating advantages were demanded and received by Great Britain and France, and by July 1, 1898, the partition of China had to all appearances begun.[73]

Here were deeds more ominous than any words could be. They touched American business sentiment in a particularly sensitive spot, for though American trade with China was, in 1897, less than two per cent of its total foreign trade, exports to China in that year were almost double those of 1896, and there was a widespread belief that China was to provide an exceedingly important market for the surplus products of the United States.[74] While some papers made light of the danger to American business presented by the Chinese crisis,[75] and others professed to see positive advantage to the United States in the development of China under European direction,[76] the less optimistic saw a probability that American trade would find itself discriminated against or excluded altogether by the partitioning powers. Mr. Charles Denby, ex-Minister to China, in a note published in the *American Banker,* warned that with the seizure of territory, American commercial treaties with China "fall to the ground, and spheres of influence hostile to American commerce spring into existence." [77] Similar alarm was voiced by numerous papers in all parts of the country,[78] by none more vehemently than the New York *Journal of Commerce.* This paper, which has been heretofore characterized as pacifist, anti-imperialist, and devoted to the development of commerce in a free-trade world, saw the foundation of its faith crumbling as a result of the threatened partition of China. Declaring that free access to the markets of China, with its 400,000,000 people, would largely solve the problem of the disposal of our surplus manufactures, the *Journal* came out not only for a stern insistence upon complete equality of rights in China, but unreservedly also for an isthmian canal, the acquisition of Hawaii, and a material increase in the navy – three measures which it had hitherto strenuously opposed.[79] Nothing could be more significant than the manner in which this paper was converted in a few weeks, justifying its change on each point by the needs of the hour in the Far East.

Finding the department of state, under Secretary Sherman, quite unimpressed by the seriousness of the Chinese situation,[80] the *Journal of Commerce* itself initiated a movement to arouse the executive to a defence of American interests. At the paper's suggestion, a committee on American interests in China was organized in New York to work for concerted action by chambers of commerce in important cities. As a direct result of this propaganda, a committee of the Chamber of Commerce of the State of New York laid before that body on February 3, 1898, a report on "American Treaty Rights in China" and a memorial to the president of the United States. The report summarized the history of the acquisition of commercial rights through treaties with the Chinese Government and argued that those rights were seriously endangered by the recent aggressions of European powers. American products, it pointed out, were already virtually excluded from French Cochin China – an omen of what was to be expected elsewhere if France and other powers made good their positions on Chinese soil. "The Administration at Washington," the report continued,

> seems to be supine about the present menace to those important interests of our citizens in China. . . . Under these circumstances it would seem that unless those concerned in our export trade take steps to agitate the matter and to have their interests safeguarded, nobody else will do it.

The memorial to the president, which was promptly adopted by the chamber, pictured the growing importance of American trade with China and the new dangers threatening it and respectfully urged that steps be taken

> for the prompt and energetic defense of the existing treaty rights of our citizens in China, and for the preservation and protection of their important commercial interests in that Empire.[81]

Within a few weeks similar action was taken by the chambers of commerce or boards of trade of Philadelphia, San Francisco, Baltimore, Boston, and Seattle.[82] Not content with this action, a group of merchants interested in the eastern trade held a meeting on March 3, at 59 Wall Street, New York, to form a permanent organization for the protection of that trade. A few days later, with the cooperation of the New York Chamber of Commerce, they took steps to organize the American China and Japan Association, to foster and safeguard the interests of citizens of the United States and others concerned in the trade with those empires and to secure and disseminate information relating thereto. The organization was not perfected until June 16. By that time the battle of Manila Bay had broadened the American outlook in the Orient, and the organization followed suit, changing its title to the American Asiatic Association and including in its field of interest American trade not only in China and Japan, but also in "the Philippine Islands, and elsewhere in Asia and Oceania." Promptly upon its organization, the association put itself into communication with the department of state, offering its services for consultation or cooperation.[83]

In the light of this widespread and intense interest in the preservation of the Chinese market, we can perhaps understand why American business, which had been, to all appearances, anti-war and anti-imperialist, was filled with sudden enthusiasm at the news of Dewey's victory at Manila Bay. Not only did the news dissipate all fears of a long and costly war and send stock prices rapidly upward; [84] still more important, it seemed to place in American hands, all unexpectedly, the key to the trade of the orient. The attack on the Spanish fleet at Manila had been anticipated for months and well advertised by the American press.[85] Some papers had speculated upon the value of the islands as an American colony and had foreseen that a victory there might greatly alter our relation to the imbroglio in China.[86] But for most, this thought did not occur until arrival of the news that the Spanish fleet was destroyed and Dewey safely in possession of Manila Bay. Then, at last, business men joined the jingoes in their acclaim of imperial conquests. Senator Lodge's exclamation — "We hold the other side of the Pacific, and the value to this country is almost beyond recognition" [87] — was matched by many a formerly conservative business journal. It was not the intrinsic value of the Philippines or their trade that most impressed American writers, though this angle of the subject was not overlooked.[88] Rather, their importance appeared to lie in their position as a gateway to the markets of eastern Asia.

It has been shown that the aggressions of the European powers in China had converted the New York *Journal of Commerce* to the belief that the United States must dig an isthmian canal, acquire Hawaii, and enlarge its navy.[89] The same paper now took the lead in insisting that the newly won vantage point in the Philippines be retained and utilized to uphold American rights in China. However disconcerting might be our possession of Manila to European plans in the Far East, we must deal with it as a "factor in the protection of our interests in that part of the world." Hitherto we had

> allowed Great Britain to fight our battle for an open market in China: with our flag floating within 500 miles of Hong Kong we shall be able to give that policy something more than merely moral support in the future.

There was thus "introduced a most formidable element of resistance to all that France and Russia at least seem to be working for in Asia." To return the islands to Spain or to dispose of them to England or any other power, said the same paper a few days later, "would be an act of inconceivable folly in the face of our imperative future necessities for a basis of naval and military force on the Western shores of the Pacific." [90]

Endorsement of these views came rapidly from all sides. "Some broad-minded men," said the *Wall Street Journal,* May 5,

> believe that the United States could retain enough interest in the Philippines to be sure of a coaling station and a naval base in Asiatic waters, under belief that the breaking up of China will make it necessary for this country to be in a position to protect, not only the existing trade with the far east, but the enormously greater trade likely to be developed in the next 25 years.

The *American Banker,* of May 11, while absolving the United States from entering the war for any selfish purpose, declared that it could not relinquish the territories which it had been forced to seize, with the result that its diplomacy would no longer be a negative quantity in European counsels, "particularly not as respects the inevitable partition of the Chinese Empire. That a war with Spain," it added, "should have transpired at precisely this time, when Europe is tending to divide a considerable section of the inhabited earth, is a coincidence which has a providential air." [91] The *Banker and Tradesman* likewise discerned the hand of Providence in bestowing the Philippines upon the United States at a time when Russia, France, and Germany were threatening American trade in China, and asked whether we could rightly throw away "a possession which would be of such great advantage to us in maintaining and defending our interests in this part of the globe." It asserted later that the answer to the question of the open door in China "was given, as European nations very well know, when Dewey entered Manilla Bay and won his glorious victory." [92] Similar views appeared in the *Age of Steel,* the *Iron Age,* the *United States Investor,* and the *Financial Record. Bradstreet's* thought the possession of Manila would greatly accelerate the growth of American trade in Asia and predicted that that city "might in time even rival Hong Kong as a distributive trade center." The New York *Commercial,* using figures supplied by the bureau of statistics in Washington, pointed out that countries closely adjacent to the Philippines contained 850,000,000 people and purchased over one billion dollars worth of goods a year, mostly articles grown or manufactured in the United States. "With the Philippines as a three-quarter way house, forming a superb trading station, the bulk of this trade should come to this country." [93] The New York Chamber of Commerce, in a report on "American Interests in China," argued that, in face of the prospect that European spheres of influence in China might become permanent territorial acquisitions, the only course by which the United States could protect its interests appeared to be active participation in politics on the "dangerous ground of the Far East" – a participation which might be "hastened and materialized through our possible occupation of the Philippine Islands." [94]

The insistence that the Philippines be retained, for the sake of their own trade and as a gateway to Asiatic markets, was confined to no one section of the country. In the south, business men saw in possession of the islands assurance of the continued growth of the marketing of American cotton goods in China.[95] The Pacific Coast very naturally displayed a lively interest. In Dewey's victory, the *Mining and Scientific Press* saw in earnest that the coast cities would be transformed from the back door to the front door of civilization. "The guns that destroyed the Spanish fleet in Manila Bay thundered a warning to the nations of our approaching commercial supremacy in the Orient." The *Commercial Bulletin of Southern California* believed acquisition of the Philippines would greatly hasten the growth of trans-Pacific trade and asserted it was with this expectation that "Pacific Coast people so generally favor territorial expansion." The *Daily Commercial News and Shipping List,* of San Francisco, thought the coast people would make determined efforts for the retention of the Philippines.[96] The Chamber of Commerce of Seattle and the Chamber of Commerce, Merchants' Association, and Manufacturers' and Producers' Association of San Francisco petitioned the president to retain not only the Philippines, but the Caroline and Ladrone Islands, "and all other lands which are now, or may hereafter be acquired in the present war with Spain," in the interests of humanity and the Oriental trade of the United States.[97] Even James J. Hill, who had been a strong opponent of the war, stated to a newspaper reporter that if it rested with him, he would retain the Philippines. "If you go back in the commercial history of the world," he was reported as saying, "you will find that the people who controlled the trade of the Orient have been the people who held the purse strings of nations." [98]

It must not be inferred that business opinion was unanimous in favor of retaining the Philippines. There was an undercurrent of opposition or indifference. The New York *Journal of Commerce,* just before the signing of the peace protocol, deplored the fact that timid people were shrinking from imperialism and that "the business men of the country are maintaining a deathlike silence." [99] The *Commercial and Financial Chronicle* was cautious, pointing out that Spain's distant possessions had proved its most vulnerable point — a fact from which the United States might learn a lesson — and hoping that the United States might yet find a way to avoid such a dangerous responsibility. The Baltimore *Journal of Commerce* was, in July, strongly opposed to annexation, and two months later held that no one yet knew whether "our position as wetnurse to Cuba, proprietors of Porto Rico and pantata to the Philippines is likely to bring us profit or loss." The *Iron Age,* which early in the summer had been strongly for expansion, was by September harboring qualms as to the real value of colonies to the business man.[100] Everett Frazar, president of the American Asiatic Association, was personally a warm supporter of annexation, but the association held upon its table for months without action a resolution on the subject.[101] The San Francisco *Call,* representing the California Hawaiian sugar interests of the Spreckels family, was strongly opposed to annexation, arguing not only that Anglo Saxons had no aptitude for tropical colonization, but also frankly warning California sugar-beet growers of the danger of competition from Philippine cane sugar.[102]

There is no way of measuring accurately the strength of business opinion for and against the retention of the Philippines. Judging opinion as best we could from the available expressions of it, it seemed safe to conclude that American business in the winter of 1897–1898 was opposed to war and either opposed to colonial expansion or oblivious to the existence of the problem. From similar evidence it seems equally safe to conclude that after the battle of Manila Bay American business became definitely imperialistic — that is, if a wish to retain the Philippines is an evidence of an imperialistic attitude. It seems certain, too, from the prominence given to the Chinese situation in nearly every discussion of the value of the islands, that the conversion of business opinion was accomplished by the combination of a European threat against the freedom of the American market in China, present and prospective, with the dramatic *coup* of the American fleet in a fine harbor so near the Chinese coast. In one paper, the New York *Journal of Commerce,* there appears with beautiful clarity the shift of position induced by the action of the European Powers in China. In November, 1897, against all schemes of colonial or naval expansion; in December, for a canal, Hawaiian annexation, and a big navy; in May and thereafter, for retention of the entire Philippine archipelago and aggressive assertion of American rights in China — the *Journal* reveals a process of thought which perhaps occurred less clearly and consciously in the minds of many business men.

Having concluded that the Philippines were wholesome and digestible, business was disposed to treat itself to more of the same diet. The venture in the Philippines strengthened immeasurably the demand for the annexation of Hawaii. "The battle of Manila Bay," said the *Journal of Commerce* May 31, "makes it imperative that we should establish permanent arrangements which will make the [Hawaiian] islands a half-way house on the road to the Philippines." When the joint resolution for annexation passed congress and received the president's signature on July 7, it was hailed not only as good in itself and in relation to the Philippines, but as the first actual step on the path of imperialism. The resolution, thought *Bradstreet's,* "gave a new direction to the impulse toward expansion, which is seldom missing among the characteristics of great nations." [103] But there were other Pacific islands that beckoned. "Bridge the Pacific!" cried the Philadelphia *Press.* "With the Philippines go the Carolines, a Spanish possession, Samoa and the Hawaiian Islands complete the chain." [104] The war in the Pacific, the prospect of new possessions there, and the voyage of the *Oregon* also gave new force to the demand for an isthmian canal.[105] In the Caribbean, business interests not only insisted that the United States needed Porto Rico for its strategic and commercial value,[106] but suggested that it might prove impossible to adhere to the

Teller Amendment, which had pledged the United States not to annex Cuba. The *Journal of Commerce,* voicing skepticism as to the capacity of the Cubans for orderly government, declared: "The Teller amendment . . . must be interpreted in a sense somewhat different from that which its author intended it to bear." The American flag must float over Cuba until law and order were assured.[107] American covetousness in the Caribbean was not limited to the Spanish islands. As early as March 31, 1898, the New York *Commercial* had advocated the purchase of St. Thomas, in the Danish West Indies, for a naval base.[108] In May, it saw signs that the British West Indies might be interested in coming under the American flag and urged that the Bahamas, Jamaica, and Bermuda be not lost sight of during the war. The *Journal of Commerce,* endorsing the same idea, remarked:

> Our people are now in an expansive mood and there is a deep and strong American sentiment that would rejoice to see the British flag, as well as the Spanish flag, out of the West Indies.[109]

Merchants and manufacturers now saw in colonies a partial solution of the disposal of the surplus of American products. European countries, prejudiced against our goods, said the New York *Commercial* (evidently recalling Count Goluchowski's speech), had acquired colonial markets while we had none; but the acquisition of the Spanish islands would supply the lack; their development by American capital would stimulate the demand for the products of our fields and factories. We should regulate their customs in a manner to favor our own industries and shipping and discourage those of other countries.[110] This procedure was condemned by the *Journal of Commerce,* the *Commercial and Financial Chronicle,* and other journals and organizations, which insisted that after urging the "open door" in China we must adhere to the same principle in our new possessions.[111] But whether the door was to be open or closed to the rest of the world, an active and lucrative trade with the new possessions was widely anticipated. "One way of opening a market is to conquer it . . ." said the *Railway World* in August. "Already our enterprising merchants are beginning to organize to take possession of the markets which our army and navy have opened to them." The Chicago *Inter-Ocean,* in a series of interviews with merchants and manufacturers in several cities, found them

> very generally waking up to the opportunities which the war has brought at a moment when the immense increase of our manufacturing capacity has rendered foreign outlets absolutely necessary to us.

The bureau of statistics reported large numbers of inquiries from all parts of the country, but chiefly from the great producing and business centers, as to the imports of Cuba and Porto Rico.[112] Not only the trade prospects but also the opportunities for American capital and skill to develop the resources of the islands excited enthusiasm. A national bank of Hawaii was organized immediately after passage of the annexation resolution. Similar plans were afoot for Porto Rico and Cuba, and enterprising Americans were studying financial conditions in the Philippines. "Railroad building may be expected to boom in all the islands which may fall under the influence of the United States," said *Rand-McNally Bankers' Monthly*. Cane sugar and tobacco growing would receive an impetus. "The forests may also be made to yield handsome returns, . . . and in fact every industry, so long under the blighting rule of Spain, will be exploited and made to show the advantages accruing from better government and wider enterprise." [113]

American business had yielded reluctantly to the necessity of a war with Spain, forced upon the United States by the distressing situation in Cuba. It had not foreseen, or if it foresaw had feared, the colonial responsibilities to which such a war might lead. But when Dewey's dramatic victory on the first of May offered a Far Eastern base from which the threatened markets in China might be defended, it had gladly accepted the result, and long before the close of the wonderful year 1898, it was building high hopes upon the supposed opportunities for trade and exploitation in a string of dependencies stretching from the Philippines to Porto Rico. As the year expired, spokesmen of the business and financial interests of the country were hailing the "incalculable expansion of the influence of the United States among other nations," [114] or declaring philosophically that the year had "witnessed a complete change in the temper and aspirations of the American people. . . . Our commercial horizon has been broadened," said one of them,

> our ideas of the work which is before us have been greatly magnified, and we have begun to be slightly conscious of the field of development into which this nation is evidently destined to enter.[115]

In no section of American opinion had the year wrought a greater transformation than in that of the business men.

That "Splendid Little War" in Historical Perspective

WALTER LAFEBER

Walter LaFeber, who studied under Fred Harvey Harrington and William A. Williams at the University of Wisconsin, is a worthy successor to the radical humanitarian tradition of his professors. His effort to synthesize the various approaches to understanding the Spanish-American War is brilliantly expressed in this short essay. Building directly on his own research — as embodied in his splendidly researched and argued The New Empire: An Interpretation of American Expansion, 1860–1898 *(Ithaca, N.Y.: Cornell University Press, 1963) — as well as on the work of his predecessors, LaFeber offers a truly integrated interpretation. Like William A. Williams, he puts economic data in a broad social framework that avoids the pitfalls of economic determinism without diluting the importance of economic factors. Moreover, he links the past to the present directly and profoundly. Some troubling problems remain. Did McKinley and his associates* accurately *assess the needs of the American system? As it became clear, over time, that the system could function and grow without China's fabled markets, why was that myth so tenaciously maintained and so selectively used?*

The "splendid little war" of 1898, as Secretary of State John Hay termed it at the time, is rapidly losing its splendor for those concerned with American foreign policy in the 1960s. Over the past decade few issues in the country's diplomatic history have aroused academics more than the causes of the Spanish-American War, and in the last several years the argument has become not merely academic, but a starting point in the debate over how the United States evolved into a great power, and more particularly how Americans got involved in the maelstrom of Asian nationalism. The line from the conquest of the Philippines in 1898 to the attempted pacification of Vietnam in 1968 is not straight, but it is quite traceable, and if Frederick Jackson Turner was correct when he observed in the

Reprinted by permission of the author and the publisher from *The Texas Quarterly,* Vol. XI, No. 4 (Winter, 1968), pp. 89–98.

1890s that "The aim of history, then, is to know the elements of the present by understanding what came into the present from the past," the causes of the war in 1898 demand analysis from our present viewpoint.

Historians have offered four general interpretations to explain these causes. First, the war has been traced to a general impulse for war on the part of American public opinion. This interpretation has been illustrated in a famous cartoon showing President William McKinley, in the bonnet and dress of a little old lady, trying to sweep back huge waves marked "Congress" and "public opinion," with a very small broom. The "yellow journalism" generated by the Hearst-Pulitzer rivalry supposedly both created and reflected this sentiment for war. A sophisticated and useful version of this interpretation has been advanced by Richard Hofstadter. Granting the importance of the Hearst-Pulitzer struggle, he has asked why these newspaper titans were able to exploit public opinion. Hofstadter has concluded that psychological dilemmas arising out of the depression of the 1890s made Americans react somewhat irrationally because they were uncertain, frightened, and consequently open to exploitation by men who would show them how to cure their frustrations through overseas adventures. In other words, the giddy minds of the 1890s could be quieted by foreign quarrels.

A second interpretation argues that the United States went to war for humanitarian reasons, that is, to free the Cubans from the horrors of Spanish policies and to give the Cubans democratic institutions. That this initial impulse resulted within ten months in an American protectorate over Cuba and Puerto Rico, annexation of the Philippines, and American participation in quarrels on the mainland of Asia itself, is explained as accidental, or, more familiarly, as done in a moment of "aberration" on the part of American policy-makers.

A third interpretation emphasizes the role of several Washington officials who advocated a "Large Policy" of conquering a vast colonial empire in the Caribbean and Western Pacific. By shrewd maneuvering, these few imperialists pushed the vacillating McKinley and a confused nation into war. Senator Henry Cabot Lodge, of Massachusetts, Captain Alfred Thayer Mahan, of the U.S. Navy, and Theodore Roosevelt, Assistant Secretary of the Navy in 1897–1898, are usually named as the leaders of the "Large Policy" contingent.

A fourth interpretation believes the economic drive carried the nation into war. This drive emanated from the rapid industrialization which characterized American society after the 1840s. The immediate link between this industrialization and the war of 1898 was the economic depression which afflicted the nation in the quarter-century after 1873. Particularly important were the 1893–1897 years when Americans endured the worst of the plunge. Government and business leaders, who were both intelligent and rational, believed an oversupply of goods created the depression. They finally accepted war as a means of opening overseas markets in order to alleviate domestic distress caused by the overproduction. For thirty years the economic interpretation dominated historians' views of the war, but in 1936 Professor Julius Pratt conclusively demonstrated that business journals did not want war in the early months of 1898. He argued instead the "Large Policy" explanation, and from that time to the present, Professor Pratt's interpretation has been pre-eminent in explaining the causes of the conflict.

As I shall argue in a moment, the absence of economic factors in causing the war has been considerably exaggerated. At this point, however, a common theme which unites the first three interpretations should be emphasized. Each of the three deals with a superficial aspect of American life; each is peculiar to 1898, and none is rooted in the structure, the bed-rock, of the nation's history. This theme is important, for it means that if the results of the war were distasteful and disadvantageous (and on this historians do largely agree because of the divisive problems which soon arose in the Philippines and Cuba), those misfortunes were endemic to episodes unique to 1898. The peculiarities of public sentiment or the Hearst-Pulitzer rivalry, for example, have not reoccurred; the wide-spread humanitarian desire to help Cubans has been confined to 1898; and the banding together of Lodge, Mahan, and Roosevelt to fight for "Large Policies" of the late 1890s was never repeated by the three men. Conspiracy theories, moreover, seldom explain history satisfactorily.

The fourth interpretation has different implications. It argues that if the economic was the primary drive toward war, criticism of that war must begin not with irrational factors or flights of humanitarianism or a few stereotyped figures, but with the basic structure of the American system.

United States foreign policy, after all, is concerned primarily with the nation's domestic system and only secondarily with the systems of other nations. American diplomatic history might be defined as the study of how United States relations with other nations are used to insure the survival and increasing prosperity of the American system. Foreign policy-makers are no more motivated by altruism than is the rest of the human race, but are instead involved in making a system function at home. Secretary of State, as the Founding Fathers realized, is an apt title for the man in charge of American foreign policy.

Turning this definition around, it also means that domestic affairs are the main determinant of foreign policy. When viewed within this matrix, the diplomatic events of the 1890s are no longer aberrations or the results of conspiracies and drift; American policymakers indeed grabbed greatness with both hands. As for accident or chance, they certainly exist in history, but become more meaningful when one begins with J. B. Bury's definition of "chance": "The valuable collision of two or more independent chains of causes." The most fruitful approach to the war of 1898 might be from the inside out (from the domestic to the foreign), and by remembering that chance is "the valuable collision of two or more independent chains of causes."

Three of these "chains" can be identified: the economic crisis of the 1890s which caused extensive and dangerous maladjustments in American society; the opportunities which suddenly opened in Asia after 1895 and in the Caribbean and the Pacific in 1898, opportunities which officials began to view as poultices, if not cure-alls, for the illnesses at home; and a growing partnership between business and government which reached its nineteenth-century culmination in the person of William McKinley. In April 1898, these "chains" had a "valuable collision" and war resulted.

The formation of the first chain is the great success story of American history. Between 1850 and 1910 the average manufacturing plant in the country multiplied its capital thirty-nine times, its number of wage-earners nearly seven times, and the value of its output by more than nineteen times. By the mid-1890s American iron and steel producers joked about their successful underselling of the vaunted British steel industry not only in world markets, but also in the vicinity of Birmingham, England, itself. The United States traded more in international markets than any nation except Great Britain.

But the most accelerated period of this development, 1873–1898, was actually twenty-five years of boom hidden in twenty-five years of bust. That quarter-century endured the longest and worst depression in the nation's history. After brief and unsatisfactory recoveries in the mid-1880s and early 1890s, the economy reached bottom in 1893. Unparalleled social and economic disasters struck. One out of every six laborers was unemployed, with most of the remainder existing on substandard wages; not only weak firms but many companies with the best credit ratings were forced to close their doors; the unemployed slept in the streets; riots erupted in Brooklyn, California, and points in between, as in the calamitous Pullman Strike in Chicago; Coxey's Army of broken farmers and unemployed laborers made their famous march on Washington; and the Secretary of State, Walter Quentin Gresham, remarked privately in 1894 that he saw "symptoms of revolution" appearing. Federal troops were dispatched to Chicago and other urban areas, including a cordon which guarded the Federal Treasury building in New York City.

Faced with the prospect of revolution and confronted with an economy that had almost ground to a stop, American businessmen and political officials faced alternative policies: they could attempt to re-examine and reorient the economic system, making radical modifications in the means of distribution and particularly the distribution of wealth; or they could look for new physical frontiers, following the historic tendency to increase production and then ferreting out new markets so the surplus, which the nation supposedly was unable to consume, could be sold elsewhere and Americans then put back to work on the production lines.

To the business and political communities, these were not actually alternatives at all. Neither of those communities has been known historically for political and social radicalism. Each sought security, not new political experiments. Some business firms tried to find such security by squashing competitors. Extremely few, however, searched for such policies as a federal income tax. Although such a tax narrowly passed through Congress in 1894, the Supreme Court declared it unconstitutional within a year and the issue would not be resurrected for another seventeen years. As a result, business and political leaders accepted the solution which was traditional, least threatening to their own power, and (apparently) required the least risk: new markets. Secretary of the Treasury John G. Carlisle summarized this conclusion in his public report of 1894: "The prosperity of our people, therefore, depends largely upon their ability to sell their surplus products in foreign markets at remunerative prices."

This consensus included farmers and the labor movement among others, for these interests were no more ingenious in discovering new solutions than were businessmen. A few farmers and laborers murmured ominously about some kind [of] political and/or economic revolution, but Richard Hofstadter seems correct in suggesting that in a sense Populism was reactionary rather than radical. The agrarians in the Populist movement tended to look back to a Jeffersonian utopia. Historians argue this point, but beyond dispute is the drive by farmers, including Populists, for foreign markets. The agrarians acted out of a long and successful tradition, for they had sought overseas customers since the first tobacco surplus in Virginia three hundred and fifty years before. Farmers initially framed the expansionist arguments and over three centuries created the context for the growing consensus on the desirability of foreign markets, a consensus which businessmen and others would utilize in the 1890s.

The farmers' role in developing this theme in American history became highly ironic in the late nineteenth century, for businessmen not only adopted the argument that overseas markets were necessary, but added a proviso that agrarian interests would have to be suppressed in the process. Industrialists observed that export charts demonstrated the American economy to be depending more upon industrial than agrarian exports. To allow industrial goods to be fully competitive in the world market, however, labor costs would have to be minimal, and cheap bread meant sacrificing the farmers. Fully comprehending this argument, agrarians reacted bitterly. They nevertheless continued searching for their own overseas markets, agreeing with the industrialist that the traditional method of discovering new outlets provided the key to prosperity, individualism, and status.

The political conflict which shattered the 1890s revolved less around the question of whether conservatives could carry out a class solution than the question of which class would succeed in carrying out a conservative solution. This generalization remains valid even when the American labor movement is examined for its response to the alternatives posed. This movement, primarily comprised of the newly-formed American Federation of Labor, employed less than 3 per cent of the total number of employed workers in nonfarm occupations. In its own small sphere of influence, its membership largely consisted of skilled workers living in the East. The AFL was not important in the West or South, where the major discontent seethed. Although Samuel Gompers was known by some of the more faint-hearted as a "socialist," the AFL's founder never dramatized any radical solutions for the restructuring of the economy. He was concerned with obtaining more money, better hours, and improved working conditions for the Federation's members. Gompers refused, moreover, to use direct political action to obtain these benefits, content to negotiate within the corporate structure which the businessman had created. The AFL simply wanted more, and when overseas markets seemed to be a primary source of benefits, Gompers did not complain. As Louis Hartz has noted, "wage consciousness," not "class consciousness," triumphed.

The first "chain of causes" was marked by a consensus on the need to find markets overseas. Fortunately for the advocates of this policy, another "chain," quite complementary to the first, began to form beyond American borders. By the mid-1890s, American merchants, missionaries, and ship captains had been profiting from Asian markets for more than a century. Between 1895 and 1900, however, the United States for the first time became a mover-and-pusher in Asian affairs.

In 1895 Japan defeated China in a brief struggle that now appears to be one of the most momentous episodes in the nineteenth century. The Japanese emerged as the major Asian power, the Chinese suddenly seemed to be incapable of defending their honor or existence, Chinese nationalism began its peculiar path to the 1960s, and European powers which had long lusted after Asian markets now seized a golden opportunity. Russia, Germany, France, and ultimately Great Britain initiated policies designed to carve China and Manchuria into spheres of influence. Within a period of months, the Asian mainland suddenly became the scene of international power politics at its worst and most explosive.

The American reaction to these events has been summarized recently by Professor Thomas McCormick: "The conclusion of the Sino-Japanese War left Pandora's box wide open, but many Americans mistook it for the Horn of Plenty." Since the first American ship sailed to sell goods in China in 1784, Americans had chased that most mysterious phantom, the China Market. Now, just at the moment when key interest groups agreed that overseas markets could be the salvation of the 1890s crisis, China was almost miraculously opening its doors to the glutted American factories and farms. United States trade with China jumped significantly after 1895, particularly in the critical area of manufactures; by 1899 manufactured products accounted for more than 90 per cent of the nation's exports to the Chinese, a quadrupling of the amount sent in 1895. In their moment of need, Americans had apparently discovered a Horn of Plenty.

But, of course, it was Pandora's box. The ills which escaped from the box were threefold. Least important for the 1890s, a nascent Chinese nationalism appeared. During the next quarter-century, the United States attempted to minimize the effects of this nationalism either by cooperating with Japan or European powers to isolate and weaken the Chinese, or by siding with the most conservative groups within the nationalist movement. Americans also faced the competition of European and Japanese products, but they were nevertheless confident in the power of their newly-tooled industrial powerhouse. Given a "fair field and no favor," as the Secretary of State phrased the wish in 1900, Americans would undersell and defeat any competitors. But could fair fields and no favors be guaranteed? Within their recently-created spheres of influence European powers began to grant themselves trade preferences, thus effectively shutting out American competition. In 1897, the American business community and the newly-installed administration of William McKinley began to counter these threats.

The partnership between businessmen and politicians, in this case the McKinley administration, deserves emphasis, for if the businessman hoped to exploit Asian markets he required the aid of the politician. Americans could compete against British or Russian manufacturers in Asia, but they could not compete against, say, a Russian manufacturer who could turn to his government and through pressure exerted by that government on Chinese officials receive a prize railroad contract or banking concession. United States businessmen could only compete against such business-government coalitions if Washington officials helped. Only then would the field be fair and the favors equalized. To talk of utilizing American "rugged individualism" and a free enterprise philosophy in the race for the China market in the 1890s was silly. There consequently emerged an American policy-making a classic example of the business community and the government grasping hands and, marching shoulder to shoulder, leading the United States to its destiny of being a major power on a Far Eastern frontier. As one high Republican official remarked in the mid-1890s: "diplomacy is the management of international business."

William McKinley fully understood the need for such a partnership. He had grown to political maturity during the 1870s when, as one Congressman remarked, "The House of Representatives was like an auction room where more valuable considerations were disposed of under the speaker's hammer than in any other place on earth." Serving as governor of Ohio during the 1890s depression, McKinley learned firsthand about the dangers posed by the economic crisis (including riots in his state which he terminated with overwhelming displays of military force). The new Chief Executive believed there was nothing necessarily manifest about Manifest Destiny in American history, and his administration was the first in modern American history which so systematically and completely committed itself to helping businessmen, farmers, laborers, and missionaries in solving their problems in an industrializing, supposedly frontierless America. Mr. Dooley caught this aggressive side of the McKinley administration when he described the introduction of a presidential speech: "Th' proceedin's was opened with a prayer that Providence might r-remain undher th' protection iv th' administration."

Often characterized as a creature of his campaign manager Mark Hanna, or as having, in the famous but severely unjust words of Theodore Roosevelt, the backbone of a chocolate eclair, McKinley was, as Henry Adams and others fully understood, a master of men. McKinley was never pushed into a policy he did not want to accept. Elihu Root, probably the best mind and most acute observer who served in the McKinley cabinets, commented that on most important matters the President had his ideas fixed, but would convene the Cabinet, direct the members toward his own conclusions, and thereby allow the Cabinet to think it had formulated the policy. In responding to the problems and opportunities in China, however, McKinley's power to exploit that situation was limited by events in the Caribbean.

In 1895 revolution had broken out in Cuba. By 1897 Americans were becoming increasingly belligerent on this issue for several reasons: more than $50,000,000 of United States investments on the island were endangered; Spaniards were treating some Cubans inhumanely; the best traditions of the Monroe Doctrine had long dictated that a European in the Caribbean was a sty in the eye of any red-blooded American; and, finally, a number of Americans, not only Lodge, Roosevelt, and Mahan, understood the strategic and political relationship of Cuba to a proposed isthmian canal. Such a canal would provide a short-cut to the west coast of Latin America as well as to the promised markets of Asia. Within six months after assuming office, McKinley demanded that the island be pacified or the United States would take a "course of action which the time and the transcendent emergency may demand." Some Spanish reforms followed, but in January 1898, new revolts wracked Havana and a month later the *Maine* dramatically sank to the bottom of Havana harbor.

McKinley confronted the prospect of immediate war. Only two restraints appeared. First, a war might lead to the annexation of Cuba, and the multitude of problems (including racial) which had destroyed Spanish authority would be dumped on the United States. Neither the President nor his close advisers wanted to leap into the quicksands of noncontiguous, colonial empire. The business community comprised a second restraining influence. By mid-1897 increased exports, which removed part of the agricultural and industrial glut, began to extricate the country from its quarter-century of turmoil. Finally seeing the light at the end of a long and treacherous tunnel, businessmen did not want the requirements of a war economy to jeopardize the growing prosperity.

These two restraints explain why the United States did not go to war in 1897, and the removal of these restraints indicates why war occurred in April 1898. The first problem disappeared because McKinley and his advisers entertained no ideas of warring for colonial empire in the Caribbean. After the war Cuba would be freed from Spain and then ostensibly returned to the Cubans to govern. The United States would retain a veto power over the more important policy decisions made on the island. McKinley discovered a classic solution in which the United States enjoyed the power over, but supposedly little of the responsibility for, the Cubans.

The second restraint disappeared in late March 1898, exactly at the time of McKinley's decision to send the final ultimatum to Madrid. The timing is crucial. Professor Pratt observed in 1936 that the business periodicals began to change their antiwar views in mid-March 1898, but he did not elaborate upon this point. The change is significant and confirms the advice McKinley received from a trusted political adviser in New York City who cabled on March 25 that the larger corporations would welcome war. The business journals and their readers were beginning to realize that the bloody struggle in Cuba and the resulting inability of the United States to operate at full-speed in Asian affairs more greatly endangered economic recovery than would a war.

McKinley's policies in late March manifested these changes. This does not mean that the business community manipulated the President, or that he was repaying those businessmen who had played vital roles in his election in 1896. Nor does it mean that McKinley thought the business community was forcing his hand or circumscribing his policies in late March. The opinions and policies of the President and the business community had been hammered out in the furnace of a terrible depression and the ominous changes in Asia. McKinley and pivotal businessmen emerged from these unforgettable experiences sharing a common conclusion: the nation's economy increasingly depended upon overseas markets, including the whole of China; that to develop these markets not only a business-government partnership but also tranquillity was required; and, finally, however paradoxical it might seem, tranquillity could be insured only through war against Spain. Not for the first or last time, Americans believed that to have peace they would have to wage war. Some, including McKinley, moved on to a final point. War, if properly conducted, could result in a few select strategic bases in the Pacific (such as Hawaii, Guam, and Manila) which would provide the United States with potent starting-blocks in the race for Asian markets. McKinley sharply distinguished between controlling such bases and trying to rule formally over an extensive territorial empire. In the development of the "chains of causes" the dominant theme was the economic, although not economic in the narrow sense. As discussed in the 1890s, business recovery carried most critical political and social implications.

Some historians argue that McKinley entered the war in confusion and annexed the Philippines in a moment of aberration. They delight in quoting the President's announcement to a group of Methodist missionaries that he decided to annex the Philippines one night when after praying he heard a mysterious voice. Most interesting, however, is not that the President heard a reassuring voice, but how the voice phrased its advice. The voice evidently outlined the points to be considered; in any case, McKinley numbered them in order, demonstrating, perhaps, that either he, the voice, or both had given some thought to putting the policy factors in neat and logical order. The second point is of particular importance: "that we could not turn them [the Philippines] over to France or Germany — our commercial rivals in the Orient — that would be bad business and discreditable. . . ." Apparently everyone who had been through the 1890s knew the dangers of "bad business." Even voices.

Interpretations which depend upon mass opinion, humanitarianism, and "Large Policy" advocates do not satisfactorily explain the causes of the war. Neither, however, does Mr. Dooley's famous one-sentence definition of American imperialism in 1898: "Hands acrost th' sea an' into somewan's pocket." The problem of American expansion is more complicated and historically rooted than that flippancy indicates. George Eliot once observed, "The happiest nations, like the happiest women, have no history." The

United States, however, endured in the nineteenth century a history of growing industrialism, supposedly closing physical frontiers, rapid urbanization, unequal distribution of wealth, and an overdependence upon export trade. These historical currents clashed in the 1890s. The result was chaos and fear, then war and empire.

In 1898, McKinley and the business community wanted peace, but they also sought benefits which only a war could provide. Viewed from the perspective of the 1960s, the Spanish-American conflict can no longer be viewed as only a "splendid little war." It was a war to preserve the American system.

CHINA: THE MISSING LINK

The Influence of Strategy upon History: The Acquisition of the Philippines

JOHN A. S. GRENVILLE AND GEORGE BERKELEY YOUNG

Almost everyone who has written about the Spanish-American War has been led, by virtue of that war's consequences if not its origins, to discuss the Far East. How, in the course of forcing stability on Cuba, did the United States end up with a Pacific empire? The disparity between cause and consequence seems vast, unaccountable. Surely somewhere such ends were already implicit in the means adopted. The three essays in this section explore the relationship between the Far East and the Caribbean from quite different perspectives.

John A. S. Grenville and George Berkeley Young, both of whom worked at Yale with Samuel Flagg Bemis, offer a sophisticated updating of Bemis's famous "great aberration" theory: The acquisition of an empire was the result of a "historical accident," the overlapping of an international Far Eastern crisis with the Spanish-American War. In the course of arguing this position, Grenville and Young also dispose of some hard-dying myths. After their research, the notion of Theodore Roosevelt as the sly architect of United States naval policy can no longer be taken seriously.

The narrow focus of Grenville and Young allows us to see events in sharp detail, but it suffers the defects of its virtues. To assert that new evidence confirms Samuel Bemis's old interpretation that "no concept of American diplomacy as it had developed before the spring of 1898 lay behind the occupation of the Philippines" is to ignore the new interpretations of old *evidence advanced by such historians as LaFeber and Williams. In this connection, the student might also want to read Richard Van Alstyne's fascinating book,* The Rising American Empire *(New York: Oxford University Press, 1960), which successfully traces aspects of the occupation of the Philippines to concepts of American diplomacy as old as the nation itself.*

Mahan studied history to distill from it the general principles of strategy. The influence of strategy on history still remains to be systematically explored. The attack on the Philippines during the Spanish-American War is a fascinating illustration of the impact of strategic decisions on the relations of the great powers. The occupation of the islands has profoundly influenced American diplomacy in the twentieth century. The significance of the event is generally acknowledged, but there is little agreement on why the United States went there in the first place. In a well-known phrase, one distinguished American diplomatic historian has referred to the event as a "great aberration." Others have sought to show that the Philippine adventure was the logical outcome of earlier American policies. To support their argument they have pointed to America's growing concern in the Far East, stimulated as it was by missionaries and merchants. But by the turn of the century optimism gave way to a more sober appreciation of the obstacles to American influence. When the Kaiser seized Kiaochow in November 1897 and Russia sent a fleet to Port Arthur, it appeared plain to everyone, and to none more so than Minister Denby in Peking, that the partition of China was at hand, and with it the possible ruin of America's future commerce. The merchants reacted strongly to this threat to their future prospects. The breach of the principle of the open door in Asia, one historian has recently concluded, "constrained the administration to make thorough preparations for offensive operations in the Pacific." [1] *

Other evidence apparently supports the notion that some Americans had cast covetous eyes on the Philippines before the battle of Manila Bay, on May 1, 1898. "The Philippines are logically our first target," Senator Albert J. Beveridge had declared in Boston on April 27, 1898.[2] A few days later, but before Dewey's victory was officially announced in Washington, Senator Lodge wrote: "If, as now seems almost certain, we have captured Manila, we ought I think, to hold that great strategic point in the

Reprinted by permission from John A. S. Grenville and George Berkeley Young, *Politics, Strategy, and American Diplomacy: Studies in Foreign Policy, 1873–1917* (New Haven: Yale University Press, 1966), pp. 267–296.
* [See pp. 169–171 for notes to this article. — Ed.]

East, which would enable us to get our share of the Pacific trade." [3] Such statements have lent support to the "conspiracy theory" — that a few men in important places had been planning for some time to seize the Philippines.

Dewey's battle of May 1 captured the imagination of the American people. The business community involved in the China trade, previously fearful that the Administration was not lending sufficient support to American interests in China, now clamored for the Philippines as a valuable market, the gateway to the Orient. We have ample reason for believing that the American interest in the Chinese market was large and vocal. But — and this is really the question — did anyone look upon American possession of the Philippines archipelago as likely to further American commercial or strategic policies in China before rumors of Dewey's impending attack on the Philippines reached the United States from Europe? There appears to be no trace of such sentiment earlier than March 1898.

Before March, the attention of the business community had been focused on China and not on the Philippines. That was also true of the State Department. When, in December 1897 and January 1898, the pressure on the Administration for a more active China policy had dramatically increased, Dewey was instructed to reconnoiter and advise on the acquisition of a Chinese, not a Philippine, base.[4] Congress and the American public meanwhile were prepared to fight for Cuba. They did not foresee that a war with Spain would change America's role in the Far East.

The dramatic story of how Roosevelt, during Secretary Long's temporary absence from the Navy Department, sent his famous telegram to Commodore Dewey on February 25, 1898, to prepare for the attack on Manila, is a commonplace of the history books. Roosevelt had not acted impulsively. He was carrying out, so we are told, a plot he and Lodge had concocted to seize the Philippines in the event of war with Spain. Commodore Dewey, so the story runs, was made privy to the secret when Lodge and Roosevelt had helped to secure his appointment to the command of the Asiatic Squadron some months earlier.[5]

This tale belongs with the legends of history. The order to attack Manila was finally sanctioned by the President at a conference in the White House on Sunday, April 24, 1898.[6] He was, moreover, acting according to a war plan worked out before Roosevelt had joined the Navy Department. This secret war plan was known to President McKinley, Secretary of the Navy Long, and the chiefs of the Navy Department; it was under constant revision during the years before the outbreak of the conflict. Neither Roosevelt nor Lodge played any part in its formulation. It was not the politicians but a group of officers in the Navy Department and at the Naval

War College who had initiated the Philippine attack. Now it might be supposed that these strategists in planning an attack on the Philippines had from the outset intended to strengthen the United States' position in the Far East. But this was not their objective, although the importance of the Far East to the United States had not been overlooked by naval officers.

American naval officers had for some years been concerned about the growing hostility of Japan toward the United States. In March 1893, soon after his retirement from the command of the Asiatic Squadron, Rear Admiral Belknap warned Secretary of the Navy Herbert that the Japanese were pursuing a plan of colonization not only in Korea and Hawaii but in Mexico and Central America as well. Japan's victory over China and her unfriendly response to the projected Hawaiian annexation sharpened these fears. In September 1897, Captain Barker, Commanding Officer of the battleship *Oregon,* warned the Navy Department that he regarded the danger from Japan as more serious than the threat of Spain. The Japanese, he claimed, had designs on the Nicaraguan Canal, Mexico, and Central and South America. He hoped his warnings would induce the Administration to send more warships to the Pacific while there was still time; the United States would have to provide adequately for the defense of Hawaii and the Pacific shore.[7] But it occurred to no naval officer to advocate the seizure of a base in the Philippines in order to defend Hawaii or the Pacific coast. Nor did American naval officers suggest that the Philippines should be annexed to strengthen American claims in China; neither missionaries nor merchants had taken an interest in the islands. In short, the attack on the islands was not influenced by any of the pressures that were increasing the American involvement in the Far East.

When Admiral McNair handed over the command of the Asiatic Squadron to Dewey in December 1897, he commented on the conditions of the ships, their disposition, and the American interests he had been charged to protect. He discussed China, Korea, and Japanese designs on Hawaii. But his reference to the Philippines was brief. "The newspapers have contained accounts, for some time past, of the rebellion in progress in the Philippine Islands. No official information has been received in relation thereto, and no information of any sort that shows American interests to be affected." [8]

The arguments employed later to persuade the Administration to retain the islands did not occur before the battle of Manila Bay. One conclusion appears to be inescapable: but for the existence of a war plan that bears the signature of Lieutenant William Wirt Kimball, the United States would not have extended her sovereignty over the Philippine Islands.

It is one of the ironies of history that the projected attack on the Philippines was no more than a secondary consideration in the general strategy of Kimball's war plan. The main purpose of the descent on Manila was not to strengthen America's commerce in the Far East but to weaken Spain by depriving it of the revenues it derived from the islands. The Asiatic Squadron was assigned the tasks first of destroying the inferior Spanish warships in Philippine waters and then of capturing Manila, and at the same time blockading all the principal ports of the islands so that, as Kimball put it, "the release of our hold on them may be used as an inducement to Spain to make peace after the liberation of Cuba." [9]

The plan was evidently not the work of Kimball alone. On Admiral Luce's suggestion, the Naval War College had in the summer of 1895 begun to study the strategic implications of a war with Spain. Replying to one of Luce's letters, Captain Taylor, President of the War College, cannily prophesied: "What you say about Cuba and Spain interests me very much and will . . . produce greater results than you fancy." [10] The plan was worked out in collaboration with the Office of Naval Intelligence; it was named after Kimball, the officer who prepared the final draft. Kimball undertook the task at the request of his immediate superior, Lieutenant Commander Richard Wainwright, Chief Intelligence Officer.[11] By a curious chance, the Office of Naval Intelligence was presided over in 1896 by the Assistant Secretary of the Navy, William McAdoo, the very man who eight years earlier had ridiculed the notion of a War College. Once in office, however, McAdoo became an enthusiastic convert to strategic planning. When handing his post over to Theodore Roosevelt in March 1897, he pointed with pride to the work done by the Naval War College and the Office of Naval Intelligence, advising Roosevelt that "in case of war or any foreign trouble it [the Office of Naval Intelligence] is the first place to go to get accurate information. The War College problems are deposited there. It is a good office, well kept up, and possibly the best anywhere . . . We are abreast, if not ahead, of some of the other countries in these matters." [12] Roosevelt took over an efficient working organization; he also inherited the war plan against Spain. The search for the "culprits" of the attack on the Philippines thus leads to the planners – Taylor, Wainwright, Kimball, and McAdoo – and not to the agents – Roosevelt and Dewey.

Lacking executive guidance about the objectives of American policy in the event of war, the officers who drew up the war plan made their own political assumptions. In 1896 they simply took for granted that the United States did not desire any of Spain's possessions for itself. Thus the war plan begins with a discussion of "the object of the war" and of "the results desired":

> It is apparent that the real cause of the war will be friction between the United States and Spain upon the Cuban question . . . Whatever may

> be the especial act which leads to the rupture of peaceful relations, it would seem to be a foregone conclusion that the object of the war to be waged by the United States would be to liberate Cuba from Spanish rule, to exact from Spain a fair war indemnity for the cost of the war, and to force a settlement of the particular question which was the direct cause of the outbreak of hostilities.

Kimball explicitly explained that he meant by the "liberation of Cuba": the establishment of a Cuban Republic. These suppositions about Cuba and the Philippines, although they did not harmonize with Olney's and McKinley's policies, influenced the basic strategy of the war. The fighting role was primarily assigned to the Navy, and not to the Army.

> [A naval campaign] would be attractive from a diplomatic or sentimental rather than a purely strategic point of view, because it would contemplate the establishment of a Cuban Republic through the efforts of its own citizens within its own borders, aided only by the extraterritorially applied sea power of the United States, instead of a conquest and occupation of Spanish territory by an organized army of invasion from this country . . . a resort to invasion would be necessary only in case naval operations alone were not effective, or required a longer time to be made so than the policy of the United States government in regard to the duration of the war could allow.[13]

When McKinley decided on the invasion of Cuba after the conflict had begun, the Army command was not equal to the task of organizing a landing quickly and efficiently. No adequate preparations had been made.

A purely naval war was attractive for other reasons. It was likely to involve the fewest American casualties and would cost less than a large-scale military operation. It was a cheap war; the successful naval campaign would cripple Spanish trade and humble Spanish pride. In any case, no other way of injuring Spain would be open to the United States should the war break out in the rainy season — so argued the naval officers.

The essence of the naval plan of operations was to make America's sea power felt wherever Spanish ships could be engaged by an equal or superior United States naval force. The immediate role of one part of the fleet was to blockade Cuba at the outset of the war. It was anticipated that the main naval battle of the war would occur when Spain sent its battlefleet to the relief of Cuba. The North Atlantic Squadron was thus assigned the task of gaining command of the Florida Strait, so that the Spanish fleet might be intercepted and destroyed before it could reach the shelter of the fortress guns in Havana harbor.

American naval superiority, the strategists believed, would also permit the United States to engage in offensive operations beyond the Caribbean theater. The Mediterranean coast of Spain was ill defended, and the seaports of Barcelona and Malaga were open to attack. In the Far East, Spanish ships guarding Manila were no match for the Asiatic Squadron. But without bases in the Far East and Europe, the difficulty of securing adequate and reliable coaling facilities presented the principal obstacle to striking at Spain and her colonies. The strategists hoped to solve the problem in Europe by chartering British colliers to meet the United States warships. But in the Far East "the difficulty of arranging a flying coaling base for such a squadron, and the strategic importance of Manila would seem to point to the latter place as a military objective to be reached even at the expense of sending an armored ship or two for its attainment." Thus injury to Spain by a strike at the Philippines involved the seizure of Manila. Kimball and his colleagues could not have thought this difficult, since they calculated that the American cruisers would only need to be reinforced by "an armored ship or two." They never dreamed that the American Army would be sent to capture and hold the principal islands. The plan merely envisaged the occupation of Manila as a hostage of war. And so it came about that a war plan helped to change the course of American history.

A group of officers who were constituted as a special War Board kept the plan for the Caribbean theater of operations under constant review during the twenty-two months that elapsed between formulation and the conflict with Spain.[14] Naval officers in Washington gave little further attention to developments in the Far East. Instead, the defenses of Havana were carefully studied, reports from Europe on the state of the Spanish Navy were evaluated, and Mahan contributed detailed proposals for the blockade of Cuba.

But two interesting questions still remain to be answered. How was it that Roosevelt secured the credit? Why did he send the famous telegram of February 25 to Dewey on that day? Roosevelt owed this good fortune to his friend Senator Lodge, who in his book *The War with Spain* first revealed how Roosevelt – with commendable foresight – had instructed Dewey to make preparations to attack Manila in good time. But it had not been Lodge's first intention to dramatize the episode. When collecting material for his book in the autumn of 1898, Lodge wrote to the Navy Department for help. He already knew the substance of the famous telegram; he had fortuitously been present in Roosevelt's office on the day it was sent. The more he studied the war preparations of the Navy Department, the more he was impressed by the Department's efficiency.

He found that the Navy Department had begun to provide for the possibility of conflict with Spain in January 1898 and placed the United States fleet in readiness. The commander-in-chief of the European station was instructed on January 11 to retain men whose enlistments were about to expire. By the third week of February the commanders of the various squadrons of the Navy had all received preliminary instructions to prepare their vessels for conflict. This fact has a bearing on the controversial instruction sent to Dewey on February 25, 1898; it should be considered in its true relation to the overall policy which the Navy Department had been following for six weeks.[15] The telegram marked a more advanced stage of war preparation, but it followed logically from the decision made earlier within the Department. Nor was the order to Dewey in any sense extraordinary. He was instructed to assemble his squadron in Hong Kong and to hold it in readiness to carry out the war plan against Spain. Similar orders were issued to the commander-in-chief of the European station on the same and following days. Secretary Long was again in active charge on February 26, and — certainly with his approval — all the United States squadrons were ordered to keep their vessels coaled and ready for instant action. It is of course true that Roosevelt had been urging the need for these preparations for several months. But he was not actually personally responsible for their adoption. The real work was done by the bureau chiefs of the Navy Department, and especially by Captain Arent Schuyler Crowninshield, Chief of the Bureau of Navigation.

Lodge wanted to give the bureau chiefs the full credit, but they were reluctant to assume public responsibility for preparing for war at a time when the President was still striving to maintain the peace. "You will probably see yourself," the Chief of the Bureau of Navigation wrote to Lodge in September 1898, that to hand over the text of the telegram of February 25 for publication "might appear to put us in a light of being almost over-prepared — in other words it might seem that the Department had as early as February 25 . . . made up its mind and that there was to be a war anyway." [16] Lodge considered the Department's caution foolish. He replied that he would have thought that the Department deserved no blame, but only unstinted praise: "My intention was simply to refer to [the telegram] as an order of the Department, but if the Secretary has the slightest objection to my doing so I will say that the order was sent by Mr. Roosevelt as Acting Secretary, and I have no doubt the Colonel of the Rough Riders will accept the responsibility of being overprepared with perfect equanimity." [17] When Lodge explained the whole story, Roosevelt was amused. He assured Lodge that he was "naturally delighted to shoulder the responsibility." [18] Lodge's popular account no doubt enhanced Roosevelt's reputation, and his standing will not suffer now. After all, his achievements rest on more solid foundations than his allegedly decisive influence on the war with Spain.

The Navy Department, as has been seen, had prepared for the war more carefully than has been supposed. Secretary Long knew nothing of tactics and strategy, but he was intelligent enough to admit to the fact and to leave such practical questions to his bureau chiefs. During the weeks immediately preceding the war, Long suffered from a recurrence of his nervous troubles; he noted in his journal that he was sleeping badly. He did not concern himself overmuch with grand strategy. Roosevelt tried to rouse him, but without success. Long recorded one of their discussions in his journal:

> Mr. Roosevelt came in, shut the door, and began in his usual emphatic and dead-in-earnest manner . . . in case of war with Spain, he intends to abandon everything and go to the front . . . He has gone so far daft in the matter that he evidently regards it as a sacred duty . . . I called him a crank, and ridiculed him to the best of my ability, but all in vain. The funny part of it all is, that he actually takes the thing seriously. Just as if there were anything in the whole business, even if it came to a scrap, that is worth serious thought. He bores me with plans of naval and military movement, and the necessity of having some scheme of attack arranged for instant execution in the case of an emergency.[19]

Long paid more attention to unimportant details. On January 15 he confided to his diary that he was "disgusted with the office boy, who prevaricates and shows the poor fiber of which he is made." Early in February he accused Roosevelt of extravagance in having spent $31 on stamps; Roosevelt responded by sending an indignant five-page reply. Later that month the *Maine* disaster badly affected Long's nerves. He now left the business of the Department entirely in the hands of his naval advisers. On February 21 he noted: "My sleep utterly broken and much nervous trouble." Four days later he felt so ill and tired he took the afternoon off.[20] Long habitually left his office punctually at 4 P.M.; he resented having to waste time talking with senators about this "carrion of patronage." He disliked the social round of Washington society; the "lengthening chain of dinners and receptions," he complained, were tiring him to death. On the eve of the war with Spain, the Navy Department was presided over by a weak man. Fortunately the bureau chiefs at this time were exceptionally able. Even so, their final and detailed strategic decisions left much to be desired.

The coordination of war planning had been placed in the hands of the Office of the Naval War Board. The War Board consisted of Assistant Secretary Roosevelt, Captain Crowninshield, and two other officers whose places were taken soon after the outbreak of hostilities by Rear Admiral

Montgomery Sicard and Mahan. The Board apparently met for the first time on March 23, 1898, in an office of the Navy Department.[21] Blankets were placed over the doors to ensure the secrecy of the proceedings. The Board advised Secretary Long to divide the warships available in the Caribbean into two squadrons. One squadron was to be assembled at Key West under the command of Rear Admiral William Sampson; at the outbreak of war it was to blockade Cuba. The second squadron, the so-called Flying Squadron, was to be placed under the command of Commodore Winfield Schley, and, with its base at Hampton Roads, was ordered to defend the eastern seaboard against the eventuality of a Spanish attack.

Little did Admiral Pascual Cervera, who was waiting off the Cape Verde islands with a ramshackle squadron of four armored cruisers and three destroyers, realize that his striking force was arousing such apprehensions in the United States that it was immobilizing two American battleships, the *Massachusetts* and *Texas,* and the cruiser *Brooklyn* with their attendant light vessels at Hampton Roads.[22] The division of the American command, moreover, was to lead a few weeks later to the unfortunate misunderstanding between Schley and Sampson at the battle of Santiago. When the Board sent its battle orders to Sampson on April 6, there was still argument about strategic objectives; Sampson balked at his defensive role of blockading Cuba and wrote to Secretary Long that he wished to attack Havana.[23] Meanwhile Dewey was waiting in Hong Kong for his battle orders. But the Board appears to have given Dewey no further thought until the British governor requested him to leave Hong Kong at the outbreak of war. Then, after a White House conference on Sunday, April 24, McKinley hastily endorsed the recommendation of the bureau chiefs that Dewey should attack the Philippines.[24] The disposition of the American fleet on the eve of the war was, despite Kimball's war plan, rather haphazard.

The United States entered the war with Spain in considerable confusion. But the failings of the detailed naval plans were as nothing compared to the chaos that reigned in the Army command. Any plans the Army might have drawn up for the invasion of Cuba did not survive among the records of the Military Information Division; probably no detailed plans existed. In any case the Secretary of War, Russell Alger, still convalescing from typhoid, and Major General Nelson A. Miles, who commanded the Army, were on the worst possible terms. It turned out that Secretary Alger could not, as he had frequently promised, put an army of 40,000 in the field on ten days' notice. General Miles was opposed to landing the Army in Cuba until the Spanish Navy had been destroyed. At a White House Conference on April 20 he insisted on at least two months to drill and prepare the Army for the invasion, and Long noted in his journal, "at present it seems as if the army were ready for nothing at all." [25] Fortunately for the United States, Spain was in worse military shape. For the United States it turned out to be, in John Hay's well-known words, a "splendid little war."

The American attack on the Spanish squadron in Manila must be rated among the worst-kept military secrets of all time. On March 2, 1898, after the Navy Department had cabled Dewey (over Roosevelt's signature), the secret instructions were known in Madrid; on March 6 the New York *Sun* was able to inform its readers of the impending attack. Was it then so obvious that the United States would strike at the Philippines at the outbreak of war? Perhaps the Spanish Government and the editor of the *Sun* had merely made a shrewd guess. The fact that Spanish ministers had received definite information is revealed by unpublished documents in the German Foreign Ministry archives. On March 2, the German consul in Hong Kong sent a sensational telegram to the Wilhelmstrasse in which he informed his superiors that according to the "strictly confidential" statement of the American consul general, "the American warships in Hong Kong harbor had received the order to prepare for an attack on Manila." Commented the Kaiser in the margin of the telegram: "At once to be passed on to Madrid where Her Majesty the Queen is to be told verbally in the form of a personal warning from me . . . the scoundrels the Yankees want war!" [26]

The Queen Regent thanked the Kaiser warmly for his message; she suggested that he could best prove his friendship by sending German warships on a friendly visit to Manila immediately. This turn of events, however, alarmed Foreign Minister Bülow, who was not averse to undermining the United States secretly but was determined to steer clear of possibly dangerous involvements. In a memorandum to the Kaiser, he suggested that Spain should ask the French for support and added, somewhat tartly, that the Kaiser's warning had been prompted by feelings of personal friendship for the Queen Regent and not by intentions to help her anti-German government.[27] During the course of the following three months, Bülow held to a cautious policy. In his attitude both to the question of possible European intervention before the war broke out and in his formulation of Germany's policy toward the Philippines, he refused to allow Germany to take the lead.[28] When in mid-May Admiral Diederichs was sent with a squadron to Manila, he was instructed merely to secure information on the situation there. Bülow firmly rejected the requests of a number of Filipino leaders for German support. They had suggested to the German consul in Manila that their independence could best be secured by the establishment of a monarchy ruled by a German prince; they had not thrown off the yoke of Spain in order to fall under American domination. But Bülow in another long memorandum to the Kaiser — who he rightly feared might be tempted — argued that the overwhelming sea power of England and the United States dominated the situation; Bülow accordingly concluded that it would be possible for Germany to reconsider its policy only if neither England nor America desired the islands.[29] Spanish hopes to secure German support were thus in vain. None of the great powers of Europe in fact was ready to antagonize the United States for the sake of Spain, with the possible exception of Austria-Hungary. Sir Julian Pauncefote, the British Ambassador, would have liked to register the moral disapprobation of Europe, but even this innocuous step was not sanctioned by Arthur Balfour, the acting British Foreign Secretary, or by the ministers in Berlin and Paris. The result of the war was never in doubt. Even the revelation of Dewey's secret plans did the Spanish government no good. American ships enjoyed an overwhelming superiority over the old, decrepit Spanish vessels anchored in Manila Bay. During the ensuing months, vital decisions were reached not on the far-flung battlefields but in the White House, the Navy Department, and on Capitol Hill.

McKinley's policy is generally depicted as being without adequate guidance and at the mercy of public opinion. His attitude to the question of taking the Philippines is used as a classical illustration of the influence of politics and public opinion on the formation of American policy.

Politics did play a large role in deciding the manner, but not the ultimate objectives, of McKinley's policy. We possess at least one vivid account of the President's outlook during the summer of 1898. William M. Laffan, who spoke to the President in July, recorded that he found him not in the least burdened by his responsibilities; on the contrary McKinley appeared confident, clearheaded, and "cheerful as a sandboy." The President declared:

> We will first take the Philippines, the Ladrones, the Carolines and Porto Rico. Then when we have possession, undisputed, we will look them all over at our leisure and do what seems to be wisest. Personally I am in favor now of keeping Luzon and fortifying Manila. We know very little about the group, but that which we do know makes it very doubtful if there would be any advantage to be derived from holding it all. I think the United States possessed of all Spain's colonies would do well to act with great magnanimity and show European governments that a lofty spirit guides us. Apart from that idea I favor the general principle of holding on to what we get. The more you look into the matter of the Philippines . . . the more doubtful you will be about keeping the whole group. If, however, as we go on it is made to appear desirable that we should retain all, then we will certainly do it.[30]

It is possible, but not likely, that a few weeks before the war with Spain McKinley may have considered retaining some portion of the Philippines if Dewey succeeded in defeating the Spanish squadron. He has left no evidence of such a view. His approach to the making of policy was pragmatic, and he took things one at a time. Until the actual outbreak of hostilities, McKinley would have preferred to preserve peace on the condition that Spain allow the Cubans to decide upon their own destiny. He certainly never would have consented to a war with the purpose of annexing either the Philippines or Cuba. It is questionable whether the United States would have interfered in Cuba if the Spanish government had accepted his terms; the Administration would certainly have taken no steps to acquire the Philippines. But the United States at war created an entirely new situation, leaving McKinley free to act entirely for the benefit of American interests.

The President's actions after April 1898 fit into a single pattern: the United States would first secure absolute control of both the Philippines and Cuba before deciding how American interests might be reconciled with the needs and wishes of the Cubans and Filipinos. What had once been the responsibility of Spain he now assumed to be the responsibility of the United States.

At a White House conference on May 8, 1898, McKinley reached the decision to dispatch an Army of Occupation both to Cuba and the Philippines. The President's instructions to the commander-in-chief of the Philippine expedition were perfectly clear: American rule was not to be severe, and local customs were to be respected; America had not come to the islands to make war on any of the natives. But the Filipinos were to understand that ultimate authority lay in the hands of the American commander acting on behalf of his President. No conflicting authority would be tolerated, for "the powers of the military occupant are absolute and supreme, and immediately operate upon the political condition of the inhabitants." If the Filipinos did not accept the fact that "the first effect of the military occupation of the enemy's territory is the severance of the former political relations of the inhabitants, and the establishment of a new political power," then the United States commander might not be able to maintain his beneficent attitude and would have to adopt "measures of a different kind" if they should prove indispensable "to the maintenance of law and order." [31] In the face of such instructions, McKinley's Philippine policy cannot be regarded as weak and indecisive. It is true that the American commander-in-chief in the Philippines received no further instructions during the difficulties that soon developed, but he had been given full authority to act on his own discretion; when it came to that point, he did so.

In Washington meantime, until the treaty of peace had been safely steered through the Senate, McKinley gave the misleading impression that he had not made up his mind about the disposition of Spain's colonies. He waited for the annexationist sentiment to win overwhelming support in the country so that the American people and the Senate might support his own firm policy.[32] To the critics who accuse him of indecision and lack of leadership, McKinley might well have replied that only a handful of senators could have wrecked his policy. Idealism was a powerful force in American life; combined with politics in this case it could have checkmated McKinley's actions. He made it appear that he had only gradually and reluctantly been driven to the conclusion that his duty to God, national honor, the Filipinos, and the Cubans demanded that the United States assume the burden of governing the Spanish colonies. The supposed "foreign designs" on the Philippines enabled the President to win congressional support. The Teller amendment, however, would have prevented McKinley from proclaiming the annexation of Cuba even if he wished to do so; as for the Philippines, he was careful to leave their future settlement open until after the Senate had sanctioned the peace treaty. Even so he won only by a narrow margin. Twenty years later President Wilson was to adopt the tactics so many critics blame McKinley for not following in 1898. McKinley's success is the best justification for the course he pursued.

The astonishing clamor for the retention of the Philippines that developed so swiftly after May 1898 has fascinated historians for several decades. Julius Pratt, Richard Hofstadter, and other scholars have already graphically described the changing mood of the American people during the 1890s.[33] The consequences of the war with Spain raise other questions of great interest.

It was an historical accident, a mere coincidence, that the Spanish-American War coincided in time with the international crisis that developed in China after the Kaiser's seizure of Kiaochow. At least three countries — England, Russia, and Japan — regarded the future of China as a matter of great concern. "It is impossible to overrate the gravity of the issue," Chamberlain, the British Colonial Secretary, declared in the town hall of Birmingham. "Our interests in China are so great, our proportion of the trade is so enormous, and the potentialities of that trade are so gigantic that I feel that no more vital question has ever been presented for the decision of the Government and the decision of the nation." [34] Many Americans shared these feelings. They wanted to secure a share of the trade in the Pacific. The United States already enjoyed overwhelming influence in the Hawaiian Republic, and during the summer of 1898 America annexed the islands. But in the western Pacific it was militarily powerless. If it came to the partition of China, the United States would have found itself excluded unless it could secure the aid of Japan, Russia, or England.

Mahan and Lodge speedily recognized the new realities of international politics. Lodge wrote to John Hay on April 21, 1898: "To me this drawing together of the English speaking people all over the world and of the two great nations seems far more momentous, more fraught with meaning to the future of mankind than the freeing of Cuba or the expulsion of Spain from this hemisphere." [35] But Lodge's conversion to an anglophile point of view was not solely due to England's friendly attitude during the crisis with Spain. Already on January 31, 1898, impressed with the importance of the Far Eastern crisis, Lodge had written to Henry White: "If I had my way I should be glad to have the United States say to England that we would stand by her in her declaration that the ports of China must be opened to all nations equally or to none." [36] By the summer, Lodge was ready to align the United States even more closely to England in the Far East.

But Americans on the whole had little interest in the military realities of foreign policy. Their education had been attempted by Mahan and a small group of politicians and naval officers, but the persuasive power of these propagandists should not be exaggerated. Dewey's victory proved to be worth more than all Mahan's books put together. It dramatically changed the nervousness that Spain might attack the eastern seaboard and the disappointment at the lack of military development in the Caribbean into a national outburst of elation and confidence. One editor even likened Dewey's victory to "the stories of the ancient battles of the Lord in the times of Joshua, David, and Jehoshaphat." [37] Overnight Dewey became the hero of the nation. The very unexpectedness of victory in the Orient added to the thrill of the occasion, and many Americans began to pore over maps to discover exactly where Manila might be. Only now, rather belatedly, business started to consider the potentialities of the Philippines as a commercial outlet for their goods and as an entrepôt for the trade of eastern Asia. But few of them could have been quite as sanguine as Senator Beveridge who, on the authority of having seen things for himself in the Philippines, described the fabulous natural resources of the islands to his fellow senators in January 1900: "the wood of the Philippines can supply the furniture for a century to come"; forty miles of Cebu's mountain chain were "practically mountains of coal." He even claimed to have picked up "a nugget of pure gold" on the banks of a Philippine creek – though he did not say exactly where.[38]

Dewey's victory transformed the narrow, intellectual movement – expansionism – into a broad and popular crusade – imperialism. The strategic implications were little understood by proponents and opponents. Carl Schurz and likeminded anti-imperialists girded themselves for battle to keep the great republic on the path of righteousness as they saw it and to a policy true to its traditions. Few anti-imperialists were as vehement as Andrew Carnegie. Secretary of State Hay in November 1898 concluded that Carnegie "really seems to be off his head." He wrote frantic letters to the Secretary of State which he signed "Your Bitterest Opponent." He threatened the President "not only with the vengeance of the voters, but with practical punishment at the hands of the mob," and he promised that he would cause the entire labor vote to be cast against the Administration.[39] But for all the high standing of the anti-imperialist leaders, for all their energy and organizational skill, and for all Carnegie's gold, the movement failed to carry with it the necessary one-third of the senators on whom the fate of the peace treaty depended.

But what of the strategists? What advice did they tender to the President? The naval officers who had first formulated the war plan of 1896 evidently did not rate Manila's strategic value to the United States highly, for in 1896 they had suggested that Manila be returned to Spain. How far did the Far Eastern crisis and the war with Spain modify these opinions? During the greater part of the war, three officers, Admiral Sicard, Commodore Crowninshield, and Captain Mahan, as members of the Naval War Board, advised the Secretary of the Navy on questions of strategy. Mahan appears to have dominated the deliberations. He had no good opinion of his colleagues and advised Secretary Long to abolish the Board and to replace it with a single officer who would act as chief of staff. (He hoped, no doubt, that this task would be entrusted to him.) In a letter to Luce, Mahan described Sicard, the President of the Board, as "a clearheaded man for Bureau work but very second or third rate for what we had to do . . . during my whole time on the Board, historical parallels to our positions were continually occurring to me. How many men in the Navy do you suppose know naval history . . . or how many, if they read this, would fail to vote me an egotistic, superannuated ass?" [40] Mahan must have been a difficult colleague to work with. Long noted on May 19 that he had attended a meeting of the Board and that "Captain Mahan is on the rampage again . . . he is very frank and manly [and] blurts out his entire dissatisfaction with the entire war board." [41] Mahan disapproved of the earlier decision to divide the battleship fleet. Already in mid-March he had advised Roosevelt (who read his letter to the President) to concentrate the fleet, "to disregard minor punishment, and devote our attention to smashing Spain in Cuba." [42] We may safely surmise that he would not have approved of Kimball's war plan and probably did not know of its existence.

His misgivings about the consequences of the Philippine adventure were not unfounded. After the battle of Manila, once the President had decided on the expedition to the Philippines, the Board was haunted by the fear that a superior force of Spanish warships might be sent to Manila and force Dewey to retire; if that happened, the American expeditionary force would be cut off. The Board recommended accordingly that the Army be supplied with modern guns to fortify the harbor.[43] In this way, no long-term strategic plan but rather the exigencies of war and faulty appraisal of Spain's naval strength led the United States into deep involvement in the Philippines.

Mahan, in fact, never wholeheartedly believed in the policy of annexing the Philippines. Writing to Lodge on July 27, 1898, he expressed his misgivings that the President might give way to public pressure to retain the islands when the war was won. The feeling about the Philippines, he wrote, "is much more doubtful . . . I myself, though rather an expansionist, have not fully adjusted myself to the idea of taking them, from our own standpoint of advantage." [44] He was inclined to hold on to no more than the island of Luzon. While serving on the War Board, Mahan was a frequent visitor to Lodge's house in Washington. Probably on Mahan's suggestion, Lodge wrote to Acting Secretary of State Day on August 11 that he was reluctant to see the United States assume the burden of holding more than the island of Luzon with Manila. The only practical solution, Lodge wrote, was to take the whole group of islands and then to cede them all, except for Luzon, to England in exchange for the Bahamas, Jamaica, and the Danish West Indies. Lodge pointed out the advantages of adopting such a course: it would free the Administration from the charge of handing back the Filipinos to Spanish oppression, relieve the Administration of the burden of governing all the islands, and leave the United States "in the Philippines associated with a friendly power with whom we should be in entire accord." [45] Lodge's suggestion reflects Mahan's caution as to the strategic difficulty of defending the Philippines, but whereas Mahan desired to see no entangling alliance, Lodge thought the defense of the Philippines should be shared with England. His proposal foreshadows at least close cooperation with England in the Far East, if not an alliance. Lodge had reached the conclusion that without England's friendship the position of the United States in the Far East might become hazardous. "We want to be very careful how far we draw out in the East," Lodge wrote to Henry White.[46] Mahan had thus, at least for a time, dampened Lodge's enthusiasm for the "foothold" in the Philippines, the archipelago whose acquisition, Lodge had written some weeks earlier, "would be of incalculable value to us." [47]

With the conclusion of the armistice on August 12, 1898, the United States found itself in occupation of Cuba, Puerto Rico, Guam, and the Philippines. But whereas the military situation in the Caribbean reinforced a concept of American policy long cherished, the state of affairs in the Philippines had been brought about largely by the adoption of Kimball's war plan, the strategic advice of the Naval War Board during the course of the conflict, and the policy McKinley followed after the outbreak of the war. No concept of American diplomacy as it had developed before the spring of 1898 lay behind the occupation of the Philippines.[48]

Ten days after the armistice was signed, the Naval War Board advised Secretary Long on the overseas bases the United States should acquire and maintain. But the geographical disposition of naval bases could not be discussed in any meaningful way without reference to the overall objectives of American diplomacy these bases were to support. It is fact that during the years from 1898 to 1917 the strategists were never once informed of the major objectives of the Administration's diplomacy. In the absence of such guidance, the strategists simply had to establish the basic premises of policy for themselves. They usually did so during the period from 1900 to 1917 by applying Mahan's lesson of history that economic rivalry was the basic cause of global conflict. This had one paradoxical result. Mahan was a confirmed anglophile, but the adoption of his principles led generations of naval officers to look upon England as a potential enemy. Obliged to work in isolation, the strategists simply imitated Mahan's historical techniques. They formulated war plans that became increasingly unsuited to the actual international conditions as they evolved in the first two decades of the twentieth century.

In August 1898 the Naval War Board postulated the premise that the United States would have to establish its supremacy in the Caribbean and over the isthmus of Central America. With the construction of the isthmian canal, the European powers would be drawn into the Caribbean. This had been one of Mahan's most insistent beliefs, and so the Board now recommended the acquisition of fortified bases commanding both entrances to the future canal. In addition, the Board also urged naval stations in Cuba (Santiago or Guantánamo), Puerto Rico (Culebra), and on St. Thomas. The construction of the canal by the United States had become a national interest, the Board stressed. In view of the defenseless position of the United States in the Pacific during the following two decades, the military policy of the United States might have been better served if the millions of dollars spent on the canal had instead been used to build a large Pacific fleet and the necessary harbor facilities to service it. But Mahan never conceived of such a solution, believing as he did that the first principle of naval strategy must be to keep the fleet undivided, able to pass from one ocean to the other as conditions might demand.

The strategic advice the Board tendered in 1898 about the Pacific Ocean was notably cautious. Here the United States could not establish its supremacy; Pago-Pago, Samoa, Hawaii, Guam, Manila, and one of the

Chusan Islands were the only bases the Board felt the United States should hold.[49] But it is difficult to see how the War Board envisaged the defense of these islands without a powerful Pacific fleet. In fact the War Board bequeathed a problem that strategists were unable to solve for half a century.

Insular Imperialism and the Open Door: The China Market and the Spanish-American War

THOMAS MCCORMICK

Thomas McCormick was, like Walter LaFeber, a student of Fred H. Harrington and William A. Williams at Wisconsin. This has led some historiographers to discern the presence of a "Wisconsin school" of interpretation. The notion is valuable only in the very loose sense that approaches to policy first delineated by scholars at Wisconsin have been further investigated by their students.

In this article, McCormick makes the most explicit link between China — its markets, politics, and people — and American foreign policy in the 1890s. China is seen as the final goal of a conscious series of policy decisions which led the United States, island by island, inexorably toward it. The seizure of the Philippines was not, according to McCormick, part of a deep-roooted quest for a colonial empire but, rather, a necessity for exploiting the markets of China. McCormick's article is, in many respects, a detailed working out of the thesis advanced by both Williams and LaFeber.

McCormick is not persuaded by arguments pointing out that, for many years, the United States did not act on its presumptive interests in Asia. In an interesting review of Paul A. Varg's The Making of a Myth: The United States and China, 1897–1912 *(East Lansing: Michigan State University Press, 1968), he argues that American businessmen could hardly be expected to "create in a twinkling . . . the kind of complex system that it took the British decades to put together and to learn to operate."*

His point, in short, is that "much of American interest in China . . . sought the preservation of a long-term option there, to see that no combination of nations or circumstances or forces pre-empted that potential market, to keep a foot in the open door too to insure that we would not find it closed in our face at some future point" ("American Expansion in China," American Historical Review, *June, 1970, pp. 1395–1396).*

The territorial expansion of the United States, as the chief of the State Department's Bureau of Foreign Commerce asserted in 1900, came as "an incident of the commercial expansion." "The recent acquisitions," he continued, "are but outposts of our future trade, and their chief importance consists not in their own resources and capabilities, but in their unquestionable value as gateways for the development of commercial intercourse with . . . the Far East." [1] *

America's insular acquisitions of 1898 were not primarily products of "large policy" imperialism. Hawaii, Wake, Guam, and the Philippines were not taken principally for their own economic worth, or for their fulfillment of the Manifest Destiny credo, or for their venting of the "psychic crisis." They were obtained, instead, largely in an eclectic effort to construct a system of coaling, cable, and naval stations into an integrated trade route which could facilitate realization of America's one overriding ambition in the Pacific – the penetration and, ultimately, the domination of the fabled China market.

These developments emerged from the cauldron of economic catastrophe. The "long depression" of the 1870's and 1880's, capped by the terrible panic of 1893, had led America's political and business leaders to embrace the heretical analysis that industrial overproduction lay at the heart of the nation's economic ills. Spurred by consequent fears of economic stagnation and social upheaval, they increasingly turned their gazes oceanward in search of outlets for their industrial glut. In essence, they sought America's new frontier in the markets of the world.

Eschewing formal imperialism, the nation's leaders chose, as the major *modus operandi* of economic expansion, the Open Door, the policy, as defined and adopted in 1895, of "keeping foreign markets open" and securing "equal and liberal trading advantages." [2] The choice, in part, re-

Reprinted from *Pacific Historical Review,* Vol. XXXII, No. 2, pp. 155–169, by permission of the author and the Branch.
* [See pp. 171–173 for notes to this article. – Ed.]

flected an aversion to the material and spiritual burdens of extensive colonialism. It also indicated, however, a buoyant assurance that American economic supremacy, given such equal commercial access, would win a sizeable share of world markets. Never rigid, the Open Door policy was to be supplemented by a limited dose of "insular imperialism" in the vast Pacific, where the technology of the day demanded island stepping-stones to the major market areas. The modification took no exception to the prevailing opinion that colonialism in large, densely-populated areas, such as China, was undesirable and unnecessary.

Many reasons propelled this economic expansion toward China. Memories of the clipper ship heyday of merchant capitalism, the influence of European writers, the blandishments of American missionaries: all played a part. Uppermost, however, was China's ignominious defeat at the hands of Japan in 1894–1895, which many American businessmen and diplomats believed would teach China "the folly of [its] exclusive and conservative policy." [3] Thus, to many influential Americans, the Sino-Japanese War heralded the long-awaited awakening of the Chinese colossus, a development which would "probably have the effect of opening vast markets to us." [4]

Subsequent developments in China belied such optimism. In 1895 and 1896, the international rivalry over Chinese indemnity loans and the completion of the Li-Lobanov pact marked an ever-quickening drive for exclusive economic privileges by the great powers. The process did not bode well for America's own inflated business hopes. So alarmed [was] the Cleveland administration that it abruptly forsook its laissez faire attitude toward American corporate interests in China and ordered its minister in Peking to use all his "personal and official influence" to win equality of economic opportunity for American "commercial enterprise." [5] This inadequate response, however, could not stem the tide, and the encroachments upon Chinese integrity reached flood-water proportions during the early McKinley administration with the famous "sphere of influence" partitioning. The "Sick Man of Asia" seemed on his deathbed, and his threatened demise promised a similar fate for the American hope of an Open Door frontier in the Celestial empire.

The growing crisis in China evoked great alarm in American business and government circles. Prompting most of the immediate apprehension were the Russian and German encroachments in Manchuria and Shantung, areas which absorbed nearly two-thirds of America's exports to China. Cognizant of this, the American minister in China, Charles Denby, cried loudly to the "Home Office" that "partition would . . . destroy our markets." He urged "an energetic protest . . . against the dismemberment of China." [6] The newly-formed Committee on American Interests in China, numerous chambers of commerce, several commercial papers, and other business groups added their fervent assent.[7]

Thus prodded, the State Department inquired pointedly of Germany and Russia as to "what would be the effect on foreign trade" of their new leases.[8] The German response concurred in the American policy of "holding China open to foreign commerce," while the Russian reply was similarly reassuring.[9] But the latter, especially, did not jibe with admonitions from the business and diplomatic communities that Russia secretly planned "the absorption of Manchuria in her Customs area." [10] So pervasive and persuasive were these suspicions that many previous promoters of Russo-American cooperation, such as Theodore Roosevelt, reversed fields and cast their lot with the administration's Anglophile elements in defining Russia as America's chief adversary in the Orient." [11]

Unassuaged then by the diplomatic responses, the McKinley administration found itself, by the spring of 1898, viewing the China problem with a critical attention second only to that of the Cuban issue. Yet the concern educed only watchful waiting (albeit, very watchful).[12] Even the dramatic British proposal for joint support of the Open Door in China could not jar American policy off its quiescent center.[13] Already preoccupied with Cuba, the United States lacked the commercial-military bases in the Pacific necessary, in the Mahanite thinking of the day, to implement a more affirmative economic and diplomatic policy. Within the year, the war with Spain was to eliminate these obstacles and pave the way for America's own Open Door policy, the policy (so Minister Denby affirmed in early 1898) of preserving equal commercial "access" and "the autonomy of China" in the hope of "an immense development of trade." [14]

From the very beginning of the Spanish-American War, the McKinley administration intended to retain a foothold in the Philippines as an "American Hong Kong," a commercial *entrepôt* to the China market and a center of American military power. Formulation of this policy commitment began seven months before hostilities with Spain; it began with Presidential examination of a Navy Department memorandum authored by Assistant Secretary Theodore Roosevelt. This multipurpose paper made one especially bold suggestion: in event of war with Spain, the Asiatic squadron "should blockade, and if possible take Manila." [15] Temporarily put in abeyance by a short-lived *detente* with Spain in late 1897, the suggestion was revived and made the basis of Roosevelt's famous February 25 orders instructing Commodore George Dewey to "start offensive operations in the Philippines" after eliminating the Spanish fleet.[16] Often viewed simply as a conspiratorial effort by "large policy" extremists, this interpretation misses two more significant facts: first, that Roosevelt's superiors accepted his orders concerning Philippine operations even though they unceremoniously countermanded fully two-thirds of the other miscellaneous orders issued concurrently by the Assistant Secretary; second, that the administration thereafter permitted the Naval War Board to incorporate the February 25 orders into its overall strategy plans for the Pacific.[17] Clearly, while Roosevelt's actions may have been precipitate, they fell within the main lines of the "larger policies" of the administration. Of these, Roosevelt, as he privately admitted, was largely "ignorant." [18]

With the outbreak of war, the McKinley administration rushed to implement its designs upon the likeliest *entrepôt,* Manila, by determining to send an army of occupation to the Philippine capital. It made this decision on May 2 before full-blown rumors of Dewey's victory at Manila Bay reached Washington, and formally issued the call for Philippine volunteers on May 4, three days before an anxious Navy Department received authoritative word that the Asiatic squadron was safe." [19] The determined size of the army force was to be "not less than twenty thousand men" — four times the number recommended by Dewey "to retain [Manila] and thus control the Philippine Islands." [20]

On May 11, McKinley and his cabinet gave definite form to American aims by approving a State Department memorandum calling for Spanish cession of a suitable "coaling station," presumably Manila. The islands as a whole were to remain with Spain.[21] Shortly thereafter, on June 3, when it had become apparent that the great distance between Manila and Honolulu demanded an intermediate coaling and cable station, the President broadened the American position to include an island in the Marianas.[22] The choice made was Guam, and the United States Navy promptly seized it.[23]

As of early June, then, administration intent envisioned only postwar control of Manila and Guam as way stations to the Orient. But dramatic events swiftly undercut this limited resolve and, for a critical fortnight, set American policy aimlessly adrift upon uncertain seas. First of all, the emergence of the Philippine insurgents as "an important factor" crystallized administration belief (as one American diplomat later noted) that "Spain cannot control; if we evacuate, anarchy rules." [24] What then; bestow the largess of Philippine independence? The mere posing of the alternative raised an even more threatening specter of European intervention against a weak, fledgling republic, an intervention warned against by American diplomats in Berlin and Paris and lent specific credibility by German actions and attitudes.[25] Either possibility — nationalistic revolution or rival intervention — might well render the isolated American position in Manila less than useful.

Between the horns of this cruel dilemma American policy lay immobilized — immobilized at a time when the growing crisis in China least afforded the luxury of prolonged indecision. On the one hand, intensified rumors that Russia regarded her South Manchurian leases as "integral portions of Russian territory" weakened the already shaky underpinnings of the Open Door in that key commercial area.[26] At the same time, England's extension of the Hong Kong settlement and her monopolistic approach to Yangtze Valley developments indicated that nation's growing estrangement from her traditional Open Door approach, and threatened to leave American policy in China diplomatically isolated.[27] In this deteriorating framework, any sustained impasse over Philippine policy incurred the obvious risk of letting America's grandiose hopes in China go by default. Against the formidable hosts of Philippine insurgency, German antagonism, and crisis in China, the American policy commitment of June 3 seemed an ineffectual one indeed. Cognizant of this, the McKinley administration, in mid-June, made a determined effort to break the bind by initiating three dramatic and interrelated moves in Hawaii, China, and the Philippines designed to increase American influence in the Western Pacific.

On June 11, the administration reactivated the sagging debate on Hawaiian annexation in the hope of strengthening America's hand in the Pacific basin. In the ensuing congressional debate, administration spokesmen hammered one theme with a greater consistency than others: "we must have Hawaii to help us get our share of China." [28] America, so the argument went, needed Hawaii not only for its own economic or cultural worth, but also for its commercial and military value as a stepping-stone to the China market. The influential Iowa congressman, William P. Hepburn, captured the themes best when he declared: "I can distinguish between the policy that would scatter all over the islands of the sea and the lands of the earth and that policy which would secure to us simply those facilities of commerce that the new commercial methods make absolutely essential." [29]

Other annexationists offered their own variations. Hawaii, they declared, would give the United States "strategic control of the North Pacific," "a permanent share in the mighty commerce which beats its wings in the waves of the broad Pacific," "this half-way house to the great markets of the East," "a harbor which will enable us to protect with our fleet our commerce in the Far East," a necessary "crossroads" for "our rapidly increasing commerce with the mighty hordes with whom we shall trade . . . across the Pacific," "our essential stepping-stone and base." [30] The theme was mainly a Republican one, but a few Democrats and one Populist bolted party lines to swell the chorus.

Significantly, anti-annexationists did not dispute the desirability of commercial expansion into Asia. Some even admitted the necessity of commercial-military bases as accoutrements to this expansion, but argued that the Pearl Harbor lease of 1886 or the Kiska holding in the Aleutians already met such needs.[31] Most, however, stressed the laissez faire, free trade approach that "commercial expansion" could best be realized "by competition of quality and price," not by "annexation of territory." [32] The point did not carry. On June 15, the House passed the annexation resolution by an overwhelming vote, 209 to 91.[33] Three weeks later, after redundant and desultory discussion, the Senate affirmed the measure by a similar ratio.[34] Thus, on July 8, with McKinley's signature, America acquired her halfway house to the Orient. The acquisition followed by four days the occupation of Wake Island, a move intended to meet the technological necessities of an additional cable point between Hawaii and Guam.

Synchronous with the push on Hawaiian annexation, the administration initiated the first step in an American economic offensive in China itself by proposing a government commercial commission to China to recommend measures for trade expansion. Secretary of State William R. Day's supporting letter to Congress made it pointedly clear that the internal economic situation necessitated a vigorous commercial expansion in China. Declaring that an industrial production "of large excess above the demands of home consumption" demanded "an enlargement of foreign markets," the Secretary concluded that "nowhere is this consideration of more interest than in its relation to the Chinese Empire." Aware that "the partition of commercial facilities" in China threatened America's "important interests," he still contended that "the United States . . . is in a position to invite the most favorable concessions to its industries and trade . . . provided the conditions are thoroughly understood and proper advantage is taken of the present situation." [35] Congress, to be sure, failed to appropriate the necessary monies. The reason, significantly, was because it considered such one-shot missions an inadequate substitute for a thoroughgoing reform of our consular representation in China. Nevertheless, the administration proposal, coupled with intensified consular activities later in the summer, served clear notice of American intent to take "proper advantage . . . of the present situation" in order to play a more active role in China.[36]

Simultaneously, on June 14, the administration capped its trio of dramatic moves by shelving the earlier decision to return the Philippines to Spain, thus opening the disposition of the islands to further examination.[37] With this open-ended shift, there began a progressive but reluctant redefinition of the desired area of American sovereignty: from Manila, to Luzon, and finally to the entire group. For two months after the June 14 move, American policy remained seemingly ambivalent on the question of extent. Even the Armistice agreement of August appeared to avoid confrontation of the issue by reserving the question of "control, disposition, and government" for final peace negotiations.[38] The ambiguity was more apparent than real, for McKinley had already crushed an internal move headed by his own secretary of state to limit American commitment to Manila.[39] In sealing this extremity, he left open only the question of how far to journey toward the other — Luzon or the entire group? The beginning of the final negotiations in early October found this problem still unresolved. While the American peace commissioners were instructed to work only for retention of Luzon, they were also to "accumulate all possible information" on the possible necessity of controlling the whole archipelago.[40] Less than one month later, on October 25, McKinley himself finally cut the knot by broadening his instructions to include all the Philippines.[41]

In this evolution of Philippine policy, America's commercial stake in China was of considerable importance. Indeed, it played the primary role in the thinking of the business and government elite that chiefly shaped McKinley's decisions. It also played a significant, though not paramount, part in the outlook of the military advisers who exercised a more limited but still crucial influence upon the President's policies.

Between June and October, business and government circles united vigorously around a policy of retaining all or part of the Philippines. Significantly, their rationale stressed the intrinsic economic worth of the islands far less than their strategic relationship to China — both as a commercial *entrepôt* and a political-military lever.[42] Moreover, it emphasized that Manila alone would not suffice for these purposes; that the United States would have to take Luzon and perhaps the whole group. In part this support for enlarged control reflected the pervading fear that native revolution or European penetration might undermine the viability of American power in Manila. It also indicated a growing belief, born of newly accumulated information, that the economic interdependence of the archipelago made efficient division most difficult. Charles H. Cramp, America's leading shipbuilder, aptly illustrated the impact of both factors upon influential Americans when he declared: "[Manila] is the emporium and the capital of the Philippines . . . and it exists because of that fact. . . . Can anyone suppose that with Manila in our hands and the rest of the Philippine territory under any other Government, that city would be of any value?" [43]

Numerous business associations, as well as prominent individual businessmen, pushed the viewpoint that trade interests in China demanded American control in the Philippines. Led by the National Association of Manufacturers and the American Asiatic Association, many special business organizations urged retention of the Philippines "for the protection and furtherance of the commercial interests of our citizens in the Far East." [44] At the same time, save for a few prominent dissasters, McKinley's many personal friends in the corporate world gave similar counsel. Typical was the advice of Irving M. Scott, manager of the Union Iron Works, that America needed the Philippines as "a point of observation at or near the centre of activity." Predicting that "the world is ours commercially" if we preserved peace and the Open Door, Scott urged that "the implements must be on hand, the position must be secured, and a vigilant watch kept on every encroachment." Noting that "the first move has been made in China," he concluded that "nothing has so effectually stopped it as the occupation of Manila." [45]

Most of McKinley's close associates in the government (many of whom were themselves products of the business community) pressed similar views upon their chief. The redoubtable Mark Hanna, State Department economic expert Frederic Emory, the American Minister to China Charles Denby, his successor Edwin H. Conger, Comptroller of the Currency Charles G. Dawes, Assistant Secretary of the Treasury Frank A. Vanderlip, to name a few, all shared in general the conviction (as Vanderlip stated) that an American-controlled Philippines would be "pickets of the Pacific, standing guard at the entrances to trade with the millions of China and Korea, French Indo-China, the Malay Peninsula, and the islands of Indonesia." [46]

Exerting a more narrow influence upon McKinley's Philippine policy was a third group, the military. In general, the President's military advisers shared the widespread concern over the strategic relationship of the archipelago to the Asian mainland. Yet, attracted by the siren's call of *imperium* (in which they would play a prominent role), many military spokesmen also promoted retention of the Philippines as the first step toward an expansive territorial imperialism.[47] In the main, their hopes were dashed as McKinley refused to heed their advice for a general American expansion into Micronesia and the islands of the South China Sea. Military advice, however, could claim one significant result: it resolved the President's ambivalence (shared by the business and government elite) between taking Luzon or the entire group by convincing him that the islands were an indivisible entity: that strategically and economically they were highly interdependent. Especially persuasive were the lengthy and articulate reports of Commander R. B. Bradford and General Francis V. Greene. Coming in late September and early October, they proved to be the decisive factors in broadening the President's instructions to their ultimate dimensions.[48]

The great repute of these business and government groups, coupled with their ready access to the Chief Executive, gave much weight to their contention (shared, in part, by the military) that American interests in China necessitated retention of the Philippines. But this view also gained a powerful though unwanted ally in the twin crisis in China itself during the fall of 1898. One side of the crisis was the intensified partitioning of railroad concessions by the European powers. Begun in the aftermath of the Sino-Japanese War, the division of concession spheres had advanced greatly by late summer of 1898. Russia and Germany had established *de facto* monopolization of Manchurian and Shantung railroads, respectively, while England bent her own efforts to strengthening her hold in the Yangtze Valley. British acceptance of the modified Open Door policy and the ratification of the Anglo-German railroad accord of September showed unmistakably that the Open Door had no current relevance to the world of railroad investments.[49] From the American point of view, the development augured ill for its own economic interests. To be sure, it did not greatly injure American investors. At this stage there was still little American financial interest in Chinese investments; and what little existed was assured profitable employment by the British in the Yangtze Valley. The solidification of railroad spheres, however, did threaten the important American export trade of Manchuria and North China by requiring American goods to travel from treaty port to market over Russian and German railroads. The prospect was not inviting, for these products might well meet railroad rate discrimination which, in raising transportation costs, would render American articles less competitive.[50]

Meanwhile, America's economic dreams faced another menace from a different quarter in China. In September of 1898, a successful coup d'etat by conservative, anti-foreign elements managed to crush the pro-western, reform party surrounding the young Chinese Emperor.[51] The new government immediately initiated administrative measures viewed by the United States as inimical to "commercial development" and the "pendulum of progress." [52] More seriously, the conservative forces failed to control anti-foreign uprisings inspired by their own *putsch*. Centered along projected Manchurian railroads, the violent and unstabilizing demonstrations offered both the excuse and the opportunity for potential Russian intervention to save her great railroad interests.[53] The mere suggestion of such a development was sufficient to conjure up visions of a further fragmented China and a vitiated Open Door.

These developments in China spawned first alarm, then action in the McKinley administration. The first move came in September with official renewal of inquiries to Russia and Germany concerning trade policies in their respective spheres. While the German response seems satisfactory, the evasive Russian declaration that her "administrative regulations" on foreign trade were still undetermined appears to be a foreboding retreat from earlier positions.[54] Thus accentuated, State Department concern germinated a second move in October with favorable action upon a textile industry petition concerning the Russian threat in China. Noting that one-half of America's cotton textile exports to China went to Russian-dominated areas, the petitioners demanded a "vigorous policy" to prevent "these markets" from being "eventually closed to our trade." Immediately, the Department responded by instructing its embassy in St. Petersburg to "use every opportunity to act energetically" against Russian adoption of discriminatory trade policies in Manchuria.[55] Quite obviously, the American government regarded the crises in China as dangerous enough to warrant substantial American reaction. Presumably, the situation was sufficiently threatening to impart added urgency and impact to the already influential opinion that America's commercial aspirations in China necessitated retention of the Philippines.

There can be no doubt that the Chinese question, illuminated by the opinion of business, government, and the military and by the growing crises in China, had progressive impact upon the shaping of America's Philippine policy. Nowhere is that fact made more significantly and dramatically apparent than in the private, candid, and lengthy exchange of opinions between McKinley and his peace commissioners at a White House meeting on September 16. The President, speaking somberly and with none of his frequent evasiveness, explained his reasons for retaining all or part of the archipelago. Almost all of them were negative, embraced with obvious reluctance. The only positive and assertive determinant was his conviction that "our tenure in the Philippines" offered the "commercial opportunity" of maintaining the Open Door, a policy which McKinley defined as "no advantages in the Orient which are not common to all." "Asking only the open door for ourselves," he told his commissioners, "we are ready to accord the open door to others." Explaining further, he made it clear that retention was no first step in an orgy of imperialism and jingoism, but simply a limited though important accoutrement to commercial expansion. "The commercial opportunity . . . associated with this opening," he declared, "depends less on large territorial possessions than upon an adequate commercial basis and upon broad and equal privileges." [56] The statement was more than rhetoric. Before the conclusion of peace, McKinley was to turn his back on jingoistic pressure to acquire all the Carolines and the Marianas from Spain, thus further illustrating that commercial needs, not Manifest Destiny, guided American decision-making in the Pacific basin; that the Open Door, not colonialism on a vast scale, was to remain the vehicle of American expansion.[57]

McKinley's linking of the Philippines question with the Open Door in China found ready favor with the majority of his peace commissioners. Indeed, the dominant triumvirate of Cushman K. Davis, William P. Frye, and Whitelaw Reid favored retention of the Philippines largely out of consideration for the future of American economic expansion in China. Reid's response to McKinley's remarks of September 16 was not atypical, when he "spoke of the great importance of the Philippines with reference to trade in China." Noting the previous acquisition of Hawaii, he concluded that "if to this we now added the Philippines, it would be possible for American energy to . . . ultimately convert the Pacific Ocean into an American Lake." [58]

Initiated then, in September, within the conscious framework of the Chinese question, the peace negotiations with Spain concluded three months later on an identical note. Article IV of the treaty made clear the intimacy that bound Philippine and China policy by keeping McKinley's earlier promise that we would accord the Open Door in the Philippines, provided we received reciprocal treatment elsewhere in the Orient. In actuality, this American Open Door was limited both in time and scope; however, administration spokesmen regarded the proviso as the key to future American policy in the Far East. Alvey A. Adee, long-time power inside the State Department, stated quite unequivocally that "the open door paragraph is the most important"; and Whitelaw Reid, dominant figure in the peace commission, insisted that the imperial "revenue tariff" for the Philippines "enables Great Britain and the United States to preserve a common interest and present a common front in the enormous development in the East that must attend the awakening of the Chinese Colossus." [59]

The final treaty arrangement on the Philippines was the outgrowth of an evolving set of circumstances dating back to 1895, when the combined impact of American depression and the Sino-Japanese War offered both the need and the hope that China might become the great absorber of America's industrial surplus. Subsequent developments, culminating in the partitioning of late 1897 and early 1898, critically threatened the hope, but in no way dissipated the need. They did, however, dictate the desirability of finding some vigorous means of safeguarding America's present and future commercial stake in the Chinese Empire. Fortuitously, perhaps, the Spanish-American War provided just such an opportunity, and the McKinley administration was quick to exploit it. The result was the effective thrust of American influence into the far Pacific. From Honolulu, through Wake and Guam, to Manila stretched a chain of potential coaling, cable, and naval stations to serve as a commercial and military avenue to the Orient. Only the construction of an isthmian canal remained to complete the system.

The grand scheme was not, in the narrow sense, imperial. The insular possessions in the Pacific were not pieces of empire, per se, but stepping-stones and levers to be utilized upon a larger and more important stage — China. Paradoxically, American expansion was designed, in part, to serve an anti-imperial purpose of preventing the colonization of China and thus preserving her for Open Door market penetration: *imperium in anti-imperio.* All this McKinley captured in his presidential message of December 5, 1898, when he declared that our "vast commerce . . . and the necessity of our staple production for Chinese uses" had made the United States a not "indifferent spectator of the extraordinary" partitioning in China's maritime provinces. Nevertheless, he continued, so long as "no discriminatory treatment of American . . . trade be found to exist . . . the need for our country becoming an actor in the scene" would be "obviated." But, he concluded, the fate of the Open Door would not be left to chance; it would be, he stated, "my aim to subserve our large interests in that quarter by all means appropriate to the constant policy of our government." [60] Quite obviously, the fruits of the Spanish-American War had enormously multiplied the "appropriate . . . means" available to American policy-makers, and had set the stage for the illusory search of America for that holy commercial grail — the China market.

American Expansion, 1870–1900: The Far East

MARILYN BLATT YOUNG

This essay on the putative link between China markets and late nineteenth-century foreign policy explores some of the differences between the approach taken by McCormick and the results of my own thinking on these problems. Having studied under Ernest R. May at Harvard, I found myself influenced both by his essentially noneconomic orientation and by the persuasive work of Williams and his students. The result is an essay marked by this tension. Like LaFeber, I make an effort to integrate various interpretations, though my conclusions are much more tentative. The essay is, perhaps, marred by this tentativeness. I recognize the importance of business interests but wish to place them in the broadest kind of ideological perspective. The specific *ties between ideology and action are, however, assumed rather than demonstrated — a fault common to historians of this period, including Williams. The essay also raises specific questions about the enthusiasm of business interests in pursuing economic oppor-*

tunities in China. The student should read this essay in close conjunction with McCormick's and attempt to frame his own synthesis.

Tragedy comes to the nationalist because the setting of *his* kingdom of fantastic ideas is unfortunately the world of reality.

Albert K. Weinberg, *Manifest Destiny*

Prompted perhaps by America's current military involvement in such traditional areas of imperialism as the Caribbean and Southeast Asia, the past five years have witnessed a resurgence of interest in the origins of American imperialism. The inevitable revisionism is often only semantic. Annexed islands are no longer colonies but (merely) naval or coaling stations, as if this rectification of names at one stroke eliminates the people living on the island and confers on the possession itself a kind of immateriality.[1] * When this is applied to a heavily populated area like the Philippines it is particularly inappropriate. It tends to hang a veil over what was involved in acquiring that "stepping stone" to China. The brutal suppression of the Filipino insurgency, comparable in many ways to the current American effort in Vietnam, hardly fits an interpretation which, by its language though not its intent, diminishes the sense of impact American imperialism had on other countries.

Several other tendencies mark the new evaluations of American foreign policy in the last three decades of the century. In 1936, Pratt remarked that his noneconomic approach to the rising expansionist philosophy of the late nineties would "controvert . . . current fashions in historical interpretation." [2] The wheel has come full circle. The attempt to explain foreign policy in terms of the demands of American businessmen and the state of the American economy is currently being pursued with greater effort, and more intelligence, than ever before. Until recently, the flurry of island-grabbing at the turn of the century was understood primarily in terms of the Spanish-American War and its unforeseen consequences. Now the interpretive process has been nearly reversed and the war is frequently explained as the logical outcome of a policy of economic expansion pursued by, but not originating with, William McKinley.[3] Convinced that America was, or would soon be, suffering from overproduction, adminis-

* [See pp. 173–175 for notes to this article. — Ed.]

trations from Grant through McKinley constantly sought to protect those markets America had and expand into those she had not. Differences of method are admitted but not stressed. The overall aim was the same: not an old-fashioned territorial empire, but a "new empire," whose rationale was commercial, whose style was "anticolonial."

The theory is an attractive, even compelling one, and my disagreement with it is as much philosophic as evidential. All its proponents give full weight to the economic rhetoric of the late 1880s and 1890s while ignoring, or playing down, the religious, political, national, and racist rhetoric which was equally prominent. Thus, because economic motives are felt to be more realistic, the policy makers studied are understood as pragmatic, hardheaded men out for the sensible main chance.

Yet even a cursory reading of the materials will demonstrate the outlandishness of many of the economic claims urged by Americans in these years; in tone and formulation they are economic corollaries of the assertions of Duty and Destiny. "What seems almost bizarre in retrospect," a recent study by two economists reflects, "is the extreme rhetoric characterizing early pronouncements of new markets." [4] Nor was this only true of the period under consideration here. In 1851 the current industrial upsurge was greeted with warnings that "the accumulations of industry furnish us with a constantly augmenting capital that must seek new channels of employment." [5] Indeed the importance of the Far Eastern and Latin American markets to the health, wealth, even survival of the United States was a commonplace long before the industrial revolution rationalized it. In 1803 an enthusiastic New England congressman declared, "Geography points us to China, Persia, India, Arabia Felix and Japan." In 1848 it was asserted that "Asia has suddenly become our neighbor with a placid intervening ocean inviting our steamships upon the track of a commerce greater than that of all Europe combined." Perry's treaty with Japan was acclaimed as "the entering wedge that will, ere long, open to us the interior wealth of these unknown lands." [6] How do we distinguish between these claims and those of an acknowledged new-empire, open-door, insular imperialist like Senator Albert J. Beveridge who, in 1900, declared, "Our largest trade henceforth must be with Asia. The Pacific is our ocean"? [7] If everyone is everyone else's forerunner, historical analysis is an infinite regression and there is no way we can understand why something happened in 1898 and not 1888.

It is true, as William Appleman Williams warns us, that the failure of expectations to be fulfilled (in regard to the China market, for example) is "beside the point; at issue is the nature of American thought and action at that time." [8] Yet surely we cannot simply dispense with the objective situation. Was the predominant economic analysis of the period correct? Did

America suffer, acutely, from overproduction? How important were foreign markets, and in particular markets in Latin America and Asia, to the survival of the economy? Unless we know the answers, it seems to me to be very difficult to evaluate the policies of McKinley and his predecessors. When the China market remained a dream only, was this because the government did not support business interests firmly enough, or because the initial analysis was incorrect? According to one study, exporters in the period 1895–1905 concentrated not on Asia or Latin America but on Europe. It was only in the following decade that underdeveloped nations became the focus of attention.[9] What was the actual capacity of China to absorb Western manufactured goods? In a largely self-sufficient village economy, how realistic were the ambitions of all Westerners in relation to their 400 million prospective customers? Despite the urgings of consular officials, business leaders, and politicians, American manufacturers in the period under discussion were slow to meet the trade demands of the Asian market. Members of the National Association of Manufacturers and the American Asiatic Association raised tireless paeans to the possibilities of a huge Asian market, yet manufacturers made little effort to adjust their products to Asian needs and the ex-Minister to China, Charles Denby, decried the unadventurous attitude of the business community which did not seem to "feel the necessity of cultivating foreign markets." [10] Exactly how important was government support to the expansion of America's export trade? One study indicates that where marketing techniques were vigorous and imaginative, American goods were able to maintain a leading position against all political odds; a lesser effort led to an early reduction of trade as the political situation became more unfavorable.[11]

These questions, which I shall not attempt to answer here, illustrate the degree to which the context of American policy remains unclear. While granting Williams' argument as to the importance of the subjective situation, it is impossible to discuss policy without a firmer grasp of the objective realities than is now available. Just as we do not accept Dean Rusk's public analysis of the causes of the Vietnam war, though recognizing the value of understanding why he believes what he does, so it would be foolish to simply accept, without further questioning, the rationale offered for their policies by the men of the late nineteenth century.

Recent analyses have stressed the peculiarly *American* nature of the empire built between 1870 and 1900. It was commercial, not colonial; it sought markets, not peoples to rule. Yet the resurgent imperialism of the Germans and English also stressed markets, investment rights, coaling stations to protect trade routes, and the like. When the Germans seized the port of Kiaochow in China it was only after a long period of abortive negotiations for a coaling station; they did not wish to colonize China. The exploitative rights which they extracted along with the port were justified in much the same way McKinley and others justified taking all of the Philippines rather than Manila alone: the security of the port and the proper enjoyment of the surrounding area.

The parochial attitude which discusses American imperialism without reference to the new imperialism of Europe is further illustrated in the persistent over-valuation of America's role in the Far East. From 1870 up to and including 1900, America was a secondary power in that area of the world, however much its nationals boasted of having "saved" China from disintegration. American policy was not without significance, but it was, at all points, less important than that of Great Britain, Russia, Japan, and even Germany. However interesting American Far Eastern policy may be in the context of the internal history of the United States, it would be a great mistake to believe that it was so regarded by other powers in the area or by China herself. The Chinese, whose foreign policy was reduced to a constant act of balancing one power against the other, used America as and when they could. To flatter the self-esteem of an American minister they might appear to throw themselves upon his mercy; at the same time identical appeals would be made to any other country which might possibly help in their current difficulty.[12] With few exceptions the Chinese found the United States unwilling to run any risks on China's behalf. Nor did American interests in China ever become substantial enough to permit an American administration basically to challenge the policy of another power for less altruistic reasons.

There can be no denying the fact that, by the late 1870s, there was widespread acceptance of the idea that expanding foreign markets were of vital importance to the nation.[13] Yet conflicts over policy did arise and it is utterly impossible to understand them if we identify anyone who advocated foreign trade as an imperialist. Differences of method were not necessarily less significant than differences of aim. Grover Cleveland's dispatch of a warship to protect American interests during the Brazilian revolution of 1893–1894 is not identical to Benjamin Harrison's scheming to acquire naval bases in Haiti and Santo Domingo, or to McKinley's dispatch of troops to the Philippines and China. I would distinguish, then, between annexationists, mild or extreme, and those who advocated expanding foreign markets through forceful diplomatic representation, the reform of the consular service, and the construction of an isthmian canal. Henry Cabot Lodge declared that he was opposed to a "widely extended system of colonization." What he did want, however, went far beyond the wishes of those looking simply to an expansion of trade. "We should take," Lodge told the Senate in 1895, "all outlying territories necessary to our own defense, to the protection of the Isthmian Canal, and to the upbuilding of our trade and commerce and to the maintenance of our military safety elsewhere. I would take and hold the outworks as we now hold the citadels of American powers." [14]

It seems clear that from the late 1870s on, there was general agreement that the government ought to concern itself with aiding American business abroad. William Evarts, Secretary of State under Hayes, was explicitly interested in expanding foreign trade and convinced of the responsibility of the government to foster its development. Through his efforts the State Department began, in 1880, to publish monthly consular reports whose statistics and assessments of trade opportunities would, it was hoped, be of substantial aid to businessmen.[15] But his view did not extend to the annexation of outlying territories, and he was unresponsive to the far-reaching plans of more aggressive State Department officials.[16] By the 1880s there may well have been a consensus view of the nation which held that the industrial revolution had effected a permanent transformation of the economy requiring a continuously rising tide of exports to maintain itself. The depression of 1893 appeared to confirm this. But the imperialists went on from this point. Their passionate demands for economic expansion were an integral part of a larger view which saw a strong navy, trade, political power, and the territory necessary, in their view, to maintain both trade and power, as complementary factors contributing to the wealth and strength of the nation.

Recent studies of the late nineteenth century continue to accept the 1890s as a major turning point in the history of American imperialism, but the forty years preceding them are also stressed. "The years between 1850 and 1889," Walter LaFeber writes, "were a period of preparation for the 1890s. These years provided the roots of empire, not the fruit." [17] Yet the gains LaFeber's overall view offers are balanced by a certain flattening out of history which it inevitably produces. One loses sight of the unique situation that each politician faced and the impact on his actions of day-to-day problems. Moreover, distinct changes are blurred as we follow the line of continuity. The policies of the Grant administration, for example, seem to me better understood as tied to the pre–Civil War type of imperialism than as an important link "in the chain of economic expansion running from Seward . . . and beyond." [18]

It was not at Grant's instigation that Commander Meade sailed grandly into the Samoan harbor of Pago Pago and signed a treaty of friendship and protection which gave the United States exclusive use of the harbor. Meade, true to the traditions of an older form of empire, was one of many American naval men who, "freely afloat at sea in different places, on their own motion cast about for stations and naval bases to serve as points of support for trade." [19] Indeed perhaps it would be better to look at Grant's foreign policy in terms of his total administration, whose dominant characteristic was one of grab. "The new capitalism," Matthew Josephson writes, "gave an immense impetus to official and political venality — *blindly*, by its own disorderliness and fiercely competitive character rather than out of regard for its own deeper interests." [20] The system of cooperation between business and politicians which began to emerge in the 1880s and reached fruition after the turn of the century [21] had yet to evolve. The very fact that the White House seemed filled with men after " '*loot* and booty . . . ready for any Mexican invasion or Caribbean annexation . . . looking to excitements and filibustering and possibly a Spanish war,' " gave imperialism in the Grant era a bad name, tainted it with corruption.[22]

The opposition to new departures in foreign policy was extraordinary and, in the wealth of imperialist moves described in recent studies, tends to be lost sight of. Blaine's interventionist and blundering pursuit of dominance in Latin America under Garfield was repudiated, and Frelinghuysen's much milder moves similarly met with staunch resistance.[23] While an aggressive foreign policy might, temporarily, serve to divert attention from domestic issues, as during the Harrison administration, ultimately the voters reacted to the overriding internal problems. Harrison's imperialist efforts were not seen as advancing the interests of rich and poor alike, but as tied to the advancement of the "plutocracy." His defeat was a result of his "failure or inability to respond to the new popular forces which were beginning to appear in American politics." [24] A public newly sensitive to issues of national honor might, as in the Valparaiso case of 1891, be whipped up to war pitch. But a more sustained and broadly based support of radical foreign policies awaited the demonstration that the benefits to be reaped would be distributed among all the people, that the strength and power of the nation redounded to the glory of all its citizens. This, in 1896, the Republican party was able to accomplish, presenting itself successfully to the country as the party of "energy and change," dedicated to advancing "economic growth" and enhancing "national power." [25] For a time, at least, imperialism became both respectable and popular.

What is interesting is the conjunction, in the 1890s, of an intellectual imperialist elite, strongly influenced by European trends, and a public, seared by depression, which found their ideas welcome. It is essential, therefore, to understand the changes which had taken place in American society during the last decade of the century, changes which make comprehensible the mingled note of fear and triumph that dominates the rhetoric of this period.

Perhaps the major psychological factor operating in the years before the turn of the century was the fact, and the awareness of that fact by most Americans, that the country was no longer (if indeed it ever had been) homogeneous and united. Signs of disorganization, even disintegration, were everywhere. For Americans, no strangers to disunion and fearful of revolution, the years from 1885 to 1897 were anxious ones.

The pace of urbanization had increased tremendously. The disrupting effect of such growth was intensified by the spectacular speed with which some cities grew. As opposed to the older urban centers, Chicago, for example, did not receive a steady flow of migrants but grew to a city of one million people in what was almost one great rush.[26] And while the service problems (such as sewage disposal, sanitation, and water supply) were no longer as serious as they had been in the cities of the early nineteenth century, the problems of social organization were much greater. Significantly, it was in the late nineteenth century that cities were first loved and cursed as "jungles."

The changing nature of immigration complicated the urban problem. A flood of impoverished alien people congregating in loathsome, sickeningly visible slums threatened and challenged the "native" American city dwellers. In every social group the city produced near-intolerable strains which each tried to meet in his own way. Everywhere clearly defined neighborhoods grew up – a geographical expression of self-definition.

People in the middle class began what proved to be a steady migration toward the suburbs where, behind white picket fences and neat lawns, they strove to demonstrate their ties with an older, simpler, native and rural America. Both upper and middle classes dissociated themselves, occasionally to the point of organized opposition, from the immigrants. For now to be an immigrant was to belong to the undifferentiated mass of unskilled workers.

The severe depression of 1893 gave actual shape to the anxieties that gripped America in its New World version of a *fin de siècle* pathology.[27] On one level, the depression weakened, perhaps destroyed, an earlier blithe belief in America's infinite material expansion. There was increased talk of economic stagnation, of overproduction, of permanent unemployment of large masses of people, of decay and decline. Fear of revolution was encouraged by two developments: the organization of the Populist party with its radical economic program, and the frequency of strikes and the actual warfare between capital and labor.

On the psychological level, the depression had an equally destructive impact. The prevailing ideology of social Darwinism, which in its most simplistic and popular form saw failure as evidence of personal inadequacy, added to the economic distress of being of being unemployed or bankrupt.

Other economic developments contributed to the tension and confusion of life in the nineties. The unorganized middle class found itself caught between two major contending forces: the nascent labor union movement and the increasingly powerful forces of big business. Reflecting in relative tranquillity some fifteen years later, Henry Adams saw the years of the great depression as ushering in "the capitalistic system with its methods; the protective tariff; the corporations and the trusts; the trades-unions and socialistic paternalism . . . the whole mechanical consolidation of force which ruthlessly stamped out the life of the class into which Adams was born." [28] The American dream of homogeneity, of an organic, infinitely progressive nation, had never before seemed so impossible of achievement.

One expression of the uneasiness that gripped American society at this time was the growth of a new, virulent, and for the first time nationwide, nativist movement. The nativism of the nineties is distinguished from earlier movements by its intensity and its conscious, extreme nationalism.[29] Nativist nationalism offered two easy verbal solutions to the painful dilemma of a changed and unstable America. By blaming disunity on the evil influence of the new immigrants, it absolved from blame and protected from criticism the more basic contradictions in the economic and social system. If immigrants were the root of the trouble, the solution was comparatively simple: keep them out. Viewed as unassimilable, revolutionary, and inherently inferior, the immigrant could be made a convenient catchall scapegoat. Secondly, by indulging in an orgy of fervent nationalism, the reality of American life could be denied, even for the moment forgotten. As John Higham points out, the "two anti-foreign movements — one international, the other internal — complemented each other, so that the jingoist atmosphere of the decade helps explain the depth and intensity of its nativism." [30]

It is in these terms that the emotional force of the Spanish-American War becomes comprehensible. The national neurosis described above was acted out in the fantastic fervor which preceded the war and perhaps made it inevitable. The pious references to "blue and grey marching together" were not empty bombast. The war was seen as a unifying force, killing Spaniards hand in hand a proof of that unity.

However, this general framework does not always explain why some policies were adopted, others rejected. In the Far East in particular, despite the tedious reiteration of the importance of Chinese markets, despite the ultra-nationalist boasts and the frequent opportunities for action, government policy was cautious in the extreme. In contrast to Latin America, where European powers were only minimally involved in a political or military way, China was a mare's-nest of rival claims. No amount of insistence on the purely commercial goals of American policy would persuade anyone; in China politics and commerce were one.

Yet this fact was only slowly acknowledged by the government and only fitfully and reluctantly acted upon. Efforts to assert American power for the benefit of American businessmen were, in contrast to European countries, noticeable by their absence. Opportunities were ignored or rejected in every case where pressure might have brought the United States into conflict with a European nation. On the other hand, pressure against China, which was helpless to resist, in areas which might advance American prestige without exciting the jealousy of other powers (as in missionary cases) was, in the 1890s, vigorously applied. For the convinced imperialist ideologues, as well as less ambitious politicians concerned only with staying in office, were faced with a fickle and unstable American public; a public not entirely convinced that its interests lay in "adventures" abroad. Moreover the business community, though always interested in government aid, was not consistently responsive to it. Everything dictated caution.

Thomas Bayard, Secretary of State in Cleveland's first administration, has been described as a "consistent Open Door expansionist." [31] He was outspoken in his assurances to American businessmen that the government would stand behind their enterprises in China.[32] Yet when he was faced with an actual enterprise, and one of vast proportions, Bayard retreated in haste. In 1886, Wharton Barker, a prominent Philadelphia banker, secured the very first concession ever granted by the Chinese government to a foreigner: the right to build long-distance telephone lines between the treaty ports. Moreover Governor-General Li Hung-chang, then at the peak of his power, hoped to establish, with Barker's help, a joint Sino-American bank which would in time finance railroads, mines, and a host of similar internal improvements.

Rumors of the Bank circulated in the foreign community in China, and the British-dominated English language press published "ponderous leaders against the scheme," calling the concessions rash, disastrous for China, tantamount to an American protectorate over the entire country.[33] Bayard's response was strictly to forbid Minister Denby to aid Barker and his partners in the face of rising European and Chinese opposition. It is true that one of Barker's colleagues was a dubious business risk and that the State Department had not been properly approached for aid by either Barker or his friends. Yet it is doubtful if these factors would have stopped the German, French, British, or Russian governments from exploiting the gains won by their nationals — however seedy.

The Sino-Japanese War of 1894–1895 revealed China's weakness to the world in all its fullness. The major powers acted swiftly to capitalize on it and within a few years the apportionment, though not the actual partition, of the country was well under way. Between the Treaty of Shimonoseki and the Boxer uprising (the period 1895–1900), China's railroads, mines, even some of her ports, were distributed among the European powers. At first, in contrast to Europe, the United States government tended to remain in the background, ready to help the curious group of Americans who arrived in Peking seeking concessions, but at no point instigating their activity.

Bayard's instructions to Minister Denby had been very strict: he was to make no representations on behalf of private Americans without prior State Department approval. Even Richard Olney's considerably liberalized instructions did not appreciably heighten the tempo of American economic activity. Without assuming any responsibility for American enterprises in the name of the government, Denby was to use his "personal and official influence and lend all proper countenance to secure reputable representatives . . . the same facilities . . . as are enjoyed by any other foreign commercial enterprise in the country." Nor should Denby feel himself tied down by State Department rules:

> It is not practicable to strictly define your duties in this connection, nor is it desirable that any instructions which may have been given should be too literally followed. . . . Broadly speaking you should employ all proper methods for the extension of American interests in China. . . .[34]

In practice this meant supporting the efforts of the American China Development Company, the only group which had successfully organized itself for a major effort in China.[35] Denby, pleased to have an opportunity to browbeat the Chinese in proper European fashion, argued the Company's case vociferously. The Company's failure to win the contract it initially bid for was due, in part, to the unwillingness of American capitalists to underbid their competitors. Although disappointed, Denby felt that the Americans were right to hold out for better terms. Control over enterprises invested in was essential and the "statesmen of China will understand" that in the case of America, "control does not mean territorial absorption nor governmental interference," as was true of European countries.[36]

The Chinese may well have understood this; but they also understood its corollary: that American businessmen were not ready to take a short-term loss in the hopes of great future benefits, nor was the government prepared (as was King Leopold in the case of the Belgians who successfully won the contract) to forcefully persuade the business community to do so. Denby himself recognized this.

> If the colonial ambitions of the Great Powers of Europe lead them to support syndicates in doubtful business undertakings . . . Americans will be greatly handicapped, because commercial matters for them in Asia cannot be mixed up with the schemes of political ambition. . . . As we have no political designs to serve in the Far East we have nothing to offer China in return for concessions. It thus happens that our great boon

> of being removed from and independent of foreign complications constitutes a correlative weakness. . . .[37]

Thus Olney's apparently forward policy still fell far short of the European style of government stimulation and support of their nationals' enterprises in China.

The concession scramble in China, reinforcing the depression-engendered fear of businessmen and politicians, turned American attention to China as never before.[38] Although the air was filled with demands that America do something, what precisely should be done was left almost entirely up to the government.

What, for example, should the government attitude be toward a man, claiming American citizenship, who had won a valuable railroad contract in China? The concession had the full support of the Chinese government; moreover it was located in an area recently seized by Germany as a "sphere of influence." Support of the claim would, at one blow, accomplish many things: it would prove to China that the American government was behind the legitimate efforts of its nationals; it would seriously hamper the European drive to stake out exclusive areas in China; it would fulfill the repeated demands of American businessmen for an active China policy which would hold that vital market for America. Yet, because the businessman involved was Chinese and his claim to citizenship therefore in question (though he had voted in all municipal, state, and federal elections since his naturalization in 1852), the State Department refused to act. Clearly, if the McKinley administration had been interested, at this time, in making a strong stand against the growing danger of spheres of influence, Yung Wing's prospective charter was an ideal occasion. Even if the State Department were unwilling to compromise the harsh consistency of the Exclusion Acts, they could have protested on Yung Wing's behalf — as an individual who had been an American, or was close to American interests. At no time, however, did the Department even weigh the issue.[39]

Charles Beresford, tireless British spokesman for the Open Door, left a tour of the United States depressed by the vagueness of the businessmen he had met. He contrasted the attitude of the "commercial classes" in Japan and America. "Both," he noted, "saw the necessity of keeping the Door open in China" but

> while on the Japanese side there was every indication of a desire to act in some practical manner . . . I could discover no desire on the part of the commercial communities in the United States to engage in any practical effort for preserving what to them might become in the future a trade, the extent of which no mortal can conjecture. On many occasions I sug-

> gested that some sort of understanding should exist between Great Britain and the United States for the mutual benefit of the two countries . . . but while receiving the most cordial support to this proposal, nothing of a definite character was suggested to me. . . .[40]

Thus, while McKinley could be sure that *some* action in regard to China would be favored by the business community, it was not clear how much action they were willing to countenance. The business community, through groups like the American Asiatic Association, helped to create a climate in which a new American China policy would be favorably received. But they did not offer prescriptions. The lineaments of policy would have to be worked out by the Secretary of State himself in the full knowledge that to overstep the limits of public tolerance for new departures was to court disaster.

However, if both government and business circles were vague about what should be done in the face of apparent European moves toward exclusive spheres, in one aspect of China policy the State Department was quite firm — the strict prosecution of antimissionary cases. Beginning in the Cleveland administration under Secretary of State Olney and pursued with thorough consistency by Secretaries Sherman, Day, and Hay, the new, firm missionary policy marked a real break with the past.

Disregarding the niceties of the separation of Church and State, which could be interpreted to preclude government intervention on behalf of sectarians, Secretary of State Olney was determined to demonstrate that the "United States government is an effective factor in securing due rights for Americans resident in China." [41] When it seemed that cooperating with other foreign powers in missionary cases, as had been done in the past, resulted in a slighting of American demands, or a delay in the proceedings, Olney was prepared to establish independent inquiry commissions despite the protests of the Chinese. Moreover, for the first time a general approach to missionary riots was worked out, one which took full advantage of the Chinese legal system and Chinese administrative norms. Thus, the highest government official of the area in which such an outbreak took place would be held responsible, though his only crime was ignorance or, on the local level, helplessness in the face of concerted mob action.[42]

In a manner reminiscent of France in the 1860s, when patronage of Roman Catholic missionaries substituted for real commercial or financial interests in China, this new missionary policy offended no European power, pleased a vested domestic interest, and served notice to China that its earlier image of America — mediating, gentle, supporting China against the rapacious world — was increasingly unattractive to Americans and certainly not to be depended upon.

The point is not that the government eschewed one approach for another, but that it acted with utmost caution in pursuit of the general goal of asserting American interest in China. Responding most directly to immediate situations and pressures, the administration was chary of any open-ended involvement, which firm support of a contested railroad contract might produce, but was ready enough to bully the Chinese on missionary cases, request firm assurances on trade, and, when the moment came, produce an all-around state paper — the Open Door Note — aimed at achieving limited objectives upon which vast claims might later be based.

Concerned, even at the height of the Cuban controversy, with the growing encroachment of European powers on China, McKinley decided, on the basis of assurances received from Russia and Germany, not to join England in a joint protest against recent Russian and German acquisitions. So long as "no discriminating treatment of American citizens and their trade" developed in the spheres of influence,[43] and so long, of course, as the United States remained fully engaged with Spain, no major diplomatic *démarche* could be expected.

The "ideal policy," John Hay wrote Henry Adams in 1900, "is . . . to do nothing, and yet be around when the watermelon is cut. Not that we want any watermelon, but it is always pleasant to be seen in smart colored circles on occasions of festivity." [44] Missionaries apart, the vagueness Beresford had complained of was characteristic of both business and government. Attempting to elucidate policy toward China in March of 1899, Hay confessed that it was "not very easy to formulate with any exactness the view of the government in regard to the present condition of things in China." Opposed to dismemberment of the Empire and convinced that "the public opinion of the United States would [not] justify the Government in taking part in the game of spoliation now going on," Hay was also concerned to keep all alternatives open.[45] Both Hay and McKinley were careful not to commit the United States to a policy of total territorial abstention in China. Discreet inquiries into the possibilities of a naval station were in fact made, for nothing in the Open Door notes precluded such an effort.

The notes themselves answered the immediate need for a policy which would satisfactorily indicate American concern to both the American public and the European powers. The first note, circulated in September 1889, was a statement of minimum demands. What America sought was *not* equality of opportunity. That, William Rockhill, Hay's chief adviser on China policy, pointed out "we cannot hope to have . . . though we should." Rather, "absolute equality of treatment" should be insisted upon.[46] In other words, America could not expect an equal opportunity for a railroad concession in the German-dominated province of Shantung; it would, however, insist that goods carried on that road should not be subject to discriminatory taxation. The aim was to lay down ground rules for the operation of trade within the spheres of influence. No one pretended that the spheres could be abolished – indeed Rockhill stressed that their existence must be accepted as *faits accomplis*. The attempt was only to limit the range of advantages enjoyed within the spheres.[47]

If America could not herself have a sphere, it was hoped that, through the Open Door Note, she might yet gain the prestige of leading a struggle to neutralize them. Whatever the modest realism Rockhill displayed when he drew up the note, he was soon making the broadest claims for it. America, he wrote a friend, "holds the balance of power in China. . . . What we have obtained will undoubtedly help to insure, for the time being, the integrity of the Chinese Empire. . . ." [48] In public statements, articles, instructions to the American legation in Peking, the same inflated notion of what the note had accomplished was pushed. The hope seemed to be that, by referring often enough to the way in which America had secured China's integrity and independence, the powers would begin to feel that they had committed themselves to it; or at least China might believe it and be suitably grateful to America. At the very least the American people might believe it and the administration could thus, at one blow, satisfy those who demanded vigorous China policy and disarm the growing anti-imperialist movement. As Rockhill's British friend and adviser Alfred Hippisley pointed out, "the announcement . . . that the U.S. had secured China's independence and so served the cause of peace and civilization would be a trump card for the Admin. and crush the life out of the anti-imperialist agitation." [49]

The greatest deterrent to the actual dismemberment of China was that no one stood to gain from it. Profit with a minimum of expensive colonial responsibility was the goal of all the powers, and the spheres-of-influence mechanism satisfied all requirements. The danger of the situation lay in its instability. An unforeseen crisis could shake the delicate balance of interests and lead to genuine partition. Again, it was not in the interest of any one of the powers to precipitate such an event. Yet each country, fearing the unknown motives of the other, might initiate a panic policy of grab that could not be easily arrested. The Boxer uprising was just such a crisis, and from its inception, American efforts were bent toward avoiding the calamity of disintegration. "The thing to do – the only thing," John Hay wrote Henry Adams, "was to localize the storm if possible. . . ." [50] Total war and partition might have occurred through accident or inertia. The vigorous diplomacy of Chinese officials in the south and central areas of the country, strongly supported by the United States, saved China for other upheavals.

McKinley's position was very delicate indeed. With the legations under siege and the fate of the American minister unknown, he clearly had to do something. But American participation in an international expedition was just the kind of danger the anti-imperialists had warned the country McKinley's policies would lead to. This was what happened when you went around annexing Pacific islands, they claimed. At the same time the crisis in China worked nicely to justify the annexation of the islands: without them effective American aid to its nationals would have been impossible. This was what we wanted the islands for, the imperialists argued. However, a formal statement of the terms under which America fought in China was essential. For McKinley had found even the most ardent imperialists unenthusiastic about American military action in China. Cushman K. Davis, for example, feared that America would find itself involved in a struggle for "partition, concessions . . . and other advantages." America's "commanding isolation" would be lost, and with it freedom of action in Asia.[51] Whitelaw Reid, owner of the powerful pro-administration *Tribune,* also believed that the United States could exert a major influence in China without the expense and danger of a military effort. Yet if "the Administration does not strain every nerve to save [Minister Conger] there will be a whirlwind." It was, he reflected, similar to the situation

> in which the country found itself after the explosion of the Maine. None of us wanted war with Spain, and yet war was inevitable. None of us want now to go into the business of killing Chinamen, and yet the country will probably not permit American troops to be absent from the column which ultimately enters Peking.[52]

With most of the Western world convinced that the Chinese had slaughtered all the inhabitants of the legations, a dramatic move was necessary to prevent the abandonment of the careful fiction under which foreign forces fought Chinese soldiers but not the Chinese government. The note circulated on July 3, 1900, was designed to meet that need. It would, it was hoped, make clear that the goal of American troops in China was the rescue of the legations and not plunder, that American policy sought only a solution which would bring the "permanent safety and peace of China, preserve Chinese territorial and administrative entity, protect all rights guaranteed to friendly powers . . . and safeguard . . . the principal of equal and impartial trade."[53] By formally and publicly stating that the powers would cooperate in every way with the efforts of those Chinese officials trying to stem the revolt, America sought to tie the powers down down to what till then had been only a very informal modus vivendi.

American participation in the Boxer expedition was the logical culmination of a China policy which had been shaping itself along interventionist lines since 1896. From that year, when antimissionary riots were met with a vigor and harshness absent from earlier American dealings with the Chinese on this subject, to the strong diplomatic representations regarding American trade made to China and the powers in 1898 and 1899, the lines of an independent, active China policy were laid down. A policy of passive cooperation with foreign forces in 1900 was impossible; no longer would an American Secretary of State leave the protection of nationals and their interests to the British. Danger to Americans now required an American armed presence, and more than that, it was hoped that an American force would give the nation increased weight and influence in the diplomatic maneuvering that was sure to follow the suppression of the antiforeign movement.

The genius, and the weakness, of American China policy was that it satisfied immediate, realistic needs through major verbal commitments. "We do not want to rob China ourselves," Hay complained

> and our public opinion will not permit us to interfere, with an army, to prevent others from robbing her. Besides, we have no army. The talk . . . about "our pre-eminent moral position giving us authority to dictate to the world" is mere flap-doodle.[54]

Yet the July 3 note talked about bringing "permanent peace" to China, and Rockhill, architect of much of the Open Door policy, spoke of America, with the acquisition of the Philippines, becoming "an eastern power and an active participator in Asiatic politics." "We had now to endeavor," he wrote, "to prevent preponderant political control within the Empire by any one foreign state, to give aid in every legitimate way to establishing a balance of power between them. . . ." [55] In fact, the United States was hardly in a position to balance powers. It took two hard years of negotiation to wring from Russia the assurance, "if assurances are to count for anything," that "no matter what happens eventually in northern China and Manchuria, the U.S will not be placed in any worse position than while the country was under the unquestioned domination of China." [56] But the impulse to attempt, from a limited base of either power or interest, to play a role in Asia, was difficult to resist.

In the late nineteenth century Americans came to feel that having influence in Asia was a categorical imperative for a world power. America, after the Spanish-American War, was a world power, *ergo* it must take a key part in Far Eastern affairs. And while the degree of actual activity, diplomatic or commercial, fluctuated widely over the years, the notion of the importance of playing a role there remained. Expectations of future power and interest were often confused with present realities. In relation to no other country did the rhetoric of politicians and businessmen, diplomats and missionaries so quickly become a force, influencing behavior, coloring reality, determining policy—or at least policy statements. However specific and realistic the response to any one situation might be (as in the dealing with Russia over Manchurian trade), whatever was accomplished was stated in the broadest possible terms. Policy decisions firmly rooted in the necessities of a particular situation (as in the two Open Door Notes) became, almost at the moment of inception, sacred doctrine.

This was due in part, at least, to the success of the propaganda of specific interest groups. Arguments intended to spur the interest of the public were accepted as facts and themselves became elements of policy in a dizzying spiral increasingly remote from reality. Thus the notion of a special friendship between China and America, of the riches of the China market, of America's role as balancer of powers in Asia, were all accepted as actual descriptions of the situation and not, as they were in fact, the possibilities merely. The American public was given to believe that its most vital national interests were involved in China, yet the commercial and financial interests which might have given substance to this claim were absent.

I have been suggesting that, for the sake of clarity, we restrict our use of the term imperialist to those who advocated the acquisition of bases and coaling stations, an aggressive foreign policy, a large navy, and the constant nurturing of American interests in the undeveloped world. Active in the period before 1893, the group reached its peak of influence and power after the disastrous effects of the depression had made their impact on the country. Influenced by Europe, the newness of their ideas consisted mainly in recognition of what was new in European imperialism and a strong desire that America follow a similar course.

In Asia, American policy clearly went beyond the simple pressure of economic facts, though fears for the health of the economy, real or imagined, were part of the imperialist argument. Unwilled events, such as the Boxer rebellion, were dealt with primarily with an eye to the domestic situation and out of a deep-seated concern that the administration neither fall behind the impulses of the public nor stand too far in the vanguard. The firm assumption was made that whatever the given state of material interests in Asia, America had a role to play there.

American policy is usually criticized for the imbalance between the broadness of its assertions and the actual military power used to back them up. America, however, did use force during the Boxer crisis. No war to safeguard Chinese integrity (as against Russian encroachments, for example) was undertaken, but neither did Britain, whose interests in the Far East were so much greater, fight any power in defense of Chinese integrity. Indeed America's restraint of arms is unique only in regard to China. The United States, in contrast to Britain, France, Germany, Japan, and Russia, was slow to use the threat of force against the Chinese government in order to gain its ends. Looked at in this light, American pacifism is hardly so startling.

A more recent approach to American policy finds it very much in balance — commercial ends were pursued diplomatically and backed by the judicious acquisition of suitable bases to protect trade. It seems to me that, perhaps disappointingly, the truth lies in between. The economic arguments used by the imperialists were an integral part of a larger complex of nationalist ideas. In a given situation, the response of the administration might well be rational, calculated, designed to avoid ultimate conflicts. Consistently, however, such a policy was presented to the public in a form likely to fulfill the self-image of the most ardent jingo. In time a sense of the importance of power in the Far East to America's very survival grew stronger so that today, when America finds herself engaged in the virtual extinction of an Asian nation, with a military force that makes the Boxer expedition look like a friendly street-corner fight, assertions of our "endangered vital interests" are everywhere, yet there seems to be no one who can spell out precisely what those interests are.

METHODS OF EMPIRE: FORMAL AND INFORMAL

Our Mylai of 1900: Americans in the Philippine Insurrection

STUART C. MILLER

Most modern empires have been mixed affairs within which different forms of control coexisted with little theoretical difficulty. The British empire, for example, included crown colonies, protectorates, and spheres of influence. The American empire also encompasses various forms of dominance — which sometimes confuses historians who believe that colonialism is the only form of imperial rule. Whatever one might argue about post–World War I America, there can be little doubt that at the turn of the century the United States had laid the groundwork (whether or not it chose to build further) for a multiform empire: outright possession of the Philippines, Hawaii, Guam, and Puerto Rico; a protectorate over Cuba; and, in the years just after the Spanish-American War, an ever-growing sphere of influence in Central America.

In seeking a full understanding of the meaning of American practice, we would do well to take a close look at its manner and consequences. Stuart Creighton Miller is an acute student of Sino-American relations whose fine study of the treatment of Chinese immigrants — The Unwelcome Immigrant: The American Image of the Chinese, 1785–1882 *(Berkeley: University of California Press, 1969) — is a painfully enlightening account of American racism. In this article, Miller fulfills one of the historian's primary tasks: to forbid a nation to forget its past.*

Few Americans are aware that 70 years ago this country fought a long and bloody war of counterinsurgency, one that was remarkably similar to our struggle today in Vietnam. Even to the well educated, this lesson seems to have been lost. Only recently, Harvard professor Lawrence Kohlberg stated that 100 years ago, or even as recently as World War II, "nobody would have raised an issue such as the Song My massacre." In fact, such an issue was raised in 1902; and what began as the court martial of a major, ended up with a general standing trial and the army's chief of staff being forced into early retirement — precisely for permitting a policy of terror against other people.

Rarely do historical events resemble each other as closely as the involvements of the United States in the Philippines in 1899 and Vietnam in 1964. The murky origins of the fighting; the quick adoption of unsuccessful Spanish techniques for suppressing the Filipinos; an unrealistically optimistic, handsome, martial-looking commander whose ineptness was rewarded with accolades from Washington; a peace movement with "teach-ins" at universities and a more activist radical faction; rumors and finally evidence of American atrocities; complaints of rainy seasons, hidden jungle entrenchments and clandestine enemy soldiers who blended with the peasants after ambushing and booby-trapping American soldiers; talk of getting our native allies to assume the burden of fighting; and, finally, a scandal involving one officer and seven top sergeants, who pocketed commissary funds — all of this should make the war in the Philippines between 1899 and 1903 sound uncannily familiar to the American of 1970. Indeed, to follow the Philippine Insurrection in old newspapers and magazines is like sitting through a shabby drama for the second time.

We are becoming accustomed to the idea that the Tonkin Gulf incident of 1964 was possibly provoked by the U.S. Navy whose destroyers were gathering electronic intelligence while their South Vietnamese allies were bombarding two islands a few miles off the coast of North Vietnam. Even so, the alleged enemy torpedo attacks "appear doubtful" in the words of the skipper of the *S.S. Maddox*. He stressed that "no actual visual sightings" had confirmed them, and they could have been invented by "over eager sonarmen" and "freak weather effects." It now seems possible that the incident that led to full-scale American intervention in Vietnam was either deliberately contrived by our military brass, who were eager to bail out their faltering allies in Saigon, or it was the product of military bumbling.

The fighting that broke out on February 4, 1899, between Filipino

Reprinted by permission from *Trans-action*, Vol. 7, No. 11 (Sept., 1970), pp. 19–28.

nationalists under the command of General Emilio Aguinaldo and American troops occupying Manila was also to the advantage of the military brass. Back in Washington anti-imperialist sentiment in the Senate was threatening to block the two-thirds vote necessary to ratify the Treaty of Paris which, apart from ending the Spanish-American War, also provided for U.S. annexation of the Philippines. The vote was scheduled for February 6 and, by presenting the Senate with a full-scale war, the military was able to stampede some undecided senators. That it was the Americans who started the action in the islands is also indicated by other circumstantial evidence that Aguinaldo was not prepared to be attacked, much less to launch one of his own. Three of his key lieutenants were away from their posts when the fighting began, and his personal secretary was visiting in Manila where he was easily captured by the Americans.

Once fighting erupted in the Philippines, General E. S. Otis assured the nation that he would speedily put down the rebellion within a few weeks, an optimistic prediction he reiterated throughout the next 12 months. General Otis's reports were filled with inflated statistics of enemy casualties and claims of spectacular American victories. Typically, they provoked headlines such as "Climax at Hand in Philippines," although a few less reverent editors wondered aloud why each optimistic report was invariably accompanied by a demand for more troops. By the end of his first year, Otis had 70,000 troops under his command (a 350 percent increase over the initial 20,000 which he had once insisted was "more than adequate"); and he was demanding an additional 30,000 to complete the job.

Less awed by the military brass than their counterparts of today, American editors at the beginning of this century openly began to question Otis's competence. Some called for an investigation of the army, and others ran headlines accusing the War Department of manufacturing statistics to conceal the actual cost of holding the Philippines. Such doubts sent Otis back to Washington to reassure Congress that, with a little more effort, victory was at hand. He was hailed as a conquering hero in the nation's capital; and all doubts were washed away in a sea of toasts and patriotic testimony. Once Otis was relieved, at his own request, it was rumored that he was slated to be the new secretary of war; but there was no cabinet shift to make room for him; and, unlike General Westmoreland, he was a "volunteer" and ineligible to become chief of staff.

Back home, Otis exchanged his sword for a pen and began to attack the anti-imperialists for encouraging the Filipinos to continue fighting after they had been obviously beaten. He also blamed the failure to end the war on his political superiors who imposed impossible limitations on his activity; nowhere was there even a suggestion of any personal responsibility. Perhaps the most striking similarity in the analogy between the

Philippines and Vietnam affairs lies in the tortured logic and the humorless, turgid, self-righteous prose in which these two generals, Otis and now Westmoreland, rationalize the successes of their enemies.

STOP THE WAR

The anti-imperialist movement, like the abolitionists a half-century earlier, was nurtured in Boston where Edward Atkinson published a magazine, *The Anti-Imperialist,* to protest the war. Atkinson featured articles entitled "The National Crime" and "Criminal Aggression: By Whom Committed?" and a July 4 issue in 1899 depicted an American flag at half-mast on the cover with the legend, "in memory and in honor of the brave soldiers of the United States whose lives have been sacrificed in the effort to subjugate the people of the Philippine Islands and to deprive them of their liberty." The postmaster general acted quickly to confiscate any copies destined for Admiral George Dewey in Manila.

In the Senate the attack on the war was led almost single-handedly at first by the distinguished and respected Republican senator from Massachusetts, George Frisbee Hoar. Like Fulbright many decades later, Hoar was in the awkward position of fighting his own party then in office. Like Fulbright too, he was not only morally indignant over the tactics being employed in the Philippines, but very practically concerned over the domestic political effects of such imperialist ventures for the United States.

Senator Hoar was joined by a good many other respected Americans, from the industrialist Andrew Carnegie to Henry Wade Rogers, president of Northwestern University. College campuses at Ann Arbor, Chicago, and Cambridge sponsored mass antiwar rallies, addressed by leading professors. "Alas, what a fall is here, my countrymen. Within the circuit of a single year to have declined from the moral leadership of mankind into the common brigandage of the robber nations of the world," Michigan professor Charles A. Towne told an assembly of colleagues, students and townsmen in Ann Arbor. At similar gatherings, Charles Elliot Norton of Harvard denounced the war; and at the University of Chicago Lawrence Laughlin evoked cries of treason when he described the Stars and Stripes as "an emblem of tyranny and butchery in the Philippines." Pro-administration newspapers, such as the *New York Times,* decried the evolution of the universities into political instruments over the Philippine affair.

In the Vietnamese conflict, Mill Valley in California's Marin County was the first local government to pass an antiwar resolution. That honor went to New York City in 1899, although a patriotic plea, asking why "Lawton's [a popular general killed early in the war] slayers" should be "upheld by representatives of New York," caused the council quickly to rescind the resolution. Attempts to get other local governments to pass antiwar resolutions were unsuccessful. Petitions to end the war were as ubiquitous 70 years ago as they are today. Senator Hoar presented one to Teddy Roosevelt shortly after he assumed the presidency; it called for an immediate end to "a contest professedly waged in the interest of humanity" but which was being "degraded into an inhuman war of extermination." This petition accused American soldiers of murdering Filipino women and children; burning down native villages; using torture to extract confessions and information from prisoners, suspects and local officials; and employing "savage allies to settle old scores under the aegis of the United States." Needless to say, Teddy was as receptive to such petitions as Nixon was when he inherited the war in Vietnam last year.

There were also some antiwar radicals who were not content with rallies, speeches and petitions to get American soldiers out of the Philippines. One group in Meadville, Pennsylvania, actually attacked Americans enlisting in the army to fight Filipinos. "Meadville seems to be afflicted by the presence of Aguinaldinos even more reckless in act and statement than those of Boston," exclaimed the *New York Times*. Other activists smuggled antiwar literature into army camps; and nine American soldiers deserted to the side of the Aguinaldo, proclaiming him to be the George Washington of the Philippines.

ENEMIES WITHOUT AND WITHIN

Today one can quickly recognize the rationalizations offered by the McKinley administration and its apologists to defend the policy in the Philippines, for they differ only in specifics from the justification for American intervention in Vietnam. We were fighting in the Philippines, they insisted, to protect the Filipino people externally from imperialistic Germans lurking by; and, internally, from Aguinaldo himself, who was attempting to enslave his countrymen. A *New York Times* editorial in 1899 explained that McKinley was "the liberator" baffling Aguinaldo, "the enslaver, the criminal aggressor, the designing tyrant." The editor denounced "the heartless indifference of the anti-imperialists to the cruel fate in store for the non-combatant natives if we fail to crush Aguinaldo." Every Atkinson pamphlet, Hoar speech, and peace rally "forges a link in the chains which Aguinaldo is trying to foster upon the wrists of his unfortunate countrymen," the editorial asserted.

To make this argument more viable, proadministration editors ran sensational stories describing "the massacre and rapine" that "marked the course of Aguinaldo." Thus, "the dearest illusion of Senator Hoar" has been "shattered by the beastly behavior of the *insurrectos* against their own countrymen," the *New York Times* commented. Ironically, the administration had to reverse itself quickly once Aguinaldo was captured early in 1901 and thereupon urged his compatriots to surrender and swear allegiance to the United States. Overnight, the "bloodthirsty tyrant" became an "honest, sincere . . . natural leader of men with considerable shrewdness and ability . . . highly respected by all." General Funston, who captured Aguinaldo, added, however, that while the Filipino commander was "a man of humane instincts," he was not always able to control his followers.

Another key rationalization for those who supported American policy in the Philippines was that only the peace movement in the United States kept the insurrection going by encouraging the Filipinos to think that the Americans would pull out of the islands short of victory. "I know from observation, confirmed by captured prisoners, that the continuance of fighting is chiefly due to reports that are sent out from America," General Lawton told a correspondent in 1899. Back home, this contention was repeated over and over, and one magazine carried a picture of Aguinaldo on a flap pasted on the cover, under which was the caption, "What is behind Aguinaldo, that *Fiend Who Has Slain American Soldiers?*" By raising the flap, the reader found a picture of William Jennings Bryan, the presidential candidate running on an anti-imperialist platform. In his chronicle of the period, *Our Times,* Mark Sullivan commented that "the spirit of America became sour" as a result of the debate over the Philippines; we taste that sourness again today.

Rumors of American atrocities were part of the peace propaganda very early in the war; but by 1900 letters from soldiers to relatives back home, describing the use of dum dum bullets, torture, retaliatory shooting of prisoners and the creation of concentration camps for civilians, began to reach the desks of local editors. One soldier bragged in a letter that Americans were shooting Filipino men, women and children "like rabbits." A Lieutenant Hall reported that General Funston had all prisoners shot as a matter of course, and described how one was dispatched on his knees still begging for his life. This disclosure dampened the administration's plans to give Funston a hero's welcome back to the United States after capturing Aguinaldo.

Another soldier freely confessed that he had used the "water cure" on 106 Filipinos, all but 26 of whom died in the process. This was the favorite method of torture. The victim was placed on his back and forced to swallow huge amounts of water, often salted. Periodically, a soldier jumped on his distended stomach; and the process was started all over again. When the victim did confess, he was usually shot and his village burned. "It is now the custom to avenge the death of an American soldier by burning to the ground all the houses and killing right and left natives who are only suspects," the *New York World* explained to its readers.

The army responded to these charges by first denying them and forcing those letter writers who were still in service to retract their statements. Private Baker, for example, publicly confessed that his statement that "we shoot people like rabbits was not so of course; and I thought they [his family] would understand it was intended as a joke." The soldier who confessed to killing scores of Filipinos with the water cure retracted his confession, claiming that it was motivated by boredom and designed to thrill a maiden aunt back in the states. "Another yarn which has failed to stand the test of time," gloated the *New York Times* in accepting the army's "proof" that such atrocities only existed in the imagination of the anti-imperialist, or, as the editor liked to call him, "the anti-everything." But not all editors were so easily convinced, and the *Springfield Republican* accused the *Times* of "suffering morally from a case of blind staggers on the Philippine question."

Not content with a simple denial, the army in the next breath usually attributed any atrocities that did occur to our Macabebe allies. The latter were scorned by most Filipinos for having served in the Spanish army before allying themselves with the Americans, just as our allies in Vietnam today once served the French. Representative John Gaines of Tennessee denounced the Macabebes on the floor of Congress as "the scum of the islands, traitors to their cause, thieves by nature and by tradition, who are hated by the Filipinos."

LIES AND EUPHEMISMS

After vigorously denying the atrocities, then attributing them to our allies, the army went on to invent euphemisms to cover these practices. The concentration camps didn't exist; but in any case they should be called "camps of instruction and sanitation" designed "to protect the natives from guerrilla bands," one official explained, apparently oblivious to the contradiction. While insisting that no "white man" ever used "the so-called water cure," General Funston went on to explain that the water cure was "by no means so severe an ordeal as would be indicated." It was merely "an unpleasant experience" for the victim. But the prize for the best euphemism produced in this war must go to President McKinley who called the process of subduing the Filipinos one of "benign assimilation."

Foreign correspondents in the Philippines began to corroborate the reports of American atrocities in spite of the crude attempts to manage the news made by General Otis and his successor, General MacArthur. A report in the *New York Journal* described how two *presidentes,* or mayors, were beaten to death by Americans with rattan rods in an unsuccessful attempt to force from them confessions of collusion with the guerrillas. Even the *New York Times* published an account of Captain Rowan's response to the assassination of a corporal in his company. Rowan not only had the assassin executed but burned his village down, and a neighboring village as well. This report was buried in the lower right-hand corner of page 6 and what the *Times* left out was that the corporal had raped the girl friend of the assassin and the second village burned was the home of the girl raped by the murdered corporal.

A front page in the *Philadelphia Ledger* carried the eye-witness account of a large-scale retaliatory killing of civilians by Americans:

> American troops have been relentless, have killed to exterminate men, women, and children, prisoners and captives, active insurgents and suspected people, from lads of 10 and up . . . have taken prisoner people who held up their hands and peacefully surrendered; and an hour later, without an atom of evidence to show that they were even insurrectos, stood them on a bridge and shot them down one by one to drop into the water below and float down as examples to those who find their bullet-riddled corpses.

Not that the correspondent was critical of such tactics. On the contrary, he attempted to justify them. "It is not civilized warfare," he conceded; "but we are not dealing with a civilized people. The only thing they know and fear is force, violence, and brutality; and we give it to them."

SAVAGES

Essentially, this was the army's last line of defense in the face of increased reports of American atrocities. After denial was no longer feasible, the military simply insisted that the tactics of the Filipinos made unorthodox methods of warfare a necessity; and, furthermore, the classification of the insurrectos as "bandits" and "criminals" legalized such methods in the eyes of the generals. "Men who participate in hostilities without being part of a regular organized force, and without sharing continuously in its operations but who do so with intermittent returns to their homes and vocations, divest themselves of the character of soldiers and, if captured, are not entitled to the privileges of war," MacArthur proclaimed in 1900. In a lengthy order "to all station commanders," a year later, General J. F. Bell carefully spelled out MacArthur's proclamation. Prefaced with the usual disclaimer that the United States had "exercised an extraordinary forbearance and patiently adhered to a magnanimous and benevolent policy toward the inhabitants," Bell accused the Filipinos of carrying out "a reign of terror" in direct violation of "the well-known laws and usages of war," as "announced in General Orders #100, Adjutant General's Office, 1863 (signed by Lincoln)." In the manner of a lawyer's brief, Bell's orders cited all the infractions and the corresponding code they violated. The Filipinos falsely swore allegiance to the United States "solely for the purpose of improving their opportunities and facilities for deceiving American officials and treacherously aiding and assisting the insurrection in violation of Section 26." It apparently never occurred to Bell that the Filipinos would not consider their lack of "special markings" and resemblance to "the ordinary peasant" a violation of any code of warfare, and certainly not Section 26 of Lincoln's orders.

What is interesting is that the charges MacArthur and Bell made against the Filipino insurrectos are almost identical to those made against the Viet Cong today. Bell accused them of constructing what today are called "booby traps." They "improvised and secreted in the vicinity of roads and trails rudely constructed infernal machines propelling poisoned arrows or darts" when triggered by an unwary American soldier. They also camouflaged pits lined with bamboo spears. These are, of course, the age-old tactics of guerrillas. Facing a superior force but enjoying popular support, the insurrectos, like the Viet Cong today, blended into peasant surroundings and resorted to ambushes, assassinations, booby traps and sabotage.

But Bell's orders would never be committed to writing by today's publicity-conscious generals. Bell ordered his commanders to "avail themselves of retaliation," to select prisoners by lot and shoot one of them for every American soldier killed. "The innocent must suffer with the guilty for the sake of speedily ending the war," his orders concluded.

Bell was an old Indian fighter, as were many of the senior army officers in the Philippines. He had never suffered any rebuke for employing such tactics against "savages" in the old Southwest. He enjoyed comparing the Filipinos to Sioux, Comanches and Apaches. "I have been in Indian campaigns where it took 100 soldiers to capture each Indian; but the problem here is more difficult on account of the inbred treachery of the people . . . and the impossibility of recognizing the actively bad from the only passively so." In endorsing Bell's orders, General Chaffee, another veteran Indian fighter, commented that "personal contact with the people and knowledge of their methods and sentiments made it [unorthodox tactics] necessary." Chaffee also warned a correspondent: "If you should hear of a few Filipinos more or less being put out of the way, don't grow too sentimental over it."

To justify further their illegal tactics, the army released a great many horror stories of atrocities committed against American prisoners. One even accused the Filipinos of injecting American prisoners with leprosy and releasing them to spread the disease among the troops. "Only a few incidents like the beheading of a captured American soldier will justify putting into effect the administration's long contemplated plan for treating the rebels not as belligerents, but as brigands; and for punishing their acts of slaughter not as war but as murder," an editorial in the *New York Times* reasoned.

Clearly, this enemy was not human, and ultimately, the key justification for using uncivilized tactics was a racist one. General S. B. Young expressed this directly when he told a group in Pittsburgh commemorating the birth of Ulysses S. Grant: "The keynote of the insurrection among the Filipinos past, present, and future is not tyranny, for we are not the tyrants. It is race. This, then, gentlemen, is the whole thing in a nutshell. If you ask me the quickest and easiest way to bring peace and good order to the Filipino, I can only say that, like the chameleon, we must put him on such a background that he can change his color!" General Young was loudly applauded by the group which included several senators, congressmen and governors, along with a bevy of retired generals. An editorial "On Filipino Character" in the *New York Times* explained that they were "veritable children" with all the weaknesses and the vices of the resourceless and unmoral human infant." Whitelaw Reid warned that the Filipinos could never attain the intelligence, morality, self-restraint and self-governing abilities "developed in the Anglo Saxon bone and fibre through all the centuries since Runnymede." General A. G. Greenwood suggested that after the war the United States could solve its racial problems by colonizing the Philippines with American blacks to mix with the "Filipino niggers." In the ranks, the soldier summed up these attitudes by referring to the Filipinos as "goo goos," who were no more human than were Indians, Negroes or Chinese.

OFFICERS ON TRIAL

By the end of 1901, it was impossible for the Senate to ignore the reports of American atrocities. A committee on Philippine affairs under the chairmanship of Senator Henry Cabot Lodge, a staunch supporter of the administration's imperialist policy, undertook an investigation. In spite of Lodge's partisan position, the testimony of witnesses called before the committee proved to be much more damaging to the administration than had been anticipated. In attempting to defend American tactics in the Philippines, a former army surgeon (Henry Howland) freely admitted to having personally administered the water cure to prisoners and suspects, as well as having witnessed prisoners being shot in retaliation. But he insisted that the "treacherous nature" of Filipinos necessitated such modes of warfare. "After so many betrayals, the men decide that the only chance of pacification lies in a wholesale cataclysm – an inundation of human blood that will purge the islands of treachery," he explained.

Another witness, ex-soldier Charles Riley, repeated charges that he had made earlier in a Northampton, Massachusetts, newspaper – the first to receive sensational treatment in the nation's press. The committee was unable to shake his testimony, and the military was unable to impugn his character as they had done to other witnesses. But most disturbing to the war department was Riley's citing a staff officer (Captain Edwin Glenn) as having personally administered the water cure on several occasions. The administration's defense that these were isolated instances and not part of policy was beginning to crumble.

To demonstrate that American crimes in the Philippines did not go unpunished, Secretary of War Elihu Root released a memorandum listing 44 trials of Americans in the islands. But this document also backfired when the press examined it more closely and discovered that one officer found guilty of assaulting and murdering prisoners had been given a reprimand and fined $300. The case of Lt. Preston Brown became a cause célèbre in the press. For murdering a Filipino, he had been dismissed from the service and sentenced to five years in prison; but the reviewing authority commuted the sentence to forfeiture of half of his pay for nine months and a loss of 35 places on the promotion list.

The yellow press that had once sensationalized Spanish atrocities in Cuba now began to raise a hue and cry over similar American tactics in the Philippines. "The hideous acts of barbarities were committed under our flag by men wearing the uniform of the United States and commanded by American officers," the *New York World* complained while the *Philadelphia North American* ran headlines on "American Atrocities in the Philippines." Overnight the charge of the anti-imperialists appeared to be vindicated. The *Boston Evening Transcript* described "a great transfer" in the "sentiments of both parties in Congress" and in editors generally. Even the *New York Times* began to express some doubts over the conduct of American troops in the islands, "Reports of cruelty, torture, and inhuman procedures in the Philippines have come to their [Americans'] ears. They have been shocked . . . when so much is known, the rest cannot remain concealed."

News that Marines on the island of Samar had summarily executed nine native bearers reached the ears of Secretary of War Root at this juncture; it appeared to be a perfect opportunity for the administration to demonstrate its ability to punish such malfeasance severely. The press, too, began to call for the head of the brigade commander, Major Littleton Waller. "Don't let the Butcher of Samar" escape, demanded a headline in the *North American*. In short, Waller was the scapegoat, and the public eagerly awaited his trial to assuage its feeling of guilt over the Philippine question.

SEARCH AND DESTROY

Waller had landed on Samar with a brigade of marines only five months earlier. This was a few months after Company C of the U.S. Ninth Infantry had been massacred in their quarters in the town of Balangiga on that island. Waller was temporarily under the command of the army's Brigadier General Jacob Smith, an old cavalryman and veteran Indian fighter known as "Hell-Roaring Jake" because his loud voice was out of proportion to his slight stature. Smith made it clear to Waller that he wanted revenge on Samar as well as pacification. He told the Major, "I want no prisoners. I wish you to kill and burn; the more you kill and burn, the more you will please me. I want all persons killed who are capable of bearing arms." Waller was no stranger to carnage. He had participated in a brutal attack on Arab cavalry at Alexandria in 1882 and had fought the Chinese Boxers only the year before. But even he was taken aback at Smith's orders and asked what "limit of age to respect." "Ten" was Smith's reply. Later Waller told his officers that they were to fight in a "civilized manner," and not make war on women and children. But, given the nature of guerrilla warfare, the racist view of the "goo goos," and the anger over the fate of Company C, who had served with Waller's men in China, it was perhaps inevitable that conventional restraints in warfare would be lost on Samar during the last few months of 1901.

The slain commander of Company C, Captain Connell, had been something of a humanitarian by army standards. To establish good relations with the natives of Balangiga, he had forbidden the use of the term "goo goo," any dealings with the women, or the bearing of arms in the town, except when officially posted as sentries. Such measures earned him the epithet "nigger lover" from his own executive officer. Waller made it clear that he was not going to repeat Connell's fatal errors. His initial orders to his officers read, "It must be impressed upon the men that the natives are treacherous, brave, and savage. No trust, no confidence can be placed in them." His concluding statement set the tone for the kind of warfare that was to follow, "We have also to avenge our late comrades in North China – the murdered men of the Ninth U.S. Infantry."

To set up what would today be called "a free fire zone," Waller ordered all natives in the interior to move to the coast; and two days later began to burn systematically every village in the interior, destroy food and hemp ready for market, kill any work animals found and sink all native boats discovered. If American uniforms or personal artifacts were discovered in any of these villages, Waller's men assumed they had belonged to Company C and simply shot down every remaining inhabitant – man, woman and child. Evidently Waller thought such behavior within the scope of "civilized warfare."

Waller also reacted harshly to the slightest infraction of his orders to the natives. When the presidente of a nearby barrio visited the brigade's headquarters at Basey without seeking Waller's permission, he was thrown in jail and his entire barrio burned to the ground. The natives retaliated by cutting the telephone cable to army headquarters elsewhere on the island, and Waller sent out repair parties with orders to shoot any natives seen in the vicinity of the line.

Waller was hardly secretive about all this. On the contrary, he made detailed reports to General Smith of every village burned, every native and carabao killed. Smith was delighted and wired back encouragement. "The interior of Samar must be made a howling wilderness," he ordered, which was to earn for the general the new nickname of "Howling Jake" in the press once Waller's court-martial began.

After a brilliant victory over the heavily fortified headquarters of the insurrectionists on Samar, Waller insisted on leading a platoon of marines on a vain, pointless and fatally miscalculated march across the island. Facing heavy rains and swollen rivers in the jungle with an inadequate food supply, only an advance party of Waller and a handful of marines made it across. The remainder turned back when they failed to receive word from Waller, losing ten men who died from exhaustion, exposure and hunger. The native bearers grew less cooperative with this group, foraging and constructing shelters of leaves for themselves and ignoring the marines. When a lieutenant threatened them with a gun, the bearers knocked him down and wounded him with a bolo. Yet, these bearers voluntarily returned to marine headquarters with a rescue party sent out by the army, only to be immediately executed. As before, Waller dutifully reported the executions to Smith; but the political climate in Washington had changed, and such behavior was no longer countenanced. At Secretary Root's insistence, General Chaffee ordered Waller court-martialed.

Represented by the same Captain Glenn who had been cited in the Senate hearings for using the water cure on prisoners, Waller freely admitted the executions, but insisted that he was following Smith's orders. While this defense won Waller an acquittal, it left the War Department with no choice but to order that Smith be court-martialed. The court found the general guilty and ordered him admonished, although Root in his review recognized extenuating circumstances in "the condition of warfare with cruel and barbarous savages." Teddy Roosevelt, too, cited "the cruelty, treachery, and total disregard of the rules and customs of civilized warfare" on the part of Filipinos to justify Smith's behavior. Nevertheless, Roosevelt astutely ordered the general to be retired from active service immediately to avoid any more unfavorable publicity.

Glenn was next to stand trial, and he fared poorly with Waller's defense. He cited the orders of Generals Bell and Chaffee to justify his use of the water cure. One telegraphed directive from Chaffee submitted in Glenn's defense read, "The Division Commander directs that no matter what measures may have to be adopted, information as to the whereabouts of the force [*insurrectos*] must be obtained." Nevertheless, Glenn was found guilty and reprimanded.

It would almost seem that Americans had had their surfeit of horror stories about the Philippine campaign by the middle of 1902. At least they seemed eager to sweep the dirt under the rug and forget it. Hence,

Glenn's trial produced few sensational headlines, nothing comparable to the "Butcher Waller Testifies to Dastardly Crimes" which appeared in the *Philadelphia North American* during the earlier trial. *The Evening Journal* in New York was roundly criticized by other newspapers for publishing a cartoon depicting American soldiers shooting women and children in the Philippines. The *New York Times* called this "a new low in yellow journalism." *Harper's* ran an article on the humanitarian aspects of the water cure and the killing of Filipino hostages; in the long run, it shortened the war and saved lives. "A choice of cruelties is the best that has been offered in the Philippines. It is not so certain that we at home can afford to shudder at the 'Water cure' unless we disown the whole job . . . the army has obeyed orders. It was sent to subdue the Filipinos. Having the devil to fight, it has sometimes used fire." The *Times* thanked *Harper's* for publishing "a particularly sane view of the situation in the Philippines."

The revelation during Glenn's trial that orders for such tactics had been endorsed all the way up the chain of command to Washington failed to provoke cries for the heads of Bell, Chaffee or their superiors. Teddy Roosevelt quietly retired the chief of staff, General Miles, but in his Memorial Day address of 1902 the president was able to say that the U.S. Army in the Philippines was "fighting for the triumph of civilization over forces which stand for the black chaos of savagery and barbarism."

Although the insurrection was officially declared over on July 4, 1902, fighting continued for another year. In 1903, the death of a Filipino priest being given the water cure by a Captain Ryan did evoke a few headlines; but the captain was acquitted by a court-martial, and the army made it clear that such tactics were necessary in order to terminate a war that was officially over. Captain Glenn was swiftly promoted to major and went on to serve many more years, attaining the rank of brigadier general. Waller served until 1920, retiring as a major general; but the notoriety of his trial clearly cost him the post of commandant of the Marine Corps.

The analogy between the two counterinsurgencies fought by Americans in the Philippines and in Vietnam six decades later is not yet complete. It will remain to be seen if Lieutenant Calley will utilize a defense similar to that of Major Waller and open up another Pandora's box for the army. Already, there are signs that higher authorities may be implicated before the trial is over. Meanwhile, Americans should realize that Vietnam is not a unique phenomenon in our history but rather the rerun of a tragic tale witnessed by our grandfathers.

The Philippine Peace

FINLEY PETER DUNNE

To Senator Albert J. Beveridge, Republican of Indiana, addressing the Senate in January, 1900, the Philippine question was deeper than partisan politics or constitutional law. "It is," he declaimed, "elemental. It is racial. God has not been preparing the English-speaking and Teutonic peoples for a thousand years for nothing but vain and idle self-contemplation and self-admiration. No! He has made us the master organizers of the world to establish system where chaos reigns." (From the speech, "Our Philippine Policy," in The Meaning of the Times *[Indianapolis: Bobbs-Merrill, 1908], p. 58.) And what of Gaelic-speaking Celts, Yiddish-speaking Slavs, Spanish-speaking Mexicans? To them Finley Peter Dunne's Irish saloonkeeper, Mr. Dooley, appearing regularly in the Chicago press, must have spoken more directly than the Senator from Indiana. Perhaps no writer, of that time or ours, has so expertly summarized the various absurdities and cruelties of America's early imperial career as Mr. Dooley. In this sketch on the Philippine peace, Dunne parodies speeches by Taft and Beveridge.*

"'Tis sthrange we don't hear much talk about th' Ph'lippeens," said Mr. Hennessy.

"Ye ought to go to Boston," said Mr. Dooley. "They talk about it there in their sleep. Th' raison it's not discussed annywhere else is that ivrything is perfectly quiet there. We don't talk about Ohio or Ioway or anny iv our other possissions because they'se nawthin' doin' in thim parts. Th' people ar-re goin' ahead, garnerin' th' products iv th' sile, sindin' their childher to school, worshipin' on Sundah in th' churches an' thankin' Hiven f'r th' blessin's iv free governmint an' th' pro-tiction iv th' flag above thim.

"So it is in th' Ph'lippeens. I know, f'r me frind Gov'nor Taft says so, an' they'se a man that undherstands con-tintmint whin he sees it. Ye can't thrust th' fellows that comes back fr'm th' jools iv th' Passyfic an' tells ye that things ar-re no betther thin they shud be undher th' shade iv th' cocoanut palm be th' blue wathers iv th' still lagoon. They mus' be satisfied

Reprinted from *Observations by Mr. Dooley* (New York: Russell, 1902), pp. 115–120.

with our rule. A man that isn't satisfied whin he's had enough is a glutton. They're satisfied an' happy an' slowly but surely they're acquirin' that love f'r th' govermint that floats over thim that will make thim good citizens without a vote or a right to thrile be jury. I know it. Guv'nor Taft says so.

"Says he: 'Th' Ph'lippeens as ye have been tol' be me young but speechful frind, Sinitor Bivridge, who was down there f'r tin minyits wanst an' spoke very highly an' at some lenth on th' beauties iv th' scenery, th' Ph'lippeens is wan or more iv th' beautiful jools in th' diadem iv our fair nation. Formerly our fair nation didn't care f'r jools, but done up her hair with side combs, but she's been abroad some since an' she come back with beautiful reddish goolden hair that a tiara looks well in an' that is betther f'r havin' a tiara. She is not as young as she was. Th' simple home-lovin' maiden that our fathers knew has disappeared an' in her place we find a Columbya, gintlemen, with machurer charms, a knowledge iv Euro-peen customs an' not averse to a cigareet. So we have pinned in her fair hair a diadem that sets off her beauty to advantage an' holds on th' front iv th' hair, an' th' mos' lovely pearl in this ornymint is thim sunny little isles iv th' Passyfic. They are almost too sunny f'r me. I had to come away.

" 'To shift me language suddintly fr'm th' joolry counther an' th' boodore, I will say that nawthin' that has been said even be th' gifted an' scholarly sinitor, who so worthily fills part iv th' place wanst crowded be Hendricks an' McDonald, does justice to th' richness iv thim islands. They raise unknown quantities iv produce, none iv which forchnitly can come into this counthry. All th' riches iv Cathay, all th' wealth iv Ind, as Hogan says, wud look like a second morgedge on an Apache wickeyup compared with th' untold an' almost unmintionable products iv that gloryous domain. Me business kept me in Manila or I wud tell ye what they are. Besides some iv our lile subjects is gettin' to be good shots an' I didn't go down there f'r that purpose.

" 'I turn to th' climate. It is simply hivenly. No other wurrud describes it. A white man who goes there seldom rayturns unless th' bereaved fam'ly insists. It is jus' right. In winter enough rain, in summer plinty iv heat. Gin'rally speakin' whin that thropical sky starts rainin' it doesn't stop till it's impty, so th' counthry is not subjected to th' sudden changes that afflict more northerly climes. Whin it rains it rains; whin it shines it shines. Th' wather frequently remains in th' air afther th' sun has been shinin' a month or more, th' earth bein' a little over-crowded with juice an' this gives th' atmosphere a certain cosiness that is indescribable. A light green mould grows on th' clothes an' is very becomin'. I met a man on th' boat comin' back who said 'twas th' finest winter climate in th' wurruld. He was be profission a rubber in a Turkish bath. As f'r th' summers they are delicious. Th' sun doesn't sit aloft above th' jools iv th' Passyfic. It comes down an' mingles with th' people. Ye have heard it said th' isles was kissed be th' sun. Perhaps bitten wud be a betther wurrud. But th' timprachoor is frequently modified be an eruption iv th' neighborin' volcanoes an' th' inthraduction iv American stoves. At night a coolin' breeze fr'm th' crather iv a volcano makes sleep possible in a hammock swung in th' icebox. It is also very pleasant to be able to cuk wan's dinner within wan.

" 'Passin' to th' pollytical situation, I will say it is good. Not perhaps as good as ye'ers or mine, but good. Ivry wanst in a while whin I think iv it, an iliction is held. Unforchnitly it usually happens that those ilicted have not yet surrindhered. In th' Ph'lippeens th' office seeks th' man, but as he is also pursooed be th' sojery, it is not always aisy to catch him an' fit it on him. Th' counthry may be divided into two parts, pollytically, — where th' insurrection continues an' where it will soon be. Th' brave but I fear not altogether cheery army conthrols th' insurrected parts be martiyal law, but th' civil authorities are supreme in their own house. Th' diff'rence between civil law an' martiyal law in th' Ph'lippeens is what kind iv coat th' judge wears. Th' raysult is much th' same. Th' two branches wurruks in perfect harmony. We bag thim in th' city an' they round thim up in th' counthry.

" 'It is not always nicessry to kill a Filipino American right away. Me desire is to idjacate thim slowly in th' ways an' customs iv th' counthry. We ar-re givin' hundherds iv these pore benighted haythen th' well-known, ol'-fashioned American wather cure. Iv coorse, ye know how 'tis done. A Filipino, we'll say, niver heerd iv th' histhry iv this counthry. He is met be wan iv our sturdy boys in black an' blue iv th' Macabebee scouts who asts him to cheer f'r Abraham Lincoln. He rayfuses. He is thin placed upon th' grass an' given a dhrink, a baynit bein' fixed in his mouth so he cannot reject th' hospitality. Undher th' inflooence iv th' hose that cheers but does not inebriate, he soon warrums or perhaps I might say swells up to a ralization iv th' granjoor iv his adoptive counthry. One gallon makes him give three groans f'r th' constitchoochion. At four gallons, he will ask to be wrapped in th' flag. At th' dew pint he sings Yankee Doodle. Occasionally we run acrost a stubborn an' rebellyous man who wud sthrain at me idee iv human rights an' swallow th' Passyfic Ocean, but I mus' say mos' iv these little fellows is less hollow in their pretintions. Nachrally we have had to take a good manny customs fr'm th' Spanyard, but we have improved on thim. I was talkin' with a Spanish gintleman th' other day who had been away f'r a long time an' he said he wudden't know th' counthry. Even th' faces iv th' people on th' sthreets had changed. They seemed glad to see him. Among th' most' useful Spanish customs is reconcenthration. Our reconcenthration camps is among th' mos' thickly popylated in th' wurruld. But still we have to rely mainly on American methods. They are always used fin'lly in th' makin' iv a good citizen, th' garotte sildom.

" 'I have not considhered it advisable to inthrajooce anny fads like thrile be jury iv ye'er peers into me administhration. Plain sthraight-forward dealin's is me motto. A Filipino at his best has on'y larned half th' jooty iv mankind. He can be thried but he can't thry his fellow man. It takes him too long. But in time I hope to have thim thrained to a pint where they can be good men an' thrue at th' inquest.

" 'I hope I have tol' ye enough to show ye that th' stories iv disordher is greatly exaggerated. Th' counthry is pro-gressin' splindidly, th' ocean still laps th' shore, th' mountains are there as they were in Bivridge's day, quite happy apparently; th' flag floats free an' well guarded over th' govermint offices, an' th' cherry people go an' come on their errands – go out alone an' come back with th' throops. Ivrywhere happiness, contint, love iv th' shtep-mother counthry, excipt in places where there ar-re people. Gintlemen, I thank ye.'

"An' there ye ar-re, Hinnissy. I hope this here lucid story will quite th' waggin' tongues iv scandal an' that people will let th' Ph'lippeens stew in their own happiness."

"But sure they might do something f'r thim," said Mr. Hennessy.

"They will," said Mr. Dooley. "They'll give thim a measure iv freedom."

"But whin?"

"Whin they'll sthand still long enough to be measured," said Mr. Dooley.

The United States in Cuba, 1898–1902

David F. Healy

Like so many of the best of the new generation of students of American foreign policy, David F. Healy did his graduate work at Wisconsin. In this concluding chapter to his book, The United States in Cuba, *Healy examines the "long and full" day enjoyed by McKinley's Cuban policy. The compromise between "altruism and annexationism," which the policy embodied, proved a far more durable model for control than did outright colonialism. Healy's examination of how the administration maneuvered among the many ambiguities of its position in Cuba touches upon most of the themes raised by other authors included in this collection: the role of "humanitarian" public opinion, business interests, racism, the balance between Congress, the Executive, and the military. McKinley's options, as Healy acknowledges, were limited by his prewar decision to dismiss the possibility of recognizing the insurgents as the proper rulers of their country as well as by the Teller Amendment, which prohibited outright annexation of the island as part of the War Resolution of April 19, 1898. The Platt Amendment of 1902, in turn, was a handy instrument of control which stretched, but did not blatantly violate, the terms under which the United States went to war.*

Healy's subtle treatment of the relationship between business interests and government decision-makers should be particularly noted: "If economic interests defined many of the broad goals to be sought, political necessities forced the specific choices of method and technique. . . ." In varying degrees, the same is no doubt true of other major policy decisions made both early and late in the history of American imperialism.

On May 20, 1902, the old Governor's Palace at Havana witnessed a ceremony in many ways similar to that which had opened the occupation more than three years before. General Wood stood with his staff in the same big, bare room, along with a number of foreign officers from warships in the harbor. Tomás Estrada Palma, the newly elected President of Cuba, headed a large group of dignitaries which included the new Cuban Congress and representatives of the insular judiciary. Outside, United States troops again drew up in the Plaza de Armas, while huge crowds jammed the streets of the city. At the stroke of noon, Wood began reading the words that transferred sovereignty to the Cuban Republic, and on flagstaffs about the city the American flag fluttered down.

The United States military government of Cuba had come to an end. For Leonard Wood, there remained only the summing-up; "The work called for and accomplished [he wrote] was the building up of a Republic, by Anglo-Saxons, in a Latin country . . . in short, the establishment, in a little over three years, in a Latin military colony, in one of the most unhealthy countries in the world, of a Republic modelled closely upon the lines of our great Republic." [1] *

From David F. Healy, *The United States in Cuba, 1898–1902: Generals, Politicians, and the Search for Policy* (Madison: The University of Wisconsin Press; © 1963 by the Regents of the University of Wisconsin), pp. 207–215.

* [See p. 175 for notes to this article. – Ed.]

Thus the Cuban intervention ended, as it had begun, in disagreement about its purposes. To Wood the real object of the intervention was the annexation of the island, if not immediately, then gradually through Americanization and close economic ties. To William McKinley the intervention had seemed necessary to prevent a chronic condition of disorder and destruction in Cuba which was injurious to important American interests. And to many Americans the purpose of the Cuban adventure had been the humanitarian one of ending suffering, anarchy, and death in a closely neighboring area.

This ambiguity of purpose had been largely resolved in fact, if not in theory, by the settlement embodied in the Platt Amendment and the Reciprocity Treaty of 1902. This was done, however, only at the cost of disavowing some earlier national commitments. The Platt Amendment, which imposed controls on Cuba, was quite clearly inconsistent with the Teller Amendment, which renounced such controls. But the Teller Amendment soon seemed inconsistent with almost any rational purpose the United States might have in Cuba. It directly forbade annexation. It also forbade the exercise of future control over Cuba. But if the United States was to end the Cuban chaos for either economic or humanitarian reasons, it could do so only by exercising some control over what happened there. The wording of the War Resolutions had implied that Cuba's ills stemmed solely from Spanish misrule and could be ended simply by the expulsion of Spanish authority, but this assumption was rapidly undermined by growing doubts of the Cubans' ability to rule their island properly after the Spanish had left it. At any rate, to go to war for the purpose of changing the Cuban situation, and at the same time to renounce all influence over that situation, did not appear to be a rational proceeding to the policy-makers of the administration.

The Teller Amendment, and the sentiments which produced it, nevertheless had a beneficial effect: they restrained the headlong annexationists from forcing any conclusive action until the nature of the situation could emerge clearly. When it did so, the administration could see that there were significant limitations on its freedom of action in Cuba. The first of these was that already imposed by the altruistic and idealistic thinking of many Americans. This element proved too strong to be openly flouted without a degree of political embarrassment. American leaders had also to consider the attitude of the Cubans themselves. The late revolution against Spain was sufficient proof that the Cuban people were capable of a formidable protest when aroused. The Philippine Insurrection served to remind the nation that such revolts were all too possible. It also introduced another political factor. The unhappy events in the Philippines had greatly depleted the reservoir of tolerance in America for colonial setbacks. Both the McKinley administration and its opponents believed that an insurrection in Cuba, coming on top of the Philippine Insurrection, would threaten the Republican expansionist program with political bankruptcy. This factor gained immediacy from the need to make some of the basic decisions about Cuba just prior to the presidential election of 1900.

The delay imposed by circumstances, and the limitations of action which this delay revealed, resulted in the step by step formation of a Cuban policy based on a growing knowledge and experience, rather than an uninformed a priori decision like that which led to the annexation of the Philippines.

It should be kept in mind, however, that the views of the Cuban situation held by even the best-informed Americans were strongly colored by the racism which was rampant at the time throughout the western world. The chief figures of national politics and of the occupation were no more inhumane from such influences than were the mass of Americans. The imperialists among them argued that the peoples of the former Spanish empire were inherently incapable of stable self-government, and that it was therefore a national duty to extend good government to them. The anti-imperialists argued that such peoples could not make worthy citizens of the United States, and thus should not be assimilated at all. The real point is that both sides assumed the innate inferiority of tropical peoples, while drawing opposite conclusions from the assumption.[2]

This added weight to the already grave doubts about the Cubans' ability for self-government. General Wilson revealed a good deal in trying to calm the fears of his fellow countrymen: "When it is remembered that the whites are to the colored in Cuba as two to one, while in the Philippines they are not more than one to fifty, the political and sociological inferiority of the Filipinos will be apparent to all." [3] In his attempts to reassure Americans about Cuba, Wilson repeatedly declared that white domination was as solidly established in Cuba as in the southern United States.

The prevalent racism, moreover, was not directed solely at non-whites, but at any ethnic group beyond the Anglo-Saxon pale. White Latin-Americans were also considered inferior to Anglo-Saxons, though perhaps less so than Negroes. The New York *Evening Post* based a part of its anti-annexation propaganda on the argument that Cuba was inhabited by a "mongrel race" which was unfit to share the benefits of United States citizenship.[4] General Ludlow thought that the Cubans were "not as we. They are Latin, and belong to a dying race" which was incapable of stable self-government.[5] Leonard Wood described them as "a race that has been steadily going down for a hundred years." [6] Elihu Root declared late in life that "all of the Latin Americans have a genius for misrepresentation." [7] Theodore Roosevelt richly exhibited this larger racism. He not only expressed contempt for the Filipinos, calling them "Malay bandits" and "Chinese halfbreeds," [8] but described the wholly white government of Colombia as "the Bogota lot of jack rabbits." [9] Such attitudes were re-inforced by the wave of anti-Catholicism which crested to a peak during the 1890's in organizations like the American Protective Association. These biases, held by both imperialists and anti-imperialists, would weigh heavily in any estimate of Cuban capabilities.

In general, it was the executive branch of the government which took the lead in creating the new Cuban policy. The War Department played by far the most significant role, with the personnel of the military occupation in the forefront, and Elihu Root making many of the pivotal decisions.

Congress also played an important part in the process, though primarily of a limiting rather than a positive nature. Not only did the legislative branch exercise an effective veto over executive policy, but from time to time it abruptly modified that policy, notably through the Teller and Foraker Resolutions. Even when Congress did nothing at all, the threat of what it might do acted as a constant brake on the actions of the executive. The executive on its side, secured Congressional adoption of its own permanent policy through the Platt Amendment and the Reciprocity Treaty of 1902.

It is less easy to define the role of economic factors in the drama. As has been shown, important economic interests were involved at every stage of the Cuban story. When a runaway Congress finally forced President McKinley to intervene in Cuba, it was to such interests that he strove to give first priority in his thinking, though purely political considerations often intervened. The economic realities of the situation all along imposed a frame of reference within which any settlement would have to be worked out, and the final settlement embodied economic as well as political arrangements.

Why, then, does "Big Business" not loom up more commandingly [in this book]? Essentially, because the necessary decisions were made, not by businessmen, but by soldiers, politicians, and civil servants. If these decision-makers sought to satisfy the desires of the business community — and obviously they did — they tried even harder to satisfy the voting public. If economic interests defined many of the broad goals to be sought, political necessities forced the specific choices of method and technique which make the Cuban settlement uniquely significant. The business world had been divided, to say the least, on the question of going to war over to Cuba in the first place. Such episodes at that of the Foraker Resolution, in which Congress temporarily impeded the penetration of Cuba by United States capital, indicate that even when the voice of business was reasonably united, it was not the only one heard at the seats of power. Indeed, in regard to reaching the specific terms of the final settlement, it is clear that political factors were of more immediate importance than any other. While American business interests soon got all they wanted in Cuba, they did so under a settlement shaped by many forces, prominent among which were the clash of domestic party politics and the demands of the oft-forgotten Cuban people.

The effects of the Cuban settlement were not limited to Cuba, but helped to set the stage for a new interpretation of the Monroe Doctrine as well. The Monroe Doctrine had begun life as a formal opposition by the United States to European intervention in American affairs. After 1900, it quickly metamorphosed into a justification *for* United States intervention in Latin-American affairs. The Platt Amendment played an important role in that metamorphosis, and in the accompanying shift to an interventionist policy on the part of the United States.[10]

In the first place, the invasion and occupation of Cuba was itself a precedent-setting intervention by the United States in a Latin-American country, while the Platt Amendment guaranteed to the United States a right to further interventions in Cuba if she should desire them. In exacting this right of intervention, however, Congress made little mention of the Monroe Doctrine. It is true that during the Senate debate on the Platt Amendment, Senator Hoar referred to it as "a proper and necessary stipulation for the application of the Monroe Doctrine," but this remark brought vigorous attacks from Senators Jones of Arkansas and Morgan of Alabama.

"This Monroe Doctrine never had anything to do with a proposition like this, the maintenance of a government adequate to the protection of life, property and individual liberty in any one of the American states. It has no connection with that," Morgan stated positively. Senator Hoar hedged and retreated, and there the matter rested.[11]

It was rather Senator Tillman who best illustrated the real connection between the passage of the Platt Amendment and the reshaping of the Monroe Doctrine, though Tillman never mentioned the doctrine at all. In the same debate, he referred to the recent entry of a German warship into a Dominican port to collect a citizen's claim. "Now," he said, "if Cuba is a kind of ward in chancery of the United States — and I think it is — we would not tolerate any European nation going there and undertaking to browbeat or to rob that people; but I can see a great deal of reason and justice in the contention that we are under some obligations to European powers to have Cuba not do such things to their citizens as will embroil her with them." [12]

In short, if the United States refused to allow European nations to enforce their rights in Cuba, then it must itself assume the responsibility for seeing that such rights were not violated there. The denial of European intervention thus involved a potential need for United States intervention.

If a parallel line of reasoning were applied to the Monroe Doctrine, which forbade European intervention in all of Latin America, it would lead to the assumption by the United States of a potential right of intervention anywhere in the hemisphere. Neither Tillman nor the other senators drew the parallel, but it was to be given expression three years later in Theodore Roosevelt's famous corollary.

If Congress would not openly tie the Platt Amendment to the Monroe Doctrine, Elihu Root did not hesitate to do so. When the committee of the Cuban constitutional convention came to Washington to confer about the Platt Amendment, Root told them that "Clause 3 is the Monroe Doctrine, but with international force." The intervention article, he said, gave the United States no rights which she did not already possess; through the Monroe Doctrine and its applications, she had for three-quarters of a century proclaimed a right before the world to intervene in Cuba. But the doctrine, being a unilateral proclamation, was not recognized in international law, while, as an agreement between two nations, the Platt Amendment would be. "Because of it," Root claimed, "European nations will not dispute the intervention of the United States in defense of the independence of Cuba." [13] The United States, in other words, would have a clear right to intervene in Cuba in order to prevent intervention from any other source. Thus Root, starting from a different position than Congress, also bridged the gap between the idea of non-intervention in Latin America by European powers and the new policy of intervention by the United States.

That tireless expansionist, Senator Beveridge, also saw the possibilities of extending the Platt Amendment beyond Cuban soil. The amendment had not only settled the Cuban question, he wrote soon after its passage, but had also paved the way for American control of other areas: "No man can now deny that the Republic may be suzerain whenever the interests of the American people or the peace of the world may make that form of control convenient." [14]

The passage of the Platt Amendment and the discussion attendent upon it had supplied a precedent, a technique, and a rhetorical defense mechanism for a general American policy of intervention. But in 1901 the man who was to make the major formal statement of that policy had not yet espoused it. Theodore Roosevelt wrote in July: "If any South American State misbehaves towards any European country, let the European country spank it." [15]

Roosevelt, however, was essentially a man of action, and when, in 1904, he wished to act, the tool was ready to his hand. He had only to add a last ingredient, an "international police power," and to synthesize the whole in the Roosevelt Corollary. "Chronic wrong-doing," he wrote, "or an impotence which results in a general loosening of the ties of civilized society, may in America, as elsewhere, ultimately require intervention by some civilized nation, and in the western hemisphere the adherence of the United States to the Monroe Doctrine may force the United States, however reluctantly, in flagrant cases of such wrong-doing or impotence, to the exercise of an international police power." [16]

Whether or not the Platt Amendment was in any part derived from the Monroe Doctrine, it provided an example and a line of reasoning which needed only to be applied to the doctrine to produce the Roosevelt Corollary. The spirit of the times insured that application would be made.

In its purely Cuban context, the Platt Amendment represented a middle course between altruism and annexationism. It was a realistic compromise designed to award each side its minimum demands. The United States allowed the Cubans nationhood and internal self-government; it demanded from them special protection for its own interests in Cuba. In the years after 1902, however, the nature of this compromise was warped by a shift in the United States' interpretation of its right of intervention. Elihu Root had declared in 1901 that United States intervention under the Platt Amendment "was not synonymous with the intermeddling or interference with the affairs of the Cuban Government." [17] But as time passed, the threat of intervention was increasingly used to coerce the Cuban government, and in fact for "intermeddling" in Cuban affairs. Root, who for years watched and privately deplored the widening applications of the right of intervention, denounced the trend as a violation of the government's original intent, and denied that it was inherent in the wording of the famous Article Three.[18]

It should also be noted that the second part of the permanent settlement, the commercial tie represented by the Reciprocity Treaty of 1902, was carried through in response to the demands of the Cuban public. It is true that American policy-makers had envisaged such an agreement as a part of their own program. But they found their original support for it in Cuba, not the United States, and it was only with the greatest difficulty that Cuban reciprocity survived the early assaults of Congress. The Americans who conceived the treaty believed it to be genuinely beneficial to both parties, Cuban as well as American, and in 1902 most Cubans would probably have agreed.

The Cuban program formulated from 1898 to 1902 was to show an impressive durability in an age of rapid change. The Platt Amendment, abrogated in 1934, was the first of its elements to disappear. The other two elements, continuing Cuban-American trade agreements and the American economic penetration of Cuba, survived for a generation longer, only to fall prey to the Castro revolution. By that time the original settlement had long since become obsolete, and the program of general Caribbean expansion which it initiated had passed its zenith and moved toward liquidation. In Haiti, in the Dominican Republic, in Nicaraugua, the Marines had come and gone, while the United States domination in Cuba appeared ended. But if the Cuban policy of Root and McKinley, of Wilson and Wood and Roosevelt, had had its day, that day was surely a long and full one.

IMPERIALISM

The Vicious Circle of American Imperialism

WILLIAM APPLEMAN WILLIAMS

Two final selections, by William A. Williams and Ernest R. May, illustrate the difficulty of getting total control over the subject of American imperialism of the 1890s or, perhaps, any other period. The first brief essay offers recent conclusions reached by William A. Williams, now professor of American history at Oregon State University. The essay modifies his earlier work, The Tragedy of American Diplomacy, *by adding to his discussion of the metropolitan industrial elite insights gained from an exhaustive study of what was happening to the agricultural majority of the country. This perspective is more fully, indeed exhaustively, developed in Williams's new book,* The Roots of the Modern American Empire (*New York: Random House, 1969*).

The essay and the book raise some old problems: Is all market expansionism, by definition, *imperialism? What was the mechanism through which so many people so thoroughly merged, and thereby corrupted, the "ideology of political freedom" with "economic nationalism"? In the conclusion to* The Tragedy of American Diplomacy *Williams writes that his essay "recommends that the frontier-expansionist explanation of American democracy and prosperity, and the strategy of the Open Door policy, be abandoned on the grounds that neither any longer bears any significant relation to reality." But did they* ever *have that relation to reality? Why do they relate less well now than they did in the past? Is it likely, as Williams believes, that capitalism can endure without the dependence upon foreign markets? Was Lenin or Hobson correct?*

Modern American imperialism is usually treated as an urban phenomenon. It is analyzed and interpreted as a manifestation of the general drive, among mature industrial countries, for markets for manufactured goods and surplus capital, for raw materials, and for military bases to secure the empire. The evidence supports this view so far as the 20th century is concerned. And it is likewise apparent that the men who *directed* America's first outward push between 1895 and 1901 acted upon an industrial conception of the economy and its needs.

The weakness of this account is that it ignores a great body of information and the great majority of the population. Once generally accepted, that is to say, the interpretation blocked off a vast preserve of facts: if imperialism was industrial, there was *ipso facto* no need to look at agriculture. The population could not so easily be ignored, however, and hence three general explanations have been offered to explain why the people supported imperialism.

Radicals and some conservatives argued that the industrial elite had the power, including control of mass media, to do as they wished. The majority was ignored when possible and manipulated when necessary. Most liberals and conservatives concluded that the majority supported expansion for reasons of humanitarianism and patriotism, thus entering their ideological caveats against the Hobson-Lenin interpretation as they resolved the intellectual problem involving the majority of the population. The more sophisticated liberals and conservatives ultimately explained the action of the majority in psychological terms. The majority opted for imperialism because it was composed of paranoiacs, other pathological sub-groups, and neurotics who, through the transfer process, dealt with their domestic frustrations by becoming imperialists.

The only trouble with all these answers is that they are theoretically crude and factually wrong. But two facts, combined with considerable research, make it possible to offer a closer approximation to reality. The first fact is a straightforward positivistic bit of data: the majority of the American population was agricultural during the period when the country embraced imperialism. Rural population in 1870 was 28.7 million as compared with 9.9 million urban; and in 1900 the figures were 45.8 rural and 30.2 urban.

The second fact is theoretical, first seen by Adam Smith: this rural majority existed in an *internal* colonial relationship vis-à-vis the domestic American metropolis (and the larger Western European metropolis of which New York is a part).

Reprinted by permission from William Appleman Williams, "The Vicious Circle of American Imperialism," *New Politics,* Vol. IV, No. 4 (Fall, 1965), pp. 48–55.

Hence the problem is defined as delineating the way that the internal colonial majority came either to accept or acquiesce in imperialism. And the answer lies in understanding that the domestic colonial majority embraced overseas economic expansion as the best way of improving its relative and absolute position within the system.

The reason for this is that the domestic colonials were commercial farmers. They did not go on the land to escape the marketplace and live a life of quiet contemplation. They turned the sod and chopped the cotton to win a healthy share of marketplace rewards. They intended to be, and they were, men of the marketplace. And they knew that, in order to improve their position, they had to have either (1) a domestic market capable of absorbing their vast production, (2) a foreign market sufficient unto their surpluses, or (3) a willingness to change their existing outlook and embrace some form of socialism.

A few of them did move toward socialism. And a good many advocated various reforms of the domestic marketplace. But the vast majority, including the reformers, turned to an expansion of the overseas market as a way of solving their problems. Hence the key to America's external imperialism lies in the way that the dynamic process of internal imperialism, through which the metropolis ruled and shaped the colonial territories south of the Potomac and west of the Appalachians (and the agriculture areas of the northeast itself), ultimately united the domestic colonials and their masters in an imperial outlook and policy that generated a drive for economic supremacy of the world.

It is textbook knowledge, of course, that the Southern cotton producer depended upon the foreign market prior to the Civil War. But it is equally important to realize that Northern and Western farmers were beginning, during the 1850s, to need the same market for their surpluses. The Civil War dramatized this in three ways. They lost their Southern consumers. They parlayed technology and westward expansion into a still greater surplus, and they became accustomed to selling that surplus in the overseas market. The Eastern dairy farmer, as well as the Western sodbuster, came to depend on the export market to provide the crucial differential between subsistence or failure, and entrepreneurial success.

This orientation toward overseas market expansion was reinforced and generalized during the years of reconstruction and the depression of the 1870s. Farmers felt the peacetime pinch within two years, and the birth of the Grange in 1867 documented the persistence of difficulties that increasingly affected more colonials in all regions. As a devastated and occupied society, the South had great difficulty reestablishing its prewar production and market position. In contrast, the Westerners suffered the consequences of their wartime boom. Their good fortune attracted new settlers and more developmental capital and those factors, added to their existing capacity, pushed output even higher. The surplus could not be absorbed even by the restored Southern market and the enlarged requirements of the metropolis, and hence they intensified their efforts to hold and enlarge their foreign markets. And to complicate their problems, they began to export cattle and dressed beef, and to extend their production of pork products.

This pattern of economic development guided the politics of the West and the South between 1865 and 1877. Cattlemen turned to the government for aid in blocking the importation of diseased animals that would ruin their herds and in turn block their exports as well as domestic sales. The Texas Grange launched a campaign for reciprocity treaties to open new markets that preceded comparable efforts by industrial and business groups in the metropolis by at least a decade. The more general agitation led by Grangers for the regulation of railroads, and the improvement of water transportation, was predicated upon the need to improve the competitive position of the colonials in the export market and to win a larger share of the existing return from that market.

These problems led to an increasing awareness of the limits imposed by England's control of the international cereal and cotton markets, and to a blunt confrontation with Britain's imperial economic power in alternate markets around the world. Southerners led the rising agitation by the agrarians for a merchant marine and an Isthmian canal built and controlled by the United States. And from the very outset the campaign by Westerners and Southerners to remonetize silver was predicated as much upon a drive to weaken Britain's world economic power, to penetrate markets dominated by Great Britain, and to enter new markets, as by a concern to increase the money supply at home.

The related aspects of this increasing involvement of the colonials with export markets were equally important. Business, financial, and political leadership in the metropolis recognized (as did the colonials) that the exports of the South and the West were paying the costs of the war, meeting the current balance of payments demands incurred by the metropolis, and rapidly providing the entire economy with a regular net credit in its dealings with the rest of the world. The vaunted turn of the trade balance was the work of the colonials, not the metropolis.

This consciousness of the role and importance of exports in the macroeconomic sense was paralleled and reinforced by a similar, if slower and less general, experience in the microeconomic sphere. Individual entrepreneurs, especially cotton textile manufacturers, turned to foreign markets as a way to survive the depression of the 1870s. The Southern mills, which concentrated from the outset on crude, rough fabrics for the export market, rapidly joined the cotton producers in demanding government action in behalf of market expansion. And the intellectual and political leaders of the metropolis responded to the example provided by the colonials by beginning to generalize that experience to the entire economy, and by concerning themselves with the demands from the Westerners and Southerners for a foreign policy geared to an expansion of the marketplace.

All these patterns of thought and action were reinforced and extended, and in turn generated further consequences, as a result of the export bonanza between 1876 and 1883. On the European side, there was the vast market created by five years of miserable weather, crop and animal diseases, and an increasing population. On the American side, there was the combination of an already sizable crop surplus further increased by immigration and internal migration, railroad expansion, and improved machinery. The result was a fantastic boom in food exports. And, during the same years, the Southerners finally reached and surpassed their prewar cotton production.

This export boom not only pulled the entire economy out of the depression, but it prompted further investments in land, improvements, and transportation, and in the associated processing industries which further increased production. The experience also served to confirm the Southern and Western colonials in their existing belief that agriculture was the foundation of all economic development and thereby reinforced their determination to obtain an equitable share of such progress.

In a similar way, the export bonanza verified the previous experience and analysis which had led the colonials to emphasize market expansion as the solution to their problems. Nor was it simply the field hands who reacted in that fashion. Thinking and acting within the framework of their cotton culture, Southerners increasingly invested capital in mills to produce rough textiles for export, and obtained funds from the North in greater quantities for the same purpose. Meat processors like Nelson Morris and Gustavus Swift launched major drives to penetrate foreign markets. Cattlemen began to pay more attention to overseas markets for beef on the hoof. And the flour companies, including those on the Pacific Coast as well as those in Wisconsin and Minnesota, intensified their efforts, first launched in 1877, to extend their foreign sales.

Watching the statistics, and evaluating the evidence, metropolitan businessmen and intellectuals increasingly devoted more attention to the fortunes of commodity and food exports, and to the relevance of that pattern for their own operations. Politicians began to act within the framework of that new metropolitan concern for market expansion as well as to respond to the colonial agitation and pressure for the same objective. Presidents James Garfield and Chester Arthur, and Secretaries of State James Blaine and Frederick Frelinghuysen, were clearly aware of what was happening; and they approached the issues of diplomacy with one eye on the general expansionist needs of the system dominated by the metropolis, and the other eye on the political consequences of failing to satisfy the demands of the colonials.

The collapse of the export boom made it very difficult to meet those demands and, at the same time, increased the pressures to provide such solutions. The end of the bonanza was caused by two factors: the recovery of European productivity, and the artificial barriers thrown up by European countries against American exports. *The colonials, not the metropolitan manufacturers or bankers, alerted the rest of the world to the challenge and the dangers of the rising power of the American economy.* Great Britain, Germany, France, and other nations retaliated with tariffs, restrictions, and even embargoes against Western commodities that jarred their economic structures and produced serious political and social dissatisfaction and even unrest. Paradoxical as it might appear, the Westerners who were colonials at home had begun to function as overseas economic expansionists who penetrated and changed foreign societies. It gave them a sense of power, and a growing conviction that America could expand without serious difficulties.

These Westerners, including the associated processors of meat and wheat, reacted to the end of the boom and the retaliation in several interrelated and mutually reinforcing patterns. They defined the European powers as enemies because they blocked existing markets and thwarted the drive for alternate markets. Great Britain was considered the chief offender in this respect, but France and Germany were seen as significant and increasingly dangerous opponents. On a broader level, the entire agricultural community saw the imperial expansion of European powers as an extension of their existing opposition to American exports, and as a swelling of their power in the world marketplace.

The fundamental connection made by Southern and Western colonials, both philosophically and psychologically, between the free marketplace and free political and social institutions was likewise applied to world affairs. European infringement upon the free marketplace was not only seen as proof of their domestic autocracy, but also — and in an increasingly important sense — as a growing threat to American freedom. And, in order to preserve and extend their own freedom in the market, which underpinned their political freedom, the colonials increasingly concluded that they had to oppose European expansion while enlarging the American marketplace.

This drive for new and alternate markets was intimately associated with the campaign for the remonetization of silver. On the one hand, Germany and France (and the Latin Union in general) were attacked for demonetizing silver and thus reinforcing Britain's power in the world economic system. For the gold standard was seen as the keystone in England's economic empire. On the other hand, the remonetization of silver was viewed as the way to break London's power. It would destroy England's special and profitable relationship with India, which was considered crucial in the commodity marketplace, and at the same time enable American exporters to deal directly with the silver using countries of Latin America and Asia. This aspect of the colonial agitation for silver was just as important to the Westerners and Southerners as their concern to increase the money supply. It became a central part of their debate with the goldbugs and illustrates how, from a very early date, the argument concerned the best *means* of economic expansion rather than the issue of whether such expansion was desirable.

The early support by colonials for a merchant marine evolved into active approval of a modern navy. Their early emphasis on commerce destroyers, and on developing the necessary technology on a nationalistic basis before undertaking a battle fleet, did not mean they were against a navy. For that matter, the Navy's own building plan called for a very similar escalation in the nature and the size of the fleet, and for mastering the construction problems prior to laying down the keels of any battleships. The crucial point about the role of the colonials in connection with the navy is that their overseas economic activity played a central role in redefining the perimeter of America's strategic security. Their involvement in the world marketplace was vital in transforming the problem from one of continental defense into one of maintaining and extending an American position in a world economic system.

By the end of the 1880s, therefore, the colonials had exerted great influence on American thinking and feeling about foreign policy. Furthermore, they played a key role in the vigorous diplomacy pursued by the administration of President Benjamin Harrison between 1889 and 1893. They exerted direct and militant pressure for action against European market restrictions, and to open alternate markets. Their general dissatisfaction with metropolitan leadership created a serious political problem for the Republicans in particular, and both Harrison and Blaine saw foreign policy as a way to meet that challenge. And through the continuing example they provided, the agrarians steadily influenced metropolitan thinking about overseas economic expansion.

Blaine was of course concerned with such expansion for industry, and for the economy as a whole, as well as for the colonials; but his fight for reciprocity treaties in 1889–1890 cannot be understood save in the context of this colonial pressure. He had originally formulated his broad policy on the basis of the agrarian example, and his specific campaign in 1890 was clearly a move to keep the Western colonials in the Republican Party as well as a drive for economic expansion in the general sense. In the process of providing the support Blaine needed, moreover, the colonials convinced William McKinley that the time had come to shift his emphasis away from pure protection toward a concern with overseas markets.

It is simply wrong to assert either that the Populists (and associated agrarian protestors) opposed such overseas economic expansion or that they turned abroad only as psychological compensation for their defeat in the election of 1896. Jeremiah Simpson of Kansas, for example, was a vigorous market expansionist who advocated free trade and silver remonetization as means to that end, and who wanted the canal dug and the merchant marine restored to its former place of dominance in world shipping. And when he was confronted with the contradiction between his free trade market expansionism modeled on the British example, and his opposition to a big navy, he admitted that America would have to build such a fleet. When the frontier was gone, he acknowledged, a battle line would become a necessity. In the meantime, moreover, he supported the construction of commerce raiders and other new ships of the intermediate class.

Senator William V. Allen of Nebraska (as well as other Populists in the upper chamber) likewise supported expansion. Allen told his colleagues bluntly that the people of the country wanted more markets and a more forceful and vigorous foreign policy, and that he supported and would act upon that analysis and feeling. When the Hawaiian Revolution offered such an opportunity, Allen stood shoulder to shoulder with Henry Cabot Lodge in demanding that the fleet be used to keep the islands under the control of the United States.

Allen was primarily concerned to establish and maintain access to the world marketplace, and to keep the marketplace itself open and competitive, so that America's great economic power could triumph within that framework. He agreed with Tom Watson that, given such conditions, the American producer could knock the hind sights off any rival. Allen realized that the old territorial colonialism was irrelevant to, if not actually subversive of, the most effective kind of market expansion. For that reason he opposed the acquisition of real estate unless it was absolutely required to establish and maintain America's position in the marketplace.

Allen's differences with other expansionists over whether Hawaii had to be annexed typified the position of the Southerners and Westerners during the entire foreign policy debate of the 1890s. They were generally against taking title to overseas territories, but they were vigorous and militant market expansionists. Allen and other colonials argued among themselves, and with metropolitan expansionists, over the means most appropriate to their common objective, but they did not oppose the creation of an overseas economic empire.

Metropolitan leaders moved rapidly during the 1890s to accept and adopt the outlook and the policy that the colonials had advocated and practiced for more than 20 years. Much of this shift was generated within the metropolitan sector itself by businessmen who needed markets, by politicians who responded to those pressures, and by intellectuals who supplied various arguments (and pressure) for such expansion. And, since the metropolis controlled the central levers of power in the system, such metropolitan leaders came increasingly to formulate and implement the expansionist policy. The diplomacy of the 1890s was conducted by metropolitan leaders, and it was finally and formally cast in terms of industrial rather than agricultural market expansion.

But none of this alters the primary role of the agrarian and colonial sector in evolving the expansionist policy per se. It was their overseas economic expansion, and their agitation in connection with that activity and policy, that defined the problem and the solution. And none of it should be allowed to obscure the continuing and important part played by the colonials during the 1890s in turning the United States into a vigorous imperial competitor in the world marketplace. They sustained their vigorous agitation for such expansion. They made significant contributions to the debate over strategy and tactics. And they were largely responsible for merging economic nationalism with the ideology of political freedom.

For better or worse, the colonials played a major part in combining economics and politics into the heady and explosive brew of expansion for freedom. As early as the 1870s the colonials had defined the world marketplace as part of the frontier which gave them freedom and prosperity, and by the 1890s their demands for sustained and effective action to extend that frontier reached a crescendo. But they were neither unique nor pathological in speaking about empire in terms of freedom. They believed in the interrelationship between expansion and freedom because their conception of expansion and empire could be demonstrated to offer better conditions than European colonialism, as well as because it could be demonstrated that more markets improved their welfare at home.

They were not flailing about in an irrational response to industrialization, or to their defeat in the election of 1896. They were merely acting on the assumptions of classical marketplace capitalism, and on the basis of an argument concerning its relationship to free and representative government.

Given the assumptions and the practice of the capitalist marketplace, these results can hardly be described as surprising or unusual. And if anything was pathological, it was the system itself rather than one element within it. But accepting what happened with the colonials as part of American history will help provide a more accurate picture of American development in the 20th century, and of the nation's present predicament. For many present-day attitudes about world affairs derive rather clearly from the attitudes and views that were evolved, agitated, and acted upon by the people of the colonial sector between 1865 and 1901. Such acceptance may also help those who view those American colonials as creators of a tradition appropriate to the contemporary crisis. For it might at the very least suggest that the problem is not so much to find an American tradition as it is to change a set of American assumptions shared by that tradition.

American Imperialism: Some Tentative Explanation

ERNEST R. MAY

Ernest R. May's conclusions about what shaped American policy in the 1890s are emphatic. At the close of his first study of the subject, Imperial Democracy *(New York: Harcourt, Brace and World, 1961), he takes a clear stand against the interpretive line pursued by Williams: "From first to last, the makers of American policy and the presumed leaders of American opinion concerned themselves either with abstract morality or with conditions inside the United States. They scarcely thought of proclaiming to the world that America was a power. They were at most only incidentally concerned about real or imagined interests abroad. They gave no sign that they meant the United States to become a factor in the international balance" (p. 269).*

May's more recent and frankly speculative essay on imperialism is designed to explore changes in American opinion that might account for the remarkable shift from decided opposition to the acquisition of a colonial empire to positive interest in it. Dealing with the problem from this angle involves a series of unproved assertions about the influence of public opinion on policy. (Current experience suggests that the flow of influence is in precisely the opposite direction.) How much do we really gain from May's explanation of elite views? What is the connection between such opinion and decision-making? May can tell us how and why segments of the American elite affirmed or resisted conclusions already reached by the McKinley administration. It is unclear that his social scientific approach can yield anything more in the way of understanding. Finally, Ernest May, like Julius Pratt, severely limits his definition of imperialism to outright acquisition of colonies. By reducing the problem to its minimal terms, does he not avoid all the truly difficult questions? As Walter LaFeber observes in his sharply critical review of the book ("Imperial Nineties," Book World, *Sept. 8, 1968), May has managed to reduce the subject to a few months — from the annexation of Hawaii in June, 1898, to the annexation of the Philippines in February, 1899. Perhaps, LaFeber wryly remarks, "We can eventually make it disappear altogether . . ." (p. 18).*

With most leaders of opinion initially opposing imperialism, how and why did a swelling public come to support the taking of the Philippines?

In trying to answer this question one has to keep in mind the factors stressed by Merk, Pratt, LaFeber, and Hofstadter. With their thoughts turned to Hawaii or the Philippines, many Americans may have called up memories of Manifest Destiny. Mentioning Jefferson, Jackson, and Polk, a San Francisco daily declared that the "virile yeomanry of the Democratic party" would not follow "bloodless pedagogues of the Mugwump stripe." Murat Halstead of the Cincinnati *Commercial* said, "The world has just grown ripe for policies of annexation by all the great powers, and we are one of them. . . . 'We the people of the United States' never lost liberty or any good thing from acquiring good land, and never will." [1] *

As Pratt discovered, many business and religious periodicals employed Social Darwinist language. Many editorials in church organs described America's alternatives as expansion or decline. Mingling Calvinism and Darwinism, many also portrayed expansion as predestined. Even the *Catholic World,* with many Irish and German-American subscribers, spoke of the dynamism of the Anglo-Saxon race leading inevitably to territorial expansion.[2]

Many periodicals also cited new conditions created by technological developments. Calling for annexation of the Philippines, the *Baptist Union* remarked, "The century that is just closing has brought with it great changes. There are no longer any far-off lands. . . . Steam and electricity have well-nigh blotted out distance." [3]

As both Pratt and LaFeber point out, the business press constantly

From *American Imperialism: A Speculative Essay* by Ernest R. May.

* [See pp. 175–178 for notes to this article. — Ed.]

emphasized the nation's need for new commercial opportunities. Echoing this theme, business organizations urged the government to help open foreign markets. The New York State Bankers' Association, for example, resolved:

> Our capacity to produce far exceeds our capacity to consume. The home market can no longer keep furnaces in blast or looms in action. That capital may earn its increment and labor be employed, enterprise must contend in the markets of the world, for the sale of our surplus products.[4]

In coming to an opinion about colonial expansion many Americans unquestionably thought of the depressed economic conditions of recent years, the shrinkage of foreign markets resulting from European tariffs, and the prospect of expanded trade if the United States had island colonies as entrepôts in the Far East.

Underlying some of the public response may have been other, less rational impulses. Several years of severe depression had brought declines in sales, fees, commissions, and salaries, causing many in the middle class to falter in their lockstep with the Joneses. Those actually falling back felt themselves encroached upon by advancing immigrant minorities, deemed to be socially inferior. As Hofstadter and others have argued, the resultant heightened anxiety could have had an influence not only on the movement for war with Spain but on later responsiveness to imperialism. Contemporary psychologists, it is true, have not had much luck in proving connections between status insecurity and aggressive stands on foreign policy issues. The best study shows equal correlations with elements of childhood history, attitudes toward parents, and certain kinds of perceptions and values.[5] Larger-scale surveys, such as the famous inquiry into "the authoritarian personality," have used questionable methods.[6] Still, it remains conceivable that worry over social status translated itself somehow into approval of colonialism, and hence the "psychic crisis" entered into play along with the Manifest Destiny tradition, Social Darwinism, technological change, and yearning for new markets.

To tick off factors encouraging expansionism is still, however, to touch only a segment of the problem. Assuming that interested citizens arrived at opinions partly through influence from others, one still has to explain how opinion in favor of expansion took root when the largest part of the establishment advised otherwise. Why were expansionist impulses not smothered in 1869–71?

The two situations, of course, differed. In the earlier period opponents of annexation had been able to recommend doing nothing. In 1898 they had to advocate returning the Filipinos to Spanish rule, handing them over to another power, or launching them on a chancy experiment with independence. While the earlier debate came in the aftermath of a long and wearing war, that of 1898 occurred with a war just begun and patriotic nationalism on the bubble. And, as Pratt and LaFeber would emphasize, many changes had meanwhile occurred in the thinking of Americans and structure of the American economy.

But not to be forgotten are changes that had come over the world scene. In 1898 the fashionableness of imperialism abroad cropped up again and again in American commentary. When Kohlsaat's Chicago *Times-Herald* came out for expansion, its editorial pointed to the English example and the proexpansionist advice of such men as Henry Norman. The *Baptist Home Mission Monthly,* speaking of Spain's expulsion from the Philippines as a *sine qua non,* asserted, "Nothing short of this will satisfy the enlightened public sentiment of this country — and of England." Albert J. Beveridge called for advancing into the world "as our mother has told us how." Hamlin Garland, the novelist, confessed to questioning the anti-imperialism current among his agrarian friends largely because of a conversation with Rudyard Kipling.[7]

Some commentary evidenced awareness of the idea, preached by Pearson and Kidd and demonstrated in practice by Chamberlain and Bismarck, that imperialism might solve social ills. The Reverend John Henry Barrows of Chicago said, "Some are rapidly perceiving that we are to have a better America through cherishing larger responsibilities," and Henry Watterson wrote in his *Louisville Courier-Journal:*

> It is true that we exchange domestic dangers for foreign dangers; but in every direction we multiply the opportunities of the people. We risk Caesarism, certainly; but even Caesarism is preferable to anarchism. . . . In short, anything is better than the pace we were going when the present forces started into life.[8]

Many opponents of imperialism attacked the foreign examples and authorities that imperialists cited. The *Congregationalist* quoted Gladstone as saying, "The idea that the colonies add to the strength of the mother country appears to me to be as dark a superstition as any that existed in the Middle Ages." The Philadelphia *Public Ledger* declared:

> One of the leading motives and incentives for the new American policy of expansion and adventure is that we shall thereby imitate England and improve trade, though many of the most thoughtful, knowing and eminent Englishmen of our own and other days have deprecated the British colonial policy.

Taking direct issue with Watterson, a St. Louis Presbyterian weekly said that he had "studied English politics to little purpose if he thinks England is not menaced by socialism and agrarianism. . . . Caesarism is no cure for the discontent of the masses." [9]

All this rebuttal had no apparent effect. Supporters of Philippine annexation made extensive use of the example of England and words from English imperialists. The antiexpansionism of prominent men at home thus found an offset in contrary expressions from prominent men abroad, and Englishmen such as Rosebery, Chamberlain, Norman, and Kipling served as leaders of opinion for Americans.

Had the American establishment stood as solidly together as in 1869–71, words of foreigners could probably have been quoted with less effect. But in 1898 a minority of the establishment, much more impressive than the minority formed by Bennett, Ward, and a few others in 1869–71, advocated expansion.

Including such men as Olney, Lodge, Capen, Holls, Mahan, Abbott, MacArthur, Roosevelt, Tree, and Hitt, this minority seemed to represent a younger generation. Of the men just mentioned, Tree was sixty-six, Olney a little over sixty, Capen and MacArthur in their fifties, the others in their forties. A similar group of antiexpansionists, such as Carnegie, Schurz, Sigel, Godkin, Low, MacVeagh, Lincoln, and Harper, would have had an average age in the mid-sixties. The chances are that, to many, the imperialists seemed more vigorous and more forward-looking, as well as more in harmony with newer currents abroad.

In 1898 the nation's opinion leadership divided. Perhaps it would be better to say that it splintered. The imperialists pressed varying lines of argument, some emphasizing power and advantage, others duty and destiny, still others ills at home worse than those that might be flown to. They and the anti-imperialists addressed themselves to more than one issue. There resulted a cacophony in which interested citizens would sometimes have found it difficult to divine who favored expansion and who did not.

The examples of Coolidge and Reid illustrate the confusion. At the outset Coolidge's position seemed clearly anti-imperialist, and on the broad issue of whether the United States should acquire a colony, his view never wavered. On the other hand, he saw Hawaiian annexation as not necessarily contravening his principles, for he could imagine Hawaii eventually becoming sufficiently Anglo-Saxonized to qualify for entry into the union. Also, he could see acquisition of a port or even maintenance of a temporary protectorate over the Philippines as providing entrepôts to markets in Asia, continuing the westward thrust, and yielding economic advantages without leaving the United States permanently in control of a subject population. Perhaps too he could envision these limited steps postponing the triumph of communism and the day when corporate bonds ceased to have value. Coolidge's opposition to annexation of the Philippines lacked sharp definition.

Reid came out not only for taking the Philippines but, in spite of the war resolution, for retaining control of Cuba. Nevertheless his views, no less than Coolidge's, defied simple categorization. An article that Reid published in *Century* magazine in September 1898 drew a direct parallel between the position of the United States in Cuba and that of Britain in Egypt. Mooting the question of whether or not intervention in Cuba had been wise, Reid asserted that, having intervened, "we made ourselves responsible for improving the situation, and . . . we cannot leave Cuba till that is done." As to the Philippines, he felt unable to present any strong argument for annexation except the absence of any alternative "consistent with our . . . honorable obligation . . . to civilization." He said candidly:

> The war is a great sorrow, and to many these results of it will seem even more mournful. They cannot be contemplated with unmixed confidence by any; and to all who think, they must be a source of some grave apprehensions. Plainly, this unwelcome war is leading us by ways we have not trod to an end we cannot surely forecast.

Reid offered some consolation. The islanders would surely benefit, he felt; construction of an interoceanic canal would come at an earlier date; and Americans could hope for "mercantile control of the Pacific Ocean." Nevertheless neither his *Century* article nor his *Tribune* editorials offered a clarion call for a colonialist movement.[10]

Some members of the establishment, to be sure, adopted simple and clear-cut stands. Charles W. Eliot helped establish the Anti-Imperialist League, which categorically opposed expansion. A number of Harvard professors joined, and so did President Rogers of Northwestern University and Von Holst of the University of Chicago. Yale's William Graham Sumner, probably the nation's best-known promoter of Social Darwinism, spoke uncompromisingly against even temporary acquisition of Philippine territory. (In opposing imperialism, it might be added, he took the same position taken by Herbert Spencer in England.) [11]

Businessmen, lawyers, and other nonacademics seemed less disposed to approach the issue as crusaders. Though Andrew Carnegie financed the Anti-Imperialist League, Carl Schurz and Lew Wallace served it as orators and pamphleteers, and Sigmund Zeisler held office in the Chicago branch, few others who have caught our eyes [in this book] played active roles in it. Its leadership came less from the foreign policy elite than from other elites usually leading campaigns for clean government or social betterment.

Similarly the establishment produced a few, but only a few, straightforward imperialists. Among them were Brooks Adams, Mahan, Judge Grosscup, and Beveridge. Perhaps one ought to add Charles A. Conant, a writer for the New York *Journal of Commerce,* Yale Professor Washburn

Hopkins, a Sanskrit scholar who argued from the example of India that a "higher morality" required Anglo-Saxons to rule the lesser races, and editor St. Clair McKelway of the Brooklyn *Eagle*.[12] On the whole, however, thoroughgoing imperialists and thoroughgoing anti-imperialists both came from the fringes of the establishment.

Most solid men of affairs resembled Coolidge and Reid in taking equivocal positions. Some opposed colonies but not expansion that would mean expansion of trade and influence. Many said, as did Depew, that colonies might turn out to be bad bargains, that the United States ought not to embark on an imperialist career, but that, all things considered, annexation of the Philippines seemed the most prudent course at present. This line of argument merged imperceptibly with Reid's — that the advantages of colonies *might* turn out to exceed the disadvantages.

By expressing ambivalent views, men of the establishment offered the interested public a wider range of choice than had the establishment of 1869–71. Also, they gave latitude to men who in other circumstances might have functioned merely as talkers. One can imagine a Bostonian such as James J. Myers or Edwin Ginn saying to his acquaintance, "Mr. Eliot says . . . but Mr. Coolidge says . . . and Mr. Olney says . . . ," and then producing his own reasons for siding with one or the other.

The more varied and unclear the statements from the establishment, the more widely leadership dispersed and the more crude and ill-informed became the reasoning employed. Those predisposed toward expansion found it easier to trot out catch phrases such as "Manifest Destiny," "survival of the fittest," and "vast markets of Asia." Those predisposed against expansion could speak less qualifiedly of need to preserve racial purity, dangers created by increasing federal patronage, the army, and government spending, and perils likely to result simply from deserting the wisdom of the founding fathers. More and more, propagandists and politicians on both sides appealed, as had the expansionists of 1869–71, to an antiestablishment public.

Some who preached expansionism pretended that the Anti-Imperialist League represented the whole establishment. . . . Some with political ambitions adopted such a line. Holls did so. Renewing his efforts to supplant Schurz, he called the veteran leader not an American at all, but an old country liberal "à la Bamberger and Eugen Richter." Beveridge sought election to the United States Senate, denouncing anti-imperialists for "disbelief in the American people." Young comers, such as James M. Beck in Philadelphia, put similar adornments on their speeches, and men already in Washington played to the patriotism and piety of citizens who did not know the world beyond their county borders. Senator Teller of Colorado, who had been responsible for the phrases in the war resolution promising independence to Cuba, shifted stance, saying, "The American flag is capable of giving to those people American law, American freedom, American progress, and enabling them to share in prosperity with us as well as in American glory." Implying that any policy except retention of the Philippines would be sacrilegious, Senator Frye of Maine declared, "God opened the door, pushed us in and closed it. No man on earth or angel in heaven can now take us out." [13]

Anti-imperialists made equally vigorous efforts to arouse some kind of antiestablishment public. They appealed to class feeling. In Senate debate, Republican William E. Mason of Illinois attributed the movement for annexing the Philippines to a conspiracy among exporters of liquor, tobacco, and textiles and importers of sugar; Democrat George G. Vest of Missouri blamed "the greed of the commercial and money-making classes"; and Democrat John L. McLaurin of South Carolina, "the trusts and the money power . . . crying out for new fields to exploit." The antiannexation bloc loudly claimed to represent American rather than foreign principles. Mason accused McKinley of imitating English rulers, and Democratic Senator Augustus O. Bacon of Georgia spoke of the administration's moving into the Far East "in order that England may carry out her schemes of foreign colonization and foreign dominion." Even members of the Anti-Imperialist League made use of this charge. A league pamphlet said, "Never was a nation so lucky as England in finding the paws of a mighty cat to put in the fire in place of her own," and so aristocratic a league member as Charles Francis Adams wrote, "Instead of finding our precedents in the experience of England or any other European power, I would suggest that the true course for this country . . . is exactly the course we have heretofore pursued." [14]

While courting a public assumed to be hostile to the establishment, imperialist and anti-imperialist politicians sought also to appeal to the establishment. Senators Platt of Connecticut and Foraker of Ohio, both given to demagoguery on other issues, showed great restraint when advocating annexation of the Philippines. Both delivered legalistic addresses, full of quotations and citations, arguing that the founding fathers and subsequent interpreters of the Constitution had envisioned the possibility of the nation's acquiring and holding colonies. On the other side, Senator Donelson Caffery of Louisiana argued against taking the Philippines, quoting extensively from Seeley and Kidd to support a contention that Anglo-Saxons did not flourish in the tropics.[15]

The administration, having decided to annex the Philippines, employed successfully the tactic with which Grant had failed in 1870. McKinley appointed a commission to survey conditions in the islands. To head it he chose an establishment man known to hold antiannexationist views. Imitating Grant to the letter, McKinley selected Andrew D. White's successor at Cornell University, Jacob Gould Schurman. Earlier, just after the

Philippine issue had arisen, the President had named as Secretary of State John Hay, a close friend not only of Lodge, Theodore Roosevelt, and their set but also of Reid, Whitney, and others in the New York establishment. With the peace treaty awaiting ratification, McKinley appointed Columbia law professor David Jayne Hill as Hay's deputy and Joseph H. Choate as ambassador to Great Britain. Coupled with official denials that ratification of the treaty would necessarily determine whether the United States kept the Philippines or eventually made them independent, these moves helped to preserve divisions and an appearance of uncertainty within the establishment. Probably, too, they helped to prevent an antiestablishment public from taking clear form as a force either for or against imperialism.

With the foreign policy elite at sixes and sevens and a much larger public taking interest in the question of whether or not to expand, the McKinley administration succeeded in doing what the Grant administration had failed to do. By using a variety of pressures, it rallied to the treaty all but two of the doubtful Republicans in the Senate. For reasons of his own, Bryan recommended that Democrats not use the two-thirds rule to block action desired by a Senate majority. As a result, the treaty with Spain, ceding the United States title to the Philippines, passed with one vote to spare.[16]

Defeat of the Dominican treaty twenty-nine years earlier had been read as an oracular national decision against expansion. Defeat of the Versailles Treaty twenty years later was to be interpreted as a binding popular verdict against collective-security arrangements. According to the custom that these two instances illustrate, the two-thirds vote in favor of annexing the Philippines should have established colonial imperialism as a new American tradition.

For a time it seemed as if this would be so. Though having denied it earlier, the President began to say that the treaty gave the United States a Philippine colony and that only a positive decree to the contrary by Congress would change the situation. Schurman came back from the islands asserting that the United States would have to remain indefinitely. Meanwhile Reid, speaking as an intimate of the President, employed much more imperialistic language than earlier. To acquire the Philippines, he said, was "to fence in the China Sea and secure [a] . . . commanding position on the other side of the Pacific – doubling our control of it and of the fabulous trade the twentieth century will see it bear." To have done otherwise, he declared, would have been to yield to "a mushy sentimentality . . . alike un-American and un-Christian." Hinting of possible future moves, Assistant Secretary of State Hill urged in the *Forum* that American policy be thought of not as expansion or imperialism but as "the extension of civilization." [17]

Such a view became more and more widely held. Though Bryan and Cleveland continued to criticize the decision to annex the Philippines, many Democrats and Democratic organs, especially those unenthusiastic about Bryan, turned toward a different position. New York financier Perry Belmont, Tammany chief Richard Croker, and former governor and senator John M. Palmer of Illinois said the United States had probably acted rightly in retaining the Philippines. Editorials in the Philadelphia *Record,* the Atlanta *Constitution,* and the New Orleans *Times-Picayune* expressed a similar judgment. Local election returns in November 1899 seemed even to the stoutly antiexpansionist New York *Evening Post* and New York *World* "a victory for imperialism." [18]

Meanwhile discussion turned to new possibilities for expansion. In late August 1899 the *Literary Digest* observed:

> Considerable change in public sentiment has appeared during the last few months with regard to Cuba's future government, and where a year and a half ago the American press was almost unanimous in calling for Cuban independence, there is now a strong undercurrent of opinion in favor of annexation.

In the autumn this undercurrent gained force. The Boston *Herald,* the New York *Journal of Commerce,* the Chicago *Inter-Ocean,* and dailies in Ohio, Minnesota, Missouri, Texas, South Dakota, and Oregon came out for reversal of the promise of independence. Kohlsaat's Chicago *Times-Herald* asserted that "annexation would be a blessing." Though McKinley did not commit himself, he said in December 1899 that Cuban independence should not be "a hasty experiment." [19]

Early in 1900 rumors circulated of secret negotiations reviving the project for purchase of the Danish West Indies. Applauding the report, Reid's New York *Tribune* remarked, "It will be a blessing to the islands if they come under our flag, and we can make them worth much more to the country than their cost." [20]

At almost the same time dispatches from the Far East told of anti-foreign violence in China and of new moves in European capitals foreshadowing that country's partitioning. The Boston *Herald* said editorially that the United States would have no choice but to take part in determining China's "future political and trade status," and the New York *Journal of Commerce* declared that the Chinese would "have . . . to establish a civilized government . . . or have one established over them." Coincidentally, books appeared by Brooks Adams, Charles A. Conant, and Josiah Strong, all forecasting ultimate American dominion over most of the Pacific and East Asia. Many signs suggested that the events of 1898–99 merely marked the beginning of America's career as a colonial power.[21]

Then the current shifted. Bryan, whose strength among Democratic state and local committees ensured him a second try at the presidency, indicated that he would make criticism of the administration's imperialism an important part of his campaign. Theretofore the play he meant to give this issue had remained uncertain. The Nebraska State Democratic platform, drafted in part by him, had called for eventual Philippine independence, but laid much more emphasis on demands for free coinage of silver and curbing of trusts. Only as convention time approached did Bryan reveal his intention. When he did, Democrats who had disagreed with him about the Philippines changed front, with Croker promising Tammany's support for an anti-imperialist campaign and Olney publishing in the *Atlantic* a jesuitical article saying that the American empire should include Cuba but not possessions in the Far East. The national party platform then named imperialism as the foremost issue, and Bryan, as the nominee, devoted his initial efforts to wooing the Anti-Imperialist League and Schurz's following among German-Americans.[22]

As if fearful that the Democrats had found a winning issue, the administration gave loud publicity to Secretary Hay's circular requesting that the powers preserve an open door for trade in China, claiming that the United States thus expressed its opposition to imperialism. Several newspapers classifying themselves as anti-imperialist, among them the Boston *Evening Transcript,* the New York *Herald,* and the New York *Evening Post,* commended McKinley and Hay for coming back toward a proper view of America's world role. Confronted with further violence in China and a rupture of communications with legations in Peking, the administration announced that it would contribute units to an international expeditionary force. At the same time, however, Hay informed the press that he had dispatched a second note, defining America's aim as the preservation of Chinese territorial and administrative integrity. This action too drew praise from anti-imperialist papers, and Republican organs close to McKinley portrayed it as proving the administration not to be imperialistic.[23]

After McKinley's renomination the White House announced that Cuban independence could be expected shortly. The three newspapers regarded as administration organs, Reid's *Tribune,* Postmaster General Charles Emory Smith's Philadelphia *Press,* and Kohlsaat's Chicago *Times-Herald,* all published editorials describing this announcement as further discrediting opposition efforts to tag the President as an imperialist. During the campaign both McKinley and vice-presidential nominee Theodore Roosevelt denied plans for further territorial acquisitions. The administration, they conceded, believed in expansion, but only in the expansion of American trade and influence.[24]

McKinley won endorsement from men who had opposed annexation of the Philippines. Though Schurz backed Bryan, Carnegie and Abram S. Hewitt came out for the President. So did Wayne MacVeagh, who said he was satisfied that McKinley's reelection would mean the nation's "return to its true mission, that of developing the rich and great American continent and dedicating it to liberty and peace." The "present tendency of President McKinley's mind," MacVeagh went on, "can be discerned in the true American policy he is now pursuing in China." [25]

Politicians judged the public to have lost enthusiasm for empire. Senator Cushman K. Davis of Minnesota wrote regretfully to Reid that "the transient people . . . have never believed in or understood the 'swelling act of the imperial theme.'" Platt of Connecticut, who still hoped the United States might keep Cuba, warned General Leonard Wood, "The whole Congress is nervous, liable to take the bit in its teeth and say we ought to get out of Cuba." [26]

Nor did professionals change their minds because of McKinley's reelection. No one remembering his campaign or Roosevelt's could interpret the Republican victory as a triumph for imperialism. Administration organs did not do so, and McKinley made no return to "the imperial theme" after being assured another term. In fact he moved almost at once, through the Platt Amendment, to give Cuba at least nominally its promised independence.

In the autumn of 1901, to be sure, the administration concluded a treaty for purchase of the Danish West Indies. But since negotiations had opened more than a year earlier, this treaty constituted a carry-over from the past. Taking it up early in 1902, after McKinley's assassination, the Senate handled it as a legacy from a martyred President and ratified with little debate. On the whole, the press eschewed comment. When the Danish Rigsdag then turned the treaty down, few expressed regret. The *Literary Digest* quoted as a typical newspaper reaction the comment of the Pittsburgh *Gazette:* "The United States has worried along without the Danish islands until this time, and can continue to do so." [27]

Once in a while came an echo of "the imperial theme" of 1898–99. When Panama seceded from Colombia and leased a canal zone to the United States, one or two newspapers mentioned the possibility of making Panama itself a colony. St. Clair McKelway continued in the Brooklyn *Eagle* to advocate annexation of Cuba and other Caribbean islands. Henry King, the editor of the St. Louis *Globe-Democrat,* campaigned for colonizing Haiti and the Dominican Republic. Theirs were, however, isolated voices.[28]

In 1904–1905 a real possibility presented itself, for the first time in over thirty years, of annexing the Dominican Republic. Divided into warring factions and pressed by both American and European creditors, Dominican political leaders invited the United States to assume some kind of control over the country's affairs. When rumors spread that Roosevelt would agree to American supervision of Dominican finances even the loyal New York *Tribune* commented, "That is a good deal to ask." When the rumor proved true and Roosevelt presented the agreement to the Senate,

Republicans as well as Democrats blocked its ratification. The President had to settle, at least temporarily, for an unratified *modus vivendi.* Neither senators nor newspaper editors exhibited appetite for a Dominican colony. Roosevelt himself commented, "I have about the same desire to annex it as a gorged boa-constrictor might have to swallow a porcupine wrong-end-to." [29]

By that time Republican leaders had begun to voice doubts even about the Philippines. On Memorial Day, 1902, Roosevelt had spoken of possible eventual independence for the islands. His words enabled one-time anti-imperialist dailies to say that a difference in principle no longer separated the administration from its former critics and that the only remaining difference concerned timing. In 1904 Elihu Root, after leaving the Secretaryship of War, prophesied that the Philippines would eventually go the way of Cuba.[30]

In 1898 the imperialist movement had been powerful, and the Senate's vote to annex the Philippines provided a starting point for a new consensus favorable to future colonial expansion. For about a year afterward such a consensus seemed in the making, foreshadowing a time when Hawaii and the Philippines would stand as merely the first members of a vast and growing colonial empire. During 1900 the new current slowed and stopped. Before long, majority opinion once again ran in the old channel. Dismissing the possibility of further colonial expansion, Lodge commented in 1903, "The American people have lost all interest in it." [31] How does one explain this reversal?

Simple lapse of time accounts for much. Without dramatic incidents to hold their attention, the members of Senator Davis' "transient public" lost interest. The possibility of their becoming engaged once again with the subject diminished as the issues became more complicated. Could tariffs be imposed on imports from the new possessions, or would the Constitution compel free entry of sugar, tobacco, and other products harvested by cheap colonial labor? Would Congress have to require that imports into the colonies pay the same tariffs as imports received on the continent? If so, the colonists would be denied cheap products from nearby lands. If not, the colonists could import goods, reexport them to the mainland, and conceivably subvert the protective system. These issues did not make their way to the decision docket of the Supreme Court until after the 1900 election. As Mr. Dooley remarked,

> Th' men that argyied that th' Constitution ought to shadow th' flag to all th' tough resorts on th' Passyfic coast an' th' men that argyied that th' flag was so lively that no Constitution cud follow it an' survive, they died or lost their jobs or wint back to Salem an' wer' f'rgotten. Expansionists

> contracted an' anti-expansionists blew up, an' little childher was born into th' wurruld an' grew to manhood an' niver heerd iv Pother Ricky except whin some wan got a job there.[32]

During the interval many deep-dyed protectionists probably lost enthusiasm for colonies.

As the interested public shrank, its composition changed. Though containing some convinced imperialists, this smaller public also contained active members of the Anti-Imperialist League and, perhaps more important, men who felt their personal interests jeopardized by colonial expansion: cane and sugar-beet growers and producers of tobacco fearing competition from tropical colonies; Irish-Americans seeing that imperialism promoted Anglo-American solidarity, reduced sympathy for the Irish cause, and weakened Irish power in American politics; and German-Americans who, for similar reasons, regretted any tightening of American ties with England and feared, in addition, increasing friction with their own aggressively expanding fatherland. When back to normal dimensions, the interested public probably possessed a large anti-imperialist component.

And some who applauded expansion in 1898–99 changed their minds as a result of the Philippine insurrection.[33] At almost the moment when the Senate approved annexation of the islands, Filipinos led by Émilio Aguinaldo opened a war for independence. Employing guerilla tactics, they eluded and harassed American forces, engaging a large part of the regular army and requiring that some wartime volunteers remain in service. Numbers of American troops fighting the guerillas grew from 30,000 in 1899 to 60,000 in 1900, with little or no evidence of headway toward pacification.

Impatient congressmen and newspaper editors called for expanding the American force to 100,000 and replacing the generals in command. Despite the approach of the election, staunch Republican papers took the President to task for his failure to bring the war to an end. Later, as reports filtered back that captives had been tortured for information, potential rebel supporters had been herded into concentration camps, and troops had been sent into one pro-rebel area with orders to make it a "howling wilderness," some of the same papers criticized the administration for tolerating such inhumanity.[34]

Anti-imperialists capitalized on discontent caused by the war, and onetime imperialists confessed chagrin at Filipino resistance to the blessings of liberty. Fear that the same kind of war might erupt in Cuba clearly had some quieting effect on ardor for annexation, especially since the army had no troops with which to fight it; and the fact that severe fighting continued in the Philippines until well into 1901 must have had an effect on all thought of possible new extensions of empire. Probably, in fact, it was the Philippine insurrection more than anything else that quelled any nascent imperialist movement.

The coincidental war between Britain and the Boer republics, which had far-reaching effects on ideas about empire within the international liberal community, was not without some impact on American thought. Opening in mid-October 1899, this war saw Britain suffer a series of humiliating defeats. It ended in a British victory, but only after hard campaigning, running into 1902, and after Britain had committed 300,000 troops to cope with an enemy numbering no more than 75,000. Watching its grim course, many Englishmen and Europeans lost their romantic ideas about imperialism.

Some so affected had friends in America. Within a month after the war's opening Cecil Spring Rice wrote Mrs. Theodore Roosevelt of having "*doubts* of all kinds which are most horrible." [35] William T. Stead, the editor of the *Pall Mall Gazette,* testified publicly to experiencing a complete change of mind about imperialism. Previously a trumpeter of England's holy imperial mission, he had visited the United States, written best sellers about crime and Christianity in Chicago and New York, and been a patron of Chicago's Columbia Exhibition. One of those crusaders against immorality whose lectures and writings combined righteousness with spiciness, he drew many American listeners and readers. When he suddenly turned against imperialism, Kohlsaat's Chicago *Times-Herald* and other American periodicals publicized the event.[36]

Day in and day out the American press also reported the powerful reaction in England within the Liberal party against Rosebery and other imperialists. Those who clung to the label "Liberal Imperialist" merely supported the war, while many others came out in open opposition, among them the party's younger, more dashing, and more imaginative leaders. By 1901 few men in English politics who commanded admiration in America still voiced the expansionist zest of the previous decade, and liberals on the continent seemed unanimous not only in decrying British imperialism but in turning away from colonialist movements in their own countries.[37]

A new anti-imperialist doctrine quite different from that of Cobden and Bright meanwhile caught the fancy of liberal intellectuals in England and elsewhere. Best represented by John A. Hobson's *Imperialism,* this doctrine held colonies to be of benefit primarily to capitalists.[38] With abundant statistics Hobson showed colonial trade to yield little for either producers or shippers. Capitalists, on the other hand, could no longer find sufficiently profitable uses at home for the large profits they earned, Hobson contended, any they therefore needed to reach into primitive lands for new opportunities to place funds in railroads, factories, and the like. Since their funds could not be safe if natives remained in charge, they wanted their own governments in control. Then they could net handsome returns.

These theses appealed to Englishmen who saw the contest in South Africa as at base a war to defend the property of Cecil Rhodes and other English and German-English investors. Many saw it thus, among them Spring Rice and Stead.[39] And Americans already disillusioned by the Philippine war and concerned about the growing power of trusts probably found Hobson's arguments especially attractive. They could return to anti-colonialism while remaining in tune with the most up-to-date thought abroad.

The complexities of the colonial issue, the Philippine insurrection, the Boer War, and the turn in foreign liberal opinion combined to have a powerful effect on members of the American establishment. Olney remarked shamefacedly that he had been "a little dazzled by our new possessions." Lyman Abbott, who published a strongly imperialist article during the campaign of 1900, confessed within a year that the Boer War had altered his opinion. Albert Shaw went through a similar change. In 1902 he counseled his friend Beveridge against saying that the United States would "never" withdraw from the Philippines.[40]

Theodore Roosevelt's letters showed a similar pattern.[41] In December 1899 he rebuked Spring Rice for signs of disillusionment. "I believe in the expansion of great nations," he wrote. "India has done an incalculable amount for the English character. If we do our work well in the Philippines and the West Indies, it will do a great deal for our character." A few months later he commented on his agreement with the *Spectator's* "disapproval of Cecil Rhodes and the capitalist gang." He also mused that the English-speaking races might have become too citified to be effective colonizers.

"The more I have looked into the Boer War," Roosevelt wrote in April 1900, "the more uncomfortable I have felt about it." Hearing of agitation in favor of America's seizing a base in the Levant, he wrote the Secretary of War opposing such a step. The United States, he warned, might find itself in worse plight than Britain in South Africa.

Though he continued to defend the decision to annex the Philippines, Roosevelt gave evidence quite early of a change of heart. Soon after the election he wrote in a private letter, "Whenever the [Philippine] islands can stand alone, I shall be only too glad to withdraw." Addressed to President Eliot of Harvard, this letter may have been insincere. Nevertheless Roosevelt showed himself much cooler than before toward projects for Cuban annexation and, in fact, never again displayed zeal for acquisition of a colony.

Not all onetime imperialists made such a quick transition. Mahan, Holls, and Beveridge continued to speak favorably of colonies long after doing so had ceased to be fashionable.[42] As early as 1902 or 1903, however, they formed as small a minority as Bennett and Ward had formed in the 1870s. The American establishment once again possessed an anticolonial consensus as firm as that which had existed in the early 1880s.

In all likelihood this fact had something to do with the shrinkage of the interested public. Had the establishment remained as divided and confused as in 1898–99, less well qualified men might have continued to figure as leaders of opinion. As it was, the words of the latter on such questions as whether or not to retain Cuba or annex the Danish West Indies and the Dominican Republic ceased to be solicited by politicians or featured in the press. Establishment men predominated in presidential and senatorial correspondence and columns of daily newspapers relating to foreign policy. Speaking again with a common voice, the establishment said clearly that tradition, economic interest, domestic conditions, and the teachings of social science all argued against colonialism.

If accurate, this description of what happened between 1898 and 1902 or 1903 has implications running beyond the subject of this essay. One is that the public interested in a given issue may vary in size according not only to the issue but also to the character of its leadership. If the establishment had been as much of one mind in 1898 as earlier and later, the Philippines might have stirred no livelier concern than Hawaii in 1893 or the Dominican Republic in 1904–1905. A high level of public interest in any question may be due no more to the importance of the question than to the presence of discord and confusion among men to whom interested citizens look for guidance.

The quality of public opinion about an issue may also depend on the clarity with which conspicuous opinion leaders express their views. In this instance emotionalism increased dramatically as leadership dispersed to men who ordinarily deferred to the establishment. Perhaps a similar loosening of customary restraints accounted in part for the Red scares of 1919 and the early 1950s. As lawyers and community leaders betrayed confusion, others took it on themselves to propose means of dealing with Communist espionage and subversion, opportunities for demagoguery arose, and politicians appealed successfully to antiestablishment publics. Certainly, as Samuel Stouffer's surveys discovered, a wide gap existed in the mid-1950s between views circulating in leadership groups and views regarded by politicians as those of the interested public.[43] Conceivably something similar could occur if the foreign policy establishment should at some point display confusion and discord about preemptive nuclear warfare. Further study of how elites shape effective public opinion thus may have other uses besides illumination of the past.

Since this essay deals with a unique moment, its generalizations do not necessarily carry far forward or far backward in time. The late nineteenth-century United States had just begun to become a complex of interdependent cities and industrial centers. Its national government had limited functions, among which the conduct of foreign relations had only newly acquired fresh importance. Congress played a large but ill-defined role in determining policy, and, for both the executive and legislative branches, methods of measuring and influencing opinion remained crude. In consequence, politicians may have gauged public views in the unfamiliar area of foreign policy by observing a small cosmopolitan elite. Earlier, when the nation had a different character, they may have made more use of other measurements. Later, when the federal machine had grown and new techniques of communication, persuasion, and opinion measurement had developed, they may have used still others. Though the suggestions offered in this essay ought to be investigated in other contexts, they remain only suggestions.

Primarily the object of this essay is to set forth a synthetic interpretation of a single episode. Trying to take account of the easily forgotten fact that public opinion is seldom if ever opinion among more than an interested minority of the electorate, it has emphasized the small group of opinion leaders that gave this minority some guidance and, perhaps more importantly, provided political leaders with evidence as to how the interested public might bend.

Though these opinion leaders seemed for an interval not to be directing or representing the public, that interval was short. Most of the time the men whom we have described as members of the foreign policy establishment served as the voices of effective opinion, and their expressed views underwent changes. Through the 1870s and 1880s they opposed America's acquiring colonies. By 1893 they had adopted a different outlook and, by and large, approved of annexing Hawaii. Only from the outbreak of the Spanish war in 1898 to some point in 1900 or 1901 did they not either concur or divide along clear lines corresponding to party lines. After 1901 they agreed once again that the United States did not need and should not want colonial possessions.

Forces that various historians have singled out account in large part for these shifts in opinion. A sense of the nation's varied traditions clearly had great importance. Few members of the establishment could even momentarily have approved colonial expansion if they had not remembered Louisiana, Florida, the Mexican cession, and Alaska, and expansionist utterances by Jefferson, Jackson, Polk, and Seward. These men did not necessarily choose the tradition of Manifest Destiny while discarding the tradition of Mission, for many who spoke for annexation of Hawaii, the Philippines, or other territories claimed to be arguing for the nation's self-fulfillment as a propagator of liberty, democracy, and progress. Accepted meanings of American traditions changed during these years. Even so, these traditions had much to do with shaping men's convictions.

Economic considerations had at least equal importance. The apparent needs of American business concerned most men in the foreign policy establishment. Few could have inclined to imperialism without believing that colonies would make the country more prosperous. Equally, however, few could have opposed imperialism except from conviction that the benefits would be meager and, in the long run, well below the costs.

All men in the establishment could see evidence of increasing productive capacity and lagging domestic consumption. Apprehensive about future internal growth and aware of European economic nationalism, all must have hoped that the millions in underdeveloped lands would become customers for American products. Adding these factors up, however, individuals arrived at different sums. Like tradition, economic logic led to no single, ineluctable conclusion, nor did Social Darwinism or the "psychic crisis."

While Social Darwinist phrases probably influenced some men in the establishment, they constituted less of a constraint than either history or economics. Certain courses of action could not be rationalized by reference to Manifest Destiny or Mission or need for new markets, but almost any course could be justified as part of a "struggle for survival." Witness the fact that extremists on both sides used this argument. Similarly, almost any action could be defended as necessary to appease or avoid exciting an irrational public. Social Darwinism and the "psychic crisis" would have colored thought but not determined the positions men took on the colonial issue.

International fashions in thought and events on the world scene could have had a decisive influence on men of the establishment.[44] Not that they attached more importance to keeping step with Europeans than to preserving tradition, furthering trade, obeying scientific laws, or preventing domestic upheaval. Quite the contrary. But knowledge of foreign thought affected their ideas about America's world mission and their understanding of Social Darwinism. Observation of foreign experience suggested to them alternative methods of promoting national prosperity and dealing with social discontent. Above all, the foreign scene provided models for imitation (reference groups and reference idols, in social science jargon). The well-traveled and well-read American could select a position on the colonial issue by identifying it with, on the one hand, Bright, Gladstone, Morley, and Richter or, on the other, Rosebery, Chamberlain, Ferry, Bismarck, or Wilhelm II. Neither the American past nor an assessment of American economic needs nor Social Darwinism nor the domestic political scene offered such guidance.

Men of the establishment belonged both to their own country and to a larger Atlantic community. Ordinarily they defined opinion for an interested public, most of whom had less familiarity with currents abroad.

Probably this fact explains in part why, when the establishment ceased to be coherent and leadership dispersed, apparent public opinion on colonies became so simplistic and emotional. It may also explain why, when the interested public appeared to be expanding, many politicians took an anti-establishment tack: they realized that a gulf separated the citizen of the Atlantic community from the citizen whose outlook comprehended only his county or state. Currents running within the larger community help to account for American public opinion not so much because they influenced a large number of Americans as because they influenced the few who set styles within a normally small foreign policy public.

As stated in the beginning, this essay does not dispute what other historians have said. On the contrary, it seeks to draw together previous interpretations by means of hypotheses about late nineteenth-century public opinion, its manifestations, and the play within it of tradition, economic interest, Social Darwinism, and psychological malaise, together with awareness of ideas and events abroad. I hope others will advance alternative hypotheses, for my aim is not to close debate but rather to reopen it by prompting new questions about this and other episodes. In the literal meaning of the term, this work is an essay.

NOTES

Why the United States Went to War with Spain in 1898, PHILIP S. FONER

[1] New York, 1961, pp. 23–24. Later in his book, Professor May forgets this statement and contradicts himself, emphasizing only that mass hysteria, developed over the Cuban situation in 1896 and again in 1897, compelled President McKinley to lead his country "unwillingly toward a war which he did not want for a cause in which he did not believe" (*ibid.*, p. 237). But he himself pictures McKinley in December, 1897, a period not marked by "mass hysteria," as having concluded that if Spain's reforms should not have brought peace to Cuba by the opening of the rainy season in the spring, intervention would be necessary. Certainly, then, when McKinley asked Congress for intervention, he was only carrying into effect a program decided upon months before.

[2] *Labour Leader,* June 4, 1898.

[3] James Louis Whitehead, "French Reaction to American Imperialism, 1895–1908," unpublished Ph.D. thesis, University of Pennsylvania, 1943, pp. 77–79.

[4] *The People,* April 24, 1898.

[5] *Ibid.*, April 17, 24, May 1, 8, 15, 22, 29, 1898.

[6] *World's Work,* January, 1902, p. 224; New York *Tribune,* March 23, 1902.

[7] While Hobson focused on symptoms of trustified expansionism, Lenin concentrated on the whole system of capitalism in its imperialist stage, showing the inevitable path which imperialism must follow. Again, whereas Hobson found it possible to reform capitalism, Lenin called for its abolition, insisting that imperialism was inevitable in capitalism and could not be reformed.

[8] J. A. Hobson, *Imperialism, A Study,* London, 1938, pp. 77–78; V. I. Lenin, *Imperialism: The Highest Stage of Capitalism,* New York, 1939, p. 15.

[9] Harold U. Faulkner, *American Economic History,* New York, 1924, pp. 624–25.

[10] Harry Elmer Barnes, *World Politics in Modern Civilization,* New York, 1930, p. 233.

[11] Charles A. Beard, *The Idea of National Interest,* New York, 1934, pp. 65–70, 78–83.

[12] Louis M. Hacker, "The Holy War of 1898," *American Mercury,* XXI (November, 1930), 326.

[13] Marcus M. Wilkinson, *Public Opinion and the Spanish-American War: A Study in War Propaganda,* Baton Rouge, La., 1932, p. 132.

[14] Joseph E. Wisan, *The Cuban Crisis as Reflected in the New York Press, 1895–1898,* New York, 1934, p. 458.

[15] George W. Auxier, Jr., "Middle Western Newspapers and the Spanish-American War, 1895–1898," *Mississippi Valley Historical Review,* XXVI (1940), 528–29. Yet in his unpublished doctoral dissertation, which is a much more careful survey of Midwestern opinion, Dr. Auxier notes that "especially from about the middle of March 1, 1898 . . . the economic motive stands out in relief as the administration papers gradually gave way to the war sentiment and the opposition editors more readily admitted the Marxian implication of our purposes." He concludes that editors of a representative cross-section of the press, though divided in their attitudes regarding Cuban belligerency, "seemed primarily interested in assisting the President bring back domestic prosperity." ("The Cuban Question as Reflected in the Editorial columns of Middle Western Newspapers, 1895–1898," unpublished Ph.D. thesis, Ohio State University, 1938, pp. 21, 209, 295–99.)

[16] These influential politicians and intellectuals were Alfred T. Mahan, Theodore

Roosevelt, Henry Cabot Lodge, Henry Adams, and his younger brother Brooks. They formed a loose coterie that vigorously sought a policy of expansion. Mahan selected the commercial needs of a great power as the foundation of his theory, and argued that a large navy and foreign bases were necessary to protect markets and a sizable merchant fleet. Applying his general theory to the United States, he pointed out that basic to American growth were annexation of Hawaii, construction and ownership of an Isthmian Canal, and control of Cuba. Lodge and Roosevelt accepted Mahan's ideas as the basis for their "large policy," which called for expansion of national interests. They set out to make their country the leading power in the Western hemisphere, "possessed of a great navy, owning and controlling an Isthmian canal, holding naval bases in the Caribbean and the Pacific, and contesting on at least even terms with the greatest powers, the naval and commercial supremacy of the Pacific Ocean and the Far East." (Julius W. Pratt, "The 'Large Policy' of 1898," *Mississippi Valley Historical Review,* XIX [1932], 223.)

Brooks Adams, related to Lodge through marriage and a friend of Roosevelt, published a volume in 1895, *The Law of Civilization and Decay,* in which he contended that an imperialistic nation was healthier than one content with its own borders, and advocated American control of the Western hemisphere and economic dominance of Asia. His brother, Henry, worked actively in Washington in favor of intervention in Cuba.

17 Julius W. Pratt, "American Business and the Spanish-American War," *Hispanic American Historical Review,* XIX (May, 1934), 163–201. See also his *Expansionists of 1898: The Acquisition of Hawaii and the Spanish Islands,* Baltimore, 1936, pp. 22, 230–316. Actually, this thesis had been somewhat casually advanced as early as 1928 by Leland H. Jenks: "If ever there was a war which the people of the country, as distinguished from their political and business leaders demanded, it was the war which the United States began on April 21, 1898." (*Our Cuban Colony: A Study in Sugar,* New York, 1928, p. 57.)

18 *Cf.* Oscar Handlin, *Chance or Destiny: Turning-points in American History,* Boston, 1945, pp. 121–42; John D. Hicks, *The American Nation,* Boston, 1949, p. 113; Sidney Hook, *The Hero in History,* Boston, 1955, pp. 53–54.

19 Charles A. Beard, *Giddy Minds and Foreign Quarrels: An Estimate of American Foreign Policy,* New York, 1939, p. 236.

20 Quoted in Foster R. Dulles, *America's Rise to World Power,* New York, 1955, p. 41.

21 New York, 1959, p. 223.

22 Compare Dulles, *America in the Pacific,* New York, 1932, pp. 227–35, with *China and America,* Princeton, N.J., pp. 101–104; *The Imperial Years,* New York, 1956, pp. 165–83; and *America's Rise to World Power,* pp. 40–41. In 1965 Dulles wrote that "economic considerations had little to do with the popular sentiment" that led to war in 1898. (*Prelude to World Power: American Diplomatic History, 1860–1900,* New York, 1965, p. 89.)

23 *The President Makers,* New York, 1940, p. 79.

24 *The Rise of Modern America, 1865–1951,* New York, 1951, p. 185.

25 *A Diplomatic History of the American People,* New York, 1950, p. 504.

26 *A Diplomatic History of the United States,* rev. ed., New York, 1936, p. 437.

27 *The Far Eastern Policy of the United States,* New York, 1938, pp. 8–9.

28 "The Needless War with Spain," in *Times of Trial,* edited by Allan Nevins, New York, 1958, pp. 179–86.

29 "Manifest Destiny and the Philippines," in *America in Crisis,* edited by Daniel Aaron, New York, 1952, pp. 188–89.

30 Arthur Barcan, "American Imperialism and the Spanish American War," unpublished M.A. thesis, Columbia University, 1940, pp. 5, 11, 81, 100–101, 108–10.

31 Ralph Dewar Bald, Jr., "The Development of Expansionist Sentiment in the United States, 1885–1895, As Reflected in Periodical Literature," unpublished Ph.D. thesis, University of Pittsburgh, 1953, pp. 121–25, 215–16.

32 *Science & Society,* XXII (Spring, 1958), 129–43.

33 Sklar does not mention it, but in connection with this important point, it is necessary to add that a change occurred in the thinking in the business community on the

cause of the Panic of 1893 and the ensuing depression. Originally it was explained as resulting from dangerous or outmoded monetary theories and policies but by 1895 there was increasing emphasis on overproduction and lack of markets as the basic cause. (See, in this connection, Thomas McCormick, "'A Fair Field and No Favor': American China Policy during the McKinley Administration, 1897–1901," unpublished Ph.D. thesis, University of Wisconsin, 1960.) [Since published as *China Market: America's Quest for Informal Empire, 1893–1901* (Chicago: Quadrangle Press, 1967).]

34 The New York *Journal* complained in 1896 that "the areas of the world" were being "taken over by naval powers," and that the world's trade routes were falling into the hands of other nations. The United States was in danger, the *Journal* felt, of being entirely excluded from its "rightful share" (February 29, 1896).

35 *Science & Society,* XXIII (Spring, 1959), 133–62.

36 New York *Daily People,* October 14, 1900.

37 William Appleman Williams, *The Tragedy of American Diplomacy, 1750–1955,* New York, 1959, pp. 31, 32–33, 34; *The Contours of American History,* Cleveland & New York, 1961, pp. 349, 363–68; *The United States, Cuba and Castro,* New York, 1962, pp. 5–6. See also Williams' review of Ernest R. May's "Imperial Democracy: The Emergence of America as a Great Power" in *Studies on the Left,* III (1963), 94–99.

38 Thomas McCormick, *op. cit.,* pp. 145–46, 153–54; "Insular Imperialism and the Open Door: The China Market and the Spanish American War," *Pacific Historical Review,* XXXII (May, 1963), 155–69.

39 Ithaca, New York, 1963, pp. 385–406.

40 Francis B. Loomis to William R. Day, November 5, 1897, William R. Day Papers, Library of Congress.

41 Alfred T. Mahan, "Strategic Features of the Caribbean Sea and the Gulf of Mexico," *Harper's New Monthly Magazine,* XCV (October, 1897), 680–91. Mahan's article and his other writings of this period show how inaccurate is Morris Levy's conclusion that Mahan had no interest in the Philippines or other Asian areas before the war with Spain. (Morris Levy, "Alfred Thayer Mahan and United States Foreign Policy," unpublished Ph.D. thesis, New York University, 1964, pp. 163–64.)

42 A. E. Orr, President of the New York State Chamber of Commerce, to William McKinley, enclosing memorial, February 3, 1898, William McKinley Papers, Library of Congress; John Sherman to A. E. Orr, February 11, 1898, John Sherman Papers, Library of Congress.

43 John J. McCook to James H. Wilson, November 17, 1896, James H. Wilson Papers, Library of Congress. Henry M. Flagler was, with John D. Rockefeller, the founder of the Standard Oil Company. "It is generally agreed that, next to Rockefeller himself, Flagler was the strongest man in the organization" (*Dictionary of American Biography,* New York, 1946, VI, 451).

John J. McCook was a New York businessman and banker who was deeply involved in Cuban affairs, especially in the floating of bonds for the Cuban *Junta* in the United States. He was also interested in the development of investments and trade in the Far East.

44 Henry Cabot Lodge to Theodore Roosevelt, May 24, 1898, *Selections from the Correspondence of Theodore Roosevelt and Henry Cabot Lodge, 1884–1918.* New York, 1925, I, 278.

45 During 1898 gigantic mergers took place in copper refining, lead, sugar, salt, tobacco, cans, whiskey, baking, street railways, cigar-making, steel, and other industries.

46 The New York *Financial Record,* however, argued that war with Spain would not depress securities nor injure business but would rather vastly increase the net earning power of every security sold on the market (November 4, 1897). The Chicago *Economist* called fallacious the argument that war would seriously hurt business (Vol. XIX, February 26, 1898). The Chattanooga *Tradesman* stated that a small prospect of war had already stimulated the iron trade in certain lines (March 1, 1898). The *Manufacturers' Record,* organ of Southern industrialists, declared in late March, 1898, that war would open vast new markets for American industry and would have no serious effect on the securities market (reprinted in *The State,* Columbia, South Carolina, March 26, 1898).

On April 23, 1898, *Bradstreet's* declared: "For nearly two months the New York banks, and the money market of the country generally, have been preparing for the events of the present week" (p. 257). On the same day, the New York *Journal of Commerce* observed: "Naturally, the business sentiment of the country has not protested with any unqualified earnestness against the influences under which we have drifted into war." On April 25 President McKinley asked Congress for a joint resolution recognizing a state of war with Spain. Both the House and the Senate passed the resolution by a voice vote the same day.

47 *Commercial and Financial Chronicle,* LXVI (February 12, 1898), 308; *Bankers' Magazine,* LVI (March, 1898), 358; John C. Spooner to Frank Bigelow, March 8, 1898, John C. Spooner Papers, Library of Congress.

48 *Wall Street Journal,* March 19, 1898; *Congressional Record,* 55th Congress, 2nd Session, pp. 5916–19; Russell Hastings to William McKinley, March 27, 1898, William McKinley Papers, Library of Congress.

49 Washington *Post,* March 27, 1898; Washington *Evening Star,* April 6, 1898.

Thomas Beer in his biography of Mark Hanna writes that his (Beer's) father "heard in Washington that Wall Street was solidly lined up against a war with Spain. He retired to New York and men grabbed his arm . . . asking what this insane Hanna meant by trying to head off the war? He noted that John Jacob Astor, John Gates, Thomas Fortune Ryan, William Rockefeller, Stuyvesant Fish, John Pierpont Morgan, and many others in Wall Street were avidly for war" (Thomas Beer, *Hanna,* New York, 1929, p. 200).

50 William C. Reick to John Russell Young, March 25, 1898, telegram, in William McKinley Papers, Library of Congress.

51 *American Banker,* LXIV (1898), 9.

52 Margaret Leech, *In the Days of McKinley,* New York, 1959, p. 180.

53 May, *op. cit.,* p. 269.

54 *Ibid.,* p 270. See also Pratt, *Expansionists of 1898,* pp. 326–27.

55 Williams, *The Contours of American History,* p. 363.

56 *American Naval Policy as Outlined in Messages of the Presidents of the United States from 1790,* Washington, D.C., 1922; Pratt, *Expansionists of 1898,* pp. 326–27; *Senate Report 681,* 56th Congress, 2nd Session, pp. 65–67.

57 John L. Offner, "President McKinley and the Origins of the Spanish-American War," unpublished Ph.D. thesis, Pennsylvania State University, 1957, p. 81.

58 Timothy McDonald, "McKinley and the Coming of the War with Spain," *The Midwest Quarterly,* VII (April, 1966), 233–35.

American Business and the Spanish-American War, JULIUS W. PRATT

1 James Ford Rhodes, *The McKinley and Roosevelt Administrations* (New York, 1922), p. 55.

2 H. U. Faulkner, *American Economic History* (New York and London, 1924), pp. 624–625.

3 This study was made possible by a grant from the Social Science Research Council.

4 *Cf. Wall Street Journal,* December 3 and 31, 1897; January 25, April 21, 1898; *Railway World* (Philadelphia, weekly), XLII. 105, 217 (January 29, February 26, 1898).

5 *Wall Street Journal,* December 31, 1897; February 17, 1898.

6 *Ibid.,* November 18, December 3, 1897; *Railway World, loc. cit.; Banker and Tradesman* (Boston, weekly), XXVI. 78 (February 23, 1898); *American Banker* (New York, weekly), LXIII. 528 (March 30, 1898); *Journal of Commerce and Commercial Bulletin* (New York), November 27, 1897; *Commercial and Financial Chronicle* (New York), LXV. 597 (October 2, 1897).

7 *Journal of Commerce and Commercial Bulletin,* February 28, 1898; *Commercial and Financial Chronicle,* April 2, 1898; *Boston Journal of Commerce,* LII. 40 (April 16, 1898);

Drugs, Oils and Paints (Philadelphia, monthly), XIII. 401 (April, 1898); *Railway World,* XLII. 241–242 (March 5, 1898); *Banker and Tradesman, loc. cit.; Daily Commercial News and Shipping List* (San Francisco), March 25, 1898.

8 Chamber of Commerce of the State of New York, *Fortieth Annual Report, 1897–98* (New York, 1898), p. 127; Boston Chamber of Commerce, *Thirteenth Annual Report, 1898* (Boston, 1899), pp. 115–116; Baltimore Board of Trade, *Report of President and Directors for Year Ending September 30, 1898* (Baltimore, 1898), p. 67; Philadelphia Board of Trade, *Sixty-Sixth Annual Report* (Philadelphia, 1899), pp. 50–51; Cleveland Chamber of Commerce, *Fiftieth Year* (Cleveland, 1898), p. 66; Indianapolis Board of Trade, *Annual Report for Year Ending June 1, 1898* (Indianapolis, 1898), p. 20. Of the resolutions printed in these reports, some spoke out strongly against war; others merely commended President McKinley's conservative course in seeking a peaceful solution of the Cuban question.

9 *American Banker, loc. cit.*

10 *Com. & Fin. Chron.*, LXVI. 641; Boston *Jour. of Comm.*, LII. 40.

11 G. H. Hull, *Industrial Depressions . . . or Iron the Barometer of Trade* (New York, 1911), pp. 161–173.

12 New York *Commercial,* January 3, 1898. The only flaw in the picture was continued depression in the cotton goods industry. For notes on this and certain other newspapers I am indebted to the kindness of Miss Bernice L. Beladeau, who allowed me to make use of some material gathered by her in preparation of a master's thesis.

13 *Com. & Fin. Chron.*, LXV. 134, 1046 (July 24, December 4, 1897).

14 *Wall Street Journal,* December 23, 1897.

15 *Banker and Tradesman,* XXVI. 297 (April 20, 1898). *Cf. American Banker,* LXIII. 178 (February 2, 1898); *Age of Steel* (St. Louis, weekly), LXXXIII. No. 1, p. 57 (January 1, 1898); *Rand-McNally Bankers' Monthly* (Chicago), XV. 19 (January 1898); *Statistical Abstract of the U.S.,* 1931, p. 488.

16 *The Iron Age,* December 9, 1897, p. 22; *Banker and Tradesman, loc. cit.; Railway World,* XLI. 837 (August 21, 1897).

17 *Daily Commercial News and Shipping List* (San Francisco), March 7, 1898.

18 *The Iron Age* (New York, weekly) December 23, 1897, pp. 19–20.

19 *Com. & Fin. Chron.*, LXV. 597–599, LXVI. 636.

20 *Banker and Tradesman,* XXVI. 328 (April 27, 1898). *Cf. ibid.,* XXVI. 130 (March 9, 1898).

21 *New Jersey Trade Review* (Newark, semi-monthly), March 1, 1898.

22 *Railway Age* (Chicago), XXV. 215, 253 (April 1, 15, 1898).

23 *Com. & Fin. Chron.*, LXVI. 308 (February 12, 1898); *Banker's Magazine,* LVI. 358 (March 1898); *U.S. Investor* (Boston, weekly) IX. 529 (April 9, 1898).

24 *Railroad Gazette* (New York, weekly) XXX. 236 (April 1, 1898). As to the position of arms and ammunition manufacturers, it is interesting to find a representative of a New York firm engaged in that trade writing to the secretary of the interior in March, 1898, in behalf of a peaceful settlement in Cuba (M. Hartley to C. N. Bliss, March 16, 17, 1898, in *Miscellaneous Letters* (Dept. of State), March, 1898, II).

25 *Iron and Steel* (Chicago, weekly), LXXII. No. 15, p. 10 (April 9, 1898). *Cf. The Iron Age,* March 17, 1898, p. 21; *The Age of Steel,* LXXXIII. No. 10 (March 5, 1898).

26 *American Wool and Cotton Reporter* (New York, weekly), XII. 439 (April 7, 1898); *Weekly Northwestern Miller* (Minneapolis), XL. 667 (April 29, 1898); *"Dixie," A Monthly Journal Devoted to Southern Industrial Interests* (Atlanta), XIV. No. 5, pp. 21–23 (May, 1898); *The Tradesman* (Chattanooga, semi-monthly), XXXIX. 60 (May 1, 1898); Portland (Ore.) *Board of Trade Journal* (monthly), XI. 6 (May, 1898).

27 *Wall Street Journal,* November 18 and December 31, 1897.

28 New York *Journal of Commerce and Commercial Bulletin,* May 21 and June 5, 1897.

29 *Com. & Fin. Chron.*, LXIV. 974, LXVI. 308 (May 22, 1897, and February 12, 1898). *Cf.* John D. Hicks, *The Populist Revolt* (Minneapolis, 1931), p. 390: "The voting of bond issues to aid in financing the war drew fire from the Populists, who would have preferred issues of treasury notes, . . ."

30 *American Banker,* LXII. 912–913; LXIII. 394 (May 26, 1897; March 9, 1898); *United States Investor,* IX. 368 (March 12, 1898); *Rand-McNally Bankers' Monthly,* XV. 294 (April, 1898). T. S. Woolsey, in his *America's Foreign Policy* (New York, 1898), pp. 13–14, remarked that currency reform would be impeded by any unusual complication, such as war, and added: "This, perhaps, will suggest a certain subtle connection between Jingoism and the flat money advocates."

31 *The Financial Record, An Investors' Manual* (New York, weekly, published by Alex C. Lassen and Co.), November 4, 17, 1897.

32 The proposal of the Kansas City Board of Trade was forwarded, with a request for endorsement, to the Philadelphia Board of Trade, which rejected it. — *Sixty-Fourth Annual Report of Philadelphia Board of Trade* (Philadelphia, 1897), p. 15.

33 *Fiftieth Annual Report* of the Cincinnati Chamber of Commerce and Merchant's Exchange (Cincinnati, 1899), p. 49.

34 *The Economist. A Weekly Financial, Commercial and Real-Estate Newspaper* (Chicago), XIX. 233, 322 (February 26 and March 19, 1898).

35 *Rand-McNally Bankers' Monthly,* XV. 199–201 (March 1898).

36 *Age of Steel,* LXXXIII. Nos. 10, 11 (March 5, 12, 1898).

37 St. Louis *Republic,* March 3, 1898.

38 *The Tradesman,* XXXIX. March 1, 1898, p. 58. The same paper, however, in its May issue, denied that any permanent good to business could result from war. *Supra,* note 26.

39 *Mining and Scientific Press* (San Francisco, weekly), LXXVI. 390 (April 9, 1898). In the issue of April 23, it remarked that war between the two chief copper-producing countries would occasion a boom in that metal (*ibid.,* LXXVI. 438).

40 *Wall Street Journal,* February 17 and 24, 1898.

41 *Dun's Review, A Weekly Review of Business and Finance* (New York), March 5 and 12, 1898. *Bradstreet's, A Journal of Trade, Finance, and Public Economy* (New York, weekly), XXVI. 161 (March 12, 1898). Similar views were expressed by the *Dry Goods Economist* (New York, weekly), April 9, 1898.

42 *Wall Street Journal,* March 19, 1898.

43 *American Banker,* LXIII. 489.

44 *Wall Street Journal,* March 31 and April 1, 1898.

45 *Miscellaneous Letters* (Dept. of State), May, 1897, II. The memorial is covered by a letter from Geo. R. Mosle (of Mosle Bros., 16 Exchange Place, New York) to Hon. John Sherman, May 17, 1897. The list of signers is headed by Lawrence Turnure & Co.; August Belmont & Co. appear near the top.

46 *Ibid.,* February, 1898, I. The memorial was signed by seventy persons or firms from New York and nearby cities; forty from Philadelphia; and sixty-four from Mobile. It was presented to the president on the morning of February 9, 1898, by George R. Mosle, Wm. Moore Carson, and George Turnure, and thereafter, at the president's suggestion, sent to Assistant Secretary Wm. R. Day. See accompanying letter from the committee to Mr. Day.

47 E. F. Atkins, *Sixty Years in Cuba* (privately printed, Cambridge, 1926), pp. 209, 212, 274, *et passim.* Atkins's attitude is illustrated by his query (p. 209) "whether the sentimental feeling of sympathy with the Cubans should outweigh the property interests amounting to some $30,000,000 of United States citizens in Cuba."

48 Juragua Iron Co., Ltd. (per Josiah Monroe, Sec'y and Treas.) to Day, Philadelphia, April 14, 1898. *Miscellaneous Letters* (Dept. of State), April, 1898, II. Spanish-American Iron Co. (per C. F. Rand, Pres.) to Day, New York, April 8, 1898. *Ibid.,* April, 1898, I.

49 Armstrong Cork Co. to Secretary Sherman, March 8, 1898. *Ibid.,* March, 1898, I. John Duer to Department of State (telegram), March 28, 1898; R. H. Clarke (Mobile) to Hon. J. Wheeler, March 26, 1898. *Ibid.,* March, 1898, III.

50 C. R. Fowles to Secretary Alger, April 23, 1898. *Ibid.,* April, 1898, III.

51 *Com. & Fin. Chronicle,* LXVI. 732 (April 16, 1898); *Journal of Commerce and Commercial Bulletin,* April 23, 1898; Boston *Journal of Commerce,* April 16, 1898; *U.S. Investor,* IX. 529 (April 9, 1898).

52 *Journal of Commerce & Commercial Bulletin,* February 24 and May 27, 1897.

[53] *Bradstreet's* XXVI. 66 (January 29, 1898). *Cf. American Banker,* LXII. 817 (May 12, 1897); *U.S. Investor,* IX. 400–401 (March 19, 1898); *Dry Goods Economist,* January 1, 1898; *American Wool and Cotton Reporter,* XII. 380 (March 24, 1898); *The Tradesman,* XXXIX. 52 (June 15, 1898). The National Board of Trade, at its annual meeting in Washington in December, 1897, recommended various measures for the further extension of export trade. — *Proceedings* of the 28th Annual Meeting of the National Board of Trade (Philadelphia, 1898), pp. 337–338.

[54] Julius W. Pratt, "The 'Large Policy' of 1898," *Mississippi Valley Historical Review,* XIX. 219–242 (September, 1932); T. S. Woolsey, *America's Foreign Policy,* pp. 1–21.

[55] The National Board of Trade, a federation of local boards of trade, chambers of commerce, etc., in all parts of the country, consistently urged construction of the canal. *Cf. Proceedings* of its 28th Annual Meeting (Philadelphia, 1898), p. 335. *Cf.* also Indianapolis Board of Trade, *Annual Report* for 1898 (Indianapolis, 1898), p. 18; Philadelphia Board of Trade, *65th Annual Report* (Philadelphia, 1898), pp. 25–26; Merchant's Exchange of St. Louis, *Annual Statement of the Trade and Commerce of St. Louis for Year 1898* (St. Louis, 1899), p. 17; Chamber of Commerce of San Francisco, *48th Annual Report* (San Francisco, 1898), p. 18. The National Association of Manufacturers, at its January, 1897, meeting, took "strong ground in favor of the Nicaragua Canal" (*Journal of Commerce and Commercial Bulletin,* January 25, 1897).

[56] *Cf. Bradstreet's* XXV. 386 (June 19, 1897); New York *Commercial,* April 30, 1898; San Francisco Chamber of Commerce, *48th Annual Report,* p. 18.

[57] Exceptions to this general rule were the *Financial Record,* which was pro-war (as shown above) and which also hailed the prospect of colonial responsibilities (June 23, 1897 and March 23, 1898); and the New York *Commercial,* which thought the United States should not only annex Cuba and Porto Rico but should also buy St. Thomas from Denmark for a naval station (March 31 and April 8, 1898). The *American Banker,* in April, 1898, thought it would be good business to buy Cuba, pay for it in silver, and set it up as an American protectorate. It remarked: "A nation that borrows foreign capital, and in fact mortgages its resources to foreigners, must expect when it becomes unable to pay to be interfered with from without" (*American Banker,* LVI. 517–520).

[58] *Com. & Fin. Chron.,* LXIV. 211–213, 1205–1207 (January 30 and June 26, 1897); *Journal of Com. & Com. Bull.,* June 17 and August 14, 1897.

[59] *Journal of Com. & Com. Bull.,* September 8, 1897.

[60] *Ibid.,* June 17 and October 21, 1897. Similarly, the *U.S. Investor* regarded Hawaiian annexation as a "menace," and the *Banker and Tradesman* thought the people of Cuba were "incapable and unfit for self-government. . . . This country does not want Cuba." *U.S. Investor,* IX. 48 (January 8, 1898); *Banker and Tradesman,* XXVI. 161 (March 16, 1898).

[61] *Com. & Fin. Chron.,* LXVI. 446–448 (March 5, 1898); *Age of Steel,* LXXXIII. No. 1, p. 57 (January 1, 1898).

[62] Baltimore Chamber of Commerce, *43rd Annual Report* (Baltimore, 1898), p. 11. Address of the president, Robert Ramsay, January 31, 1898.

[63] *Jour. of Com. & Com. Bull.,* January 24, 1896.

[64] *Com. & Fin. Chron.,* LXV. 1147–1148 (December 18, 1897).

[65] An analysis of biographies of business men of the time points to the same conclusion. *Cf.* Pratt, *op. cit.,* p. 237 and note 55.

[66] *Jour. of Com. & Com. Bull.,* May 27, 1897. Similar apprehension was expressed by the *American Banker,* LXII. 817 (May 12, 1897), and the *Railway World,* XLI. 572 (June 5, 1897).

[67] *American Banker,* LXII. 2328–2329 (December 1, 1897); *Dry Goods Economist,* January 15, 1898.

[68] *The Iron Age,* December 23, 1897; *American Machinist,* quoted in *Daily Com. News & Shipping List* (San Francisco), September 17, 1898. *Cf. Drugs, Oils and Paints,* XIV. p. 88 (August, 1898), which argued that while protective tariffs might be useful, the proper object of such a tariff was to make itself unnecessary, and that many American industries which had hitherto been dependent upon protection had now reached a "stage where the tariff neither protects the industry nor profits the Government."

69 *The Tradesman,* XXXIX. 52 (June 15, 1898); Baltimore Chamber of Commerce, *43rd Annual Report,* p. 11.

70 *Literary Digest,* XV. 964 (December 11, 1897).

71 *Atlanta Constitution,* Philadelphia *Ledger,* Houston *Post,* in *ibid.,* XV. 965; New York *Commercial,* January 27, 1898; *Com. & Fin. Chron.,* LXV. 1147–1148 (December 18, 1897).

72 *Jour. of Com. & Com. Bull.,* November 30, 1897.

73 H. B. Morse, *The International Relations of the Chinese Empire* (London and New York, 1910–1918), III. 105–127; J. Van A. MacMurray, *Treaties and Agreements with and concerning China, 1894–1919* (New York, 1921), I. 112–116, 119–121, 128–130, 152–153; P. Joseph, *Foreign Diplomacy in China, 1894–1900* (London, 1928), chaps. 9–14.

74 Tyler Dennett, *Americans in Eastern Asia* (New York, 1922), 579–582; *Jour. of Com. & Com. Bull.,* May 15, 1896, February 22, December 23, 1897, January 8, 1898. Of all markets for American manufactures, said the paper on the last date, "China is incomparably the greatest."

75 San Francisco *Bulletin,* January 4, 1898; *Financial Record,* December 29, 1897.

76 *American Banker,* LXIII. 9 (January 5, 1898); New York *Commercial,* January 5 and 22, 1898; Baltimore *Sun,* Kansas City *Journal* in *Literary Digest,* XVI. 31–33 (January 8, 1898); *Com. & Fin. Chron.,* LXVI. 106–107 (January 15, 1898).

77 *American Banker,* LXII. 2489 (December 29, 1897).

78 New Orleans *Picayune,* in *Literary Digest, loc. cit.; Age of Steel,* January 8, 29, 1898; The *Nation* (New York), LXVI. 122–123 (February 17, 1898).

79 *Jour. of Com. & Com. Bull.,* December 28, 1897 and January 7, 1898.

80 *Ibid.,* January 5, 1898. Secretary Sherman had been interviewed by the Philadelphia *Press* and was quoted as saying that if the powers should partition China, it would not interest us materially, "as the powers would gladly seize the opportunity to trade with us. Our commercial interests would not suffer, as far as I can see, in the least—quite the contrary." Such remarks seemed to the editor of the *Journal of Commerce* to suggest "serious intellectual limitations." For confirmation of Secretary Sherman's indifference to the partitioning of China, see S. F. Bemis (ed.), *American Secretaries of State and Their Diplomacy* (10 vols., N.Y., 1927–1929), IX. 15, 18, 122.

81 These documents were printed in a small pamphlet entitled *Commercial Rights of the United States in China,* a copy of which is in department of state, *Miscellaneous Letters,* June, 1898, II, accompanying a letter of E. Frazar to Secretary Day, June 17, 1898. Another document there printed is a communication from about seventy mercantile and manufacturing firms and individuals in New York, Philadelphia, Pittsburgh, Paterson, etc., urging the New York chamber to bring the situation in China to the attention of the department of state. The original of the memorial to the president is in *Misc. Letters,* February 1898, I. The part played by the *Journal of Commerce* is related in the issue of June 18, 1898.

82 Philadelphia Board of Trade to the President, February 25, 1898; San Francisco Chamber of Commerce to same, March 8, 1898; Baltimore Chamber of Commerce to Secretary Sherman, March 17, 1898; Boston Chamber of Commerce to the President, March 30, 1898; Seattle Chamber of Commerce to same, April 14, 1898.—Dept. of State, *Misc. Letters,* February-April, 1898.

83 E. Frazar to Day, June 17, 1898 (Dept. of State, *Misc. Letters,* June, 1898, II). Accompanying the letter is a printed constitution of the Association. *Cf.* for first steps New York *Commercial,* March 10, 1898.

84 *Dun's Review,* May 7, 1898, said railway stocks had advanced on the average of $2.79 per share since the news, adding: "One day's work by the officers and men at Manila has given many days' work to thousands of people at home. . . . and has placed all American industries and interests on a stronger footing for any conceivable future." *Cf. Jour. of Com. & Com. Bull.,* May 3, 1898; *Com. & Fin. Chron.,* LXVI. 874 (May 7, 1898).

85 New York *Sun,* November 8, 1897 and March 13, 1898.

[86] The *U.S. Investor,* IX. 624 (April 30, 1898) thought that such a victory, even if we did not retain the islands, "might pave the way for future interventions on the part of the United States in the affairs of the East." The *Financial Record,* May 5, 1898 (in an editorial written before receipt of the news of the battle), thought the Philippines "would be good trading material for getting our share of what is going in Asia." *Cf.* New York *Commercial,* April 27, 1898; New York *Sun,* April 29, 1898.

[87] Allan Nevins, *Henry White, Thirty Years of Diplomacy* (New York, 1930), p. 136.

[88] The New York *Commercial,* May 7, 1898, declared the Philippines were "treasure islands" — "the richest islands in the world." Their development by American capital, it said (June 7), would stimulate the trade of the Pacific Coast and promote the establishment of new industries in the west. The *Daily Commercial News and Shipping List* of San Francisco also saw great possibilities of trade with the islands (May 13) and hailed the prospect of "Gold in the Philippines" (June 17). *Cf.* Chattanooga *Tradesman,* May 15, 1898.

[89] Subsequently the paper had reverted at least partially to its earlier opposition to the canal and Hawaiian annexation. Issues of April 2 and June 25, 1898. But on May 31 it urged that control of the Hawaiian islands was "imperative."

[90] *Jour. of Com. & Com. Bull.,* May 3, 4, and 11, 1898. The paper held consistently to this position. August 24, 1898, it said: "We can establish ourselves as one of the Oriental powers by acquiring a really important stake in the Philippines, or we may resign ourselves to seeing the open door shut gradually in our faces." *Cf. ibid.,* February 1, 1899.

[91] *American Banker,* LXIII. 785.

[92] *Banker and Tradesman,* XXVI. 456 and 776 (June 1 and Aug. 24, 1898).

[93] *Age of Steel,* May 21, 1898; *Iron Age,* June 23, 1898; *U.S. Investor,* IX. 953, 1017 (July 2 and 16, 1898); *Financial Record,* June 15, 1898; *Bradstreet's,* XXVI. 356 (June 4, 1898); N.Y. *Commercial,* June 1, 1898.

[94] *Jour. of Com. & Com. Bull.,* June 17, 1898.

[95] *The Tradesman,* June 15, September 1, 1898; *"Dixie,"* XIV. No. 6, p. 27 (June, 1898). *Cf.* New Orleans *Picayune,* quoted in New York *Jour. of Com. & Com. Bull.,* May 18, 1898.

[96] *Mining and Scientific Press,* LXXVI. 534 and 643 (May 21 and June 18, 1898); *Com. Bull. of Sou. Cal.* (Los Angeles, weekly), June 17, December 23, 1898; *Daily Com. News & Shipping List,* August 10, 1898.

[97] Seattle *Post-Intelligencer,* August 8, 1898, Chamber of Commerce of San Francisco, *49th Annual Report* (San Francisco, 1899), pp. 23–24. The quotation is from resolutions adopted July 29, 1898, by the San Francisco Chamber of Commerce in conjunction with the other bodies named above. On the other hand, the Los Angeles Chamber of Commerce, at its meeting on August 4, 1898, voted strongly against annexing the Philippines. *Daily Com. News & Shipping List,* August 6, 1898.

[98] Seattle *Post-Intelligencer,* June 1, 1898. *Cf.* J. G. Pyle, *Life of James J. Hill* (2 vols., Garden City, New York, 1917), II. 77.

[99] *Jour. of Com. & Com. Bull.,* August 11, 1898.

[100] *Com. & Fin. Chron.,* LXVI. 876–878 and 922–924 (May 7 and 14, 1898); Baltimore *Journal of Commerce,* July 16 and September 10, 1898; *Iron Age,* September 29 and November 24, 1898. By August, the *Chronicle* had come to regard annexation as inevitable (LXVII. 401, August 27, 1898).

[101] Everett Frazar to Pres. McKinley, November 11, 1898 (Dept. of State, *Misc. Letters,* November, 1898, I). Other business men wrote McKinley opposing annexation of the Philippines. T. G. Bush, president of the Mobile and Birmingham Railroad Co., thought all we needed was a coaling and naval station in the Philippines. Wharton Barker, of Philadelphia, thought trade could best be built up by reciprocity with the Americas, not by expansion in the Far East. Bush to McKinley, July 30, 1898. *Ibid.,* July, 1898, III. Barker to McKinley, August 25, 1898. — *Misc. Letters sent to the Pres. & the Secretary of State,* Paris, Peace Commission, 1898.

[102] San Francisco *Call,* September 10 and 17 and December 15, 1898.

[103] *Bradstreet's,* XXVI. 450 (July 16, 1898). *Cf. Financial Record,* July 13, 1898, and *Com. & Fin. Chron.,* LXVII. 96 (July 16, 1898), which thought that "whether wisely done or not, the annexation of Hawaii has settled the general principle."

[104] Quoted in New York *Commercial,* May 13, 1898. Propaganda for annexation of the Carolines arose from religious rather than business sources. Spain had expelled American missionaries from the islands and closed their schools. *Cf.* Toledo *Blade,* quoted in New York *Commercial,* April 27, 1898; also a memorial to the American peace commission from the Board of the Hawaiian Evangelical Association, September 12, 1898 (Dept. of State, *Misc. Letters,* September, 1898, I). Dr. Edward Van Dyke Robinson was active in the same cause. See copy of letter from him to Captain Bradford, September 27, 1898, in *Misc. Letters sent to Members of the Peace Commission, 1898* (MSS., Dept. of State), and another letter to Congressman R. R. Hitt of Illinois, December 20, 1898, in Dept. of State, *Misc. Letters,* December, 1898, III.

[105] *Cf.* resolutions of San Francisco Chamber of Commerce, May 4, 1898, in *Daily Commercial News and Shipping List,* May 6, 1898.

[106] The *Journal of Commerce* (May 11, 1898) thought either Porto Rico or Cuba was necessary for reasons similar to those dictating the retention of the Philippines. "We want no acquisitions other than those needful for strategic purposes, but whatever territory of that nature falls into our hands must never be parted with." Letters from business men to the department of state urged the annexation of Porto Rico as a "garden spot," capable of contributing greatly to American commerce. J. H. Hamlin & Son, Portland, Me., to McKinley, May 11, 1898. Dept. of State, *Misc. Letters,* May, 1898, II. T. G. Bush, Anniston, Ala., to McKinley, July 30, 1898. *Ibid.,* July, 1898, III.

[107] *Jour. of Com. & Com. Bull.,* May 24, 1898. Similarly, the *American Banker* (LXIII. 986, June 8, 1898) thought conditions in Cuba might force the United States to abandon its pledge as to the independence of the island; and the *Banker and Tradesman* (XXVI. 688, July 27, 1898) believed it might be necessary to "take absolute possession of the island, and put down the insurgents." Similar views were expressed by T. G. Bush (above, note 106), and by the *Wall St. Journal,* May 5, 1898.

[108] The same paper on April 14 stated that negotiations for purchase of St. Thomas had been suspended, presumably because of opposition of a St. Thomas newspaper.

[109] New York *Commercial,* May 12, 1898; *Jour. of Com. & Com. Bull.,* August 25, 1898. Senator Lodge suggested that the United States receive from Spain the entire Philippine group, retain Luzon, and trade the remainder to England "in exchange for the Bahamas and Jamaica and the Danish Islands, which I think we should be entitled to ask her to buy and turn over to us" (Lodge to Secretary Day, August 11, 1898, in Dept. of State, *Misc. Letters,* August, 1898, II). Lodge's labors in behalf of the acquisition of the Danish West Indies are treated in C. C. Tansill, *The Purchase of the Danish West Indies* (Baltimore, 1932), pp. 208–216.

[110] New York Commercial, May 9, June 8 and August 4, 1898.

[111] *Jour. of Com. & Com. Bull.,* May 31 and July 13, 1898, and January 6 and February 1, 1899; *Com. & Fin. Chron.,* LXVI. 922–924, LXVII. 290, 401, 1082–3 (May 14, August 13 and 27, and November 26, 1898; *U.S. Investor,* IX. 1704–1705 (November 26, 1898); *Rand-McNally Bankers' Monthly,* XVI. 464 (December 1898). The American Asiatic Association, in a set of resolutions adopted January 5, 1899, called for the application of the "open door" policy in the Philippines (American Asiatic Association to Secretary Hay, January 7, 1899 in Dept. of State, *Misc. Letters,* January, 1899, I).

[112] *Railway World,* XLII. 861 (August 6, 1898); Chicago *Inter-Ocean* quoted in Portland *Morning Oregonian,* September 14, 1898; *Rand-McNally Bankers' Monthly,* XVI. 199 (September 1898), for bureau of statistics. Similar enthusiasm for the markets offered by the new possessions is found in *The American Exporter* (New York, monthly), XLIII. No. 1, p. 10 (December, 1898), and *ibid.,* No. 2, p. 10 (January, 1899), and in the *Financial Record,* December 21, 1898.

[113] *Bankers Magazine,* LVII. 171–173 (August 1898); *Rand-McNally Bankers' Monthly,* XVI. 107–108 (August 1898); *cf.* also *The Tradesman,* November 15, 1898, pp. 60–61.

[114] *Dun's Review,* December 31, 1898.

[115] *Banker and Tradesman,* XXVI. 1186 (December 28, 1898).

The Influence of Strategy upon History:
The Acquisition of the Philippines,
JOHN A. S. GRENVILLE AND GEORGE BERKELEY YOUNG

1 LaFeber, *The New Empire,* p. 362. Richard Warner Van Alstyne, in his perceptive book *The Rising American Empire* (Oxford, Blackwell, 1960), stresses the continuity of policy. Samuel Flagg Bemis, in his *A Diplomatic History of the United States* (New York, Holt, 1936), refers to the acquisition of the Philippines as "The Great Aberation of 1898."

2 Quoted and discussed in Pratt, *Expansionists,* p. 228.

3 Lodge to L. S. Amonson, May 3, 1898. Lodge MSS.

4 Memorandum by Long, Feb. 1, 1898. Navy Department, R. G. 45, area 10 file. For the "China lobby" of businessmen, see esp. Charles S. Campbell, Jr., *Special Business Interests and the Open Door Policy* (New Haven, Yale University Press, 1951).

5 For example, A. Whitney Griswold, *The Far Eastern Policy of the United States* (New York, Harcourt, Brace, 1938), pp. 11 ff. Historians have tended to accept the idea of Roosevelt's "plot" rather uncritically.

6 Long to Agnes Long, Oct. 9, 1898. Long MSS. This describes the immediate origins of the dispatch: "The war was declared Thursday, April 21st. I immediately went to the President and told him that it was the judgment of the Department and the leading officers there that he should order Dewey immediately to Manila to attack the Spanish forces. He preferred to consider the matter a little longer. On the following Sunday morning I went over again and took with me the despatch, as it was afterwards signed and sent. Even I did not write the despatch. It was written in the Bureau of Navigation, as a matter of routine work. The President did not dictate a word of it. No Cabinet officer was consulted about it. No one would have objected to it if he had been. The President ordered it sent, and it went that afternoon."

7 Belknap to Herbert, March 17, 1893. Navy Department, R. G. 45, area 10 file. Barker to Navy Department, Sept. 15, 1897; Aug. 30, 1897. Navy Department, *Miscellaneous letters.*

8 McNair to Dewey, Dec. 31, 1897. Navy Department, R. G. 45, area 10 file.

9 "War with Spain, 1896, General Considerations of the War, the Results desired, and the Consequent Kind of Operations To Be Undertaken." Plan by W. W. Kimball, Lt. U.S. Navy, Staff Intelligence Officer, June 1, 1896, R. G. 313, Naval Operating Forces, North Atlantic Station, Entry 43, Box 11. Navy Department, National Archives, Washington, D.C.

10 Taylor to Luce, Aug. 5, 1895. Luce MSS.

11 Richard Wainwright three years later, the Executive Officer of the *Maine,* was one of the few survivors of the disaster.

12 McAdoo to Roosevelt, "Memorandum Regarding Naval Attachés Abroad," and "Memorandum Regarding the War College," April 15, 1897, R. G. 80, Entry 124, Records of the Assistant Secretary of the Navy, Letterpress, 5, National Archives, Washington, D.C.

13 Kimball, "War with Spain, 1896."

14 O.N.I. to Commander-in-Chief North Atlantic Squadron, May 25, 1897. Navy Department, O.N.I. The members of the war board in 1897 were the Commander-in-Chief of the North Atlantic Squadron, the chiefs of the Bureaus of Navigation and Ordnance, the President of the Naval War College, and the Chief Intelligence Officer. The Board reported to the Secretary of the Navy.

15 The chronological sequence of orders sent by the Navy Department is shown in a memorandum preserved in the papers of Senator Lodge. Lodge MSS.

16 Crowninshield to Lodge, Sept. 19, 1898. Lodge MSS.

17 Lodge to Crowninshield, Sept. 12, 21, and 26, 1898. Lodge MSS.

18 Lodge to Roosevelt, Sept. 21, 1898. Lodge MSS. Roosevelt to Lodge, Sept. 26, 1898. Morison, ed., *Letters of Roosevelt,* 2, 880.

19 Long Journal, Jan. 13, 1898. Long MSS.

20 Long Journal, Jan. 15, Feb. 13, 21, 1898. Long MSS.

21 The origins of this board are somewhat obscure. As has been already noted, Kimball's war plan had been studied during the previous year and had been adopted by a board of officers who coordinated their work with the Office of Naval Intelligence. It seems to have been an ad hoc arrangement; judging by Theodore Roosevelt's contemporary letters, no permanent strategy board was in existence early in March 1898. When Mahan that month offered his services as strategic adviser to the Department and asked Roosevelt for advice on whether in the present crisis he ought not to cancel his trip to Europe, Roosevelt told him not to alter his plans, adding that he did not believe the Cuban crisis would end in war. Nevertheless, and in the circumstances it appears rather odd, on the very next day after writing to Mahan, Roosevelt sent a note to Captain Richardson Clover informing him that he had been appointed by the secretary as "a member of the Board to formulate a plan of campaign." Perhaps the decision to constitute the War Board had been reached that very day; all the same Mahan was not recalled from Europe until April 25. Possibly Long had been averse to employing Mahan, for he noted on May 9, the day Mahan joined the Board, "I doubt very much whether he will be of much value practically." Long Journal, May 9, 1898. Long MSS. One thing is certain: Mahan, a strong advocate of treating all units of the fleet as one great battle squadron, would not have approved the division of the United States fleet as decided upon by the War Board on the eve of the war.

22 For an interesting comment on the strategic decisions taken by the Naval War Board, see Mahan's report of Oct. 29, 1966, "A History of the Naval War Board of 1898," General Board Study, 401–02, *General Board Records,* Navy Department. He regarded the retention of the Flying Squadron off Hampton Roads as the only possible error.

23 Sampson to Secretary of the Navy, April 9, 1898. Navy Department, R. G. 45, area 8 file.

24 See p. 270, n.

25 Long Journal, April 20, 1898. Long MSS. For a good discussion of the inadequacy of the Army plans, see Leech, *In the Days of McKinley,* pp. 201 ff.

26 Bülow to the Kaiser, telegram, March 2, 1898; German consul in Hong Kong to German Foreign Ministry, telegram, March 3, 1898. Microfilms of German Foreign Ministry Archives, Public Record Office, London, G.F.M. 13/141.

27 Radowitz to German Foreign Ministry, telegram, March 4, 1898; memorandum by Bülow, March 5, 1898. German Foreign Ministry Archives, G.F.M. 13/141.

28 For the attitude of the European powers in general, see May, *Imperial Democracy,* pp. 196–239. This may be supplemented as far as the British attitude is concerned by Grenville's *Salisbury,* chap. 9. See also R. G. Neale, *Britain and American Imperialism* (Brisbane, University of Queensland Press, 1965).

29 German consul in Manila to German Foreign Ministry, telegram, received in Berlin, May 12, 1898; memorandum by Bülow, various drafts, May 14, 1898; Bülow to Admiral Tirpitz, May 18, 1898. German Foreign Ministry Archives, G.F.M. 13/123.

30 William M. Laffan to Lodge, July 14, 1898. Lodge MSS.

31 McKinley to Secretary of War, May 19, 1898. Copy in Navy Department, R. G. 45, area 10 file.

32 On this important point the authors have independently reached the same conclusion as Wayne Morgan, *William McKinley and His America,* esp. pp. 379–99.

33 See Pratt, *Expansionists,* for a brilliant analysis, and also Richard Hofstadter, "Manifest Destiny and the Philippines," in Daniel Aaron, ed., *America in Crisis* (New York, Harcourt, Brace, 1952), which however repeats the legend of Roosevelt's responsibility for the seizure of the Philippines.

34 Grenville, *Salisbury,* p. 169.

35 Lodge to Hay, April 21, 1898. Lodge MSS.

36 Lodge to Henry White, Jan. 31, 1898. Lodge MSS.

37 Pratt, *Expansionists,* pp. 289 ff.

38 Claude G. Bowers, *Beveridge and the Progressive Era* (New York, The Literary Guild, 1952), p. 120.

39 Hay to Reid, Nov. 29, 1898. Hay MSS.

[40] Mahan to Luce, n.d., Mahan MSS; the first page of this interesting letter is unfortunately missing.

[41] Long's journal, May 19, 1898. Long MSS.

[42] Mahan to Roosevelt, March 14, 1898. Mahan MSS.

[43] Sicard to the Secretary of the Navy, May 30, 1898. R.G. 45, Entry 371, Naval War Board Letterpress, pp. 145–47.

[44] Mahan to Lodge, July 27, 1898. Lodge MSS.

[45] Lodge to Day, Aug. 11, 1898. Lodge MSS.

[46] Lodge to Henry White, Aug. 12, 1898. Lodge MSS.

[47] Lodge to Charles G. Fall, May 5, 1898. Lodge MSS.

[48] On the basis of this new evidence, the authors have thus reached a conclusion similar to that expressed by Samuel Flagg Bemis.

[49] Sicard, Crowninshield, and Mahan to Long, August 1898. R.G. 45, Entry 371, Naval War Board Letterpress, pp. 335–54.

Insular Imperialism and the Open Door: The China Market and the Spanish-American War,

THOMAS MC CORMICK

[1] Frederic Emory, "Our Growth as a World Power," *The World's Work,* I (1900), 65.

[2] Instruction, Edwin Uhl to Charles Denby, June 9, 1895, National Archives, Record Group 59 (hereafter denoted as NA, RG 59).

[3] John W. Foster to Charles Denby, Sept. 26, 1894, James H. Wilson MSS.

[4] Frederic Emory to Thomas Bayard, May 28, 1895, Bayard MSS.

[5] Instruction, Richard Olney to Denby, Dec. 13, 1896, NA, RG 59.

[6] Dispatch, Denby to John Sherman, Jan. 31, 1898, NA, RG 59.

[7] See Charles S. Campbell, *Special Business Interests and the Open Door Policy* (Baltimore, 1957), 34–35; also, Committee of American Merchants in Shanghai to President of the New York Chamber of Commerce, March 16, 1898, Miscellaneous Letters, NA, RG 59.

[8] Sherman to Andrew D. White, Feb. 11, 1898, W. W. Rockhill MSS; Instruction, Sherman to E. A. Hitchcock, March 17, 1898, NA, RG 59.

[9] Dispatch, White to Sherman, Feb. 28, 1898, NA, RG 59; Dispatch, Hitchcock to Sherman, March 19, 1898, NA, RG 59.

[10] For example, see: Dispatch, John Hay to Sherman, March 25, 1898, NA, RG 59; *The Commercial-Financial Chronicle,* XLVI (April 2, 1898), 642.

[11] For example, see: James H. Wilson to John J. McCook, Feb. 11, 1898, Letterbook, Wilson MSS; Theodore Roosevelt to Baron H. S. von Sternburg, Jan. 17, 1898, Letterbook, Roosevelt MSS.

[12] Dispatch, Henry White to Sherman, March 5, 1898, NA, RG 59 (notations by A. A. Adee and William R. Day).

[13] Enclosure, March 8, 1898, Hay MSS.

[14] Dispatch, Denby to Sherman, April 3, 1898, NA, RG 59.

[15] Theodore Roosevelt to Henry Cabot Lodge, Sept. 21, 1897, Letterbook, Roosevelt MSS.

[16] George Dewey, *Autobiography of George Dewey* (New York, 1913), 179.

[17] Margaret Long, ed., *The Journal of John D. Long* (Rindge, N.H., 1956), 217. Margaret Leech, *In the Days of McKinley* (New York, 1959), 195.

[18] Roosevelt to B. F. Tracy, April 18, 1898, Letterbook, Roosevelt MSS.

[19] Russell A. Alger, *The Spanish-American War* (New York and London, 1901), 326; *San Francisco Chronicle,* May 4, 1898, p. 1; Leech, *op. cit.,* 210.

[20] George Dewey to John D. Long, May 13, 1898, McKinley MSS; Henry C. Lodge, ed., *Selections from the Correspondence of Theodore Roosevelt and Henry Cabot Lodge, 1884–1918* (New York and London, 1925), I, 299.

[21] State Department memorandum, May 9, 1898, John B. Moore MSS; J. B. Moore memorandum, undated, Moore MSS.

[22] Instruction, William R. Day to Hay, June 3, 1898, NA, RG 59.

[23] Leech, *op. cit.,* 212, 261.

[24] Instruction, Day to Hay, June 14, 1898, NA, RG 59; Consular Dispatch, O. F. Williams to Day, Sept. 5, 1898, NA, RG 59.

[25] Dispatch, Horace Porter Sherman, June 10, 1898, NA, RG 59; Andrew D. White to Day, June 18, 1898, Moore MSS.

[26] Dispatch, Denby to Sherman, June 6, 1898, NA, RG 59.

[27] *Loc. cit.;* Philip Joseph, *Foreign Diplomacy in China, 1894–1900* (London, 1928), 337, 357–358. This uncertainty over British policy may have been the motivating factor in John Hay's attempt to renew discussion of the earlier proposal for joint support of the Open Door policy. Though McKinley discouraged the attempt, he did attempt to encourage the British to hold the line on their China policy by obliquely prophesying that "the outcome of our struggle with Spain" might develop "the need of extending and strengthening our interests in the Asiatic Continent": Day to Hay, July 14, 1898, Hay MSS.

[28] See George F. Hoar, *Autobiography of 70 Years* (New York, 1903), II, 308.

[29] *Cong. Record,* 55 Cong., 2 Sess., 6017.

[30] *Ibid.,* 5772, 5775, 5782, 5783, 5879, 5895, 5897, 5916, 5988, 5989.

[31] *Ibid.,* 5780, 5924, 5925.

[32] *Ibid.,* 5904.

[33] *Ibid.,* 6019.

[34] *Ibid.,* 6712.

[35] *House Doc. 536,* 55 Cong., 2 Sess.

[36] Instruction, Moore to Edwin H. Conger, Aug. 30, 1898, NA, RG 59; Dispatch, Conger to Hay, Oct. 12, 1898, NA, RG 59.

[37] Instruction, Day to Hay, June 14, 1898, NA, RG 59.

[38] *Spanish Diplomatic Correspondence and Documents, 1896–1900* (translation, Washington, D.C., 1905), 213–214.

[39] Charles S. Olcott, *The Life of William McKinley* (Boston, 1916), II, 63.

[40] Reid Diaries, Sept. 16, 1898, Whitelaw Reid MSS.

[41] McKinley to Day, Letterbook, Oct. 25, 1898, McKinley MSS; *Papers Relating to the Foreign Relations of the United States 1898* (Washington, D.C., 1899), 935.

[42] See especially Benjamin H. Williams, *Economic Foreign Policy of the United States* (New York, 1926), 325–326.

[43] Charles H. Cramp to Charles Emory Smith, undated, Whitelaw Reid MSS.

[44] See especially Campbell, *op. cit.,* 16; *Journal of the American Asiatic Association,* I (Aug. 25, 1898), 1.

[45] Irving M. Scott to Charles A. Moore, Aug. 4, 1898, McKinley MSS.

[46] Campbell, *op. cit.,* 16; memorandum, Sept. 16, 1898, McKinley MSS; Reid Diaries, September 15, 1898, Reid MSS; Dispatch, Conger to Day, Aug. 26, 1898, NA, RG 59; Charles G. Dawes to McKinley, Aug. 10, 1898, McKinley MSS; Moorfield Storey and Marcial P. Lichuaco, *The Conquest of the Philippines by the United States* (New York and London, 1926), 38.

[47] See especially Leech, *op. cit.,* 339–341; and Earl S. Pomeroy, *Pacific Outpost, American Strategy in Guam and Micronesia* (Stanford, 1951), 3–19.

[48] Leech, *op. cit.,* 327, 330, 334–336, 339–341.

[49] Joseph, *op. cit.,* 339, 346–347, and 363–364; Dispatch, Conger to Day, Sept. 16, 1898, NA, RG 59.

[50] Campbell, *op. cit.,* 39–40.

[51] See Lim Boon Keng, *The Chinese Crisis From Within* (London, 1901), 48–67; Meribeth E. Cameron, *The Reform Movement in China, 1898–1912* (Stanford, 1931), 23–55; and George Nye Steiger, *China and the Occident: Origin and Development of the Boxer Movement* (New Haven, 1927), 87–106.

[52] Dispatch, Conger to Day, Sept. 24, 1898, and Conger to Day, Oct. 14, 1898, NA, RG 59.

[53] Instruction, Hay to Conger, Oct. 10, 1898, NA, RG 59.

[54] Dispatch, Hitchcock to Day, Sept. 29, 1898, NA, RG 59.

[55] Campbell, *op. cit.*, 47–48.

[56] Reid Diaries, Sept. 16, 1898, Reid MSS; *Foreign Relations 1898*, pp. 907–908.

[57] Reid Diaries, Dec. 4, 1898, Reid MSS.

[58] *Ibid.*, Sept. 16, 1898.

[59] A. A. Adee to Hay, Dec. 13, 1898, Hay MSS; Whitelaw Reid, *Problems of Expansion* (New York, 1900), 18.

[60] *Foreign Relations 1898*, p. lxxii.

American Expansion, 1870–1900: The Far East,

MARILYN BLATT YOUNG

[1] Thomas McCormick, "Insular Imperialism and the Open Door: The China Market and the Spanish-American War," *Pacific Historical Review*, XXXII, 156, talks of this " 'insular imperialism' " and its use of "island stepping-stones."

[2] Julius W. Pratt, *Expansionists of 1898: The Acquisition of Hawaii and the Spanish Islands* (Quadrangle edition; Chicago, 1964), p. 22.

[3] Walter LaFeber, *The New Empire, An Interpretation of American Expansion, 1860–1898* (Ithaca, N.Y., 1963), Ch. I.

[4] Matthew Simon and David E. Novack, "Commercial Responses to the American Export Invasion, 1871–1914: An Essay in Attitudinal History," *Essays in Entrepreneurial History*, 2nd Ser. (Winter 1966), p. 139.

[5] *Hunt's Merchant Magazine*, quoted in LaFeber, *New Empire*, p. 24.

[6] Quoted in William L. Neumann, *America Encounters Japan* (Baltimore, 1963), pp. 4–5, 23, 46.

[7] Quoted in Norman K. Graebner, ed. *Ideas and Diplomacy: Readings in the Intellectual Tradition of American Foreign Policy* (New York, 1964), p. 370.

[8] William A. Williams, *The Tragedy of American Diplomacy*, rev. and enlarged ed. (New York, 1962), p. 35.

[9] Simon and Novack, "Commercial Responses," pp. 138–39.

[10] Charles Denby, *China and Her People* (Boston, 1906), II, 38.

[11] Dana C. Munro, *American Commercial Interests in Manchuria*, American Academy of Political and Social Science. Publication No. 654. Reprinted from the *Annals*, January, 1912. Munro shows that Standard Oil successfully resisted Russian and Japanese discrimination for some time, in contrast to cotton interests, which made no effort to retain the American import lead in Manchuria through proper marketing techniques.

[12] See for example Chinese diplomacy during the Sino-Japanese War as reflected in the dispatches of Charles Denby to the State Department, National Archives, *China: Dispatches*, Vols. 97 and 98.

[13] LaFeber, *New Empire*, pp. 17–24.

[14] Quoted in Merze Tate, *The United States & the Hawaiian Kingdom, A Political History* (New Haven, Conn., 1965), pp. 262–63.

[15] Edward C. Kirkland notes that, in its requests for aid, "Private enterprise was asking the government to do what it had failed to accomplish." *Industry Comes of Age: Business, Labor and Public Policy, 1860–1897* (New York, 1961), p. 303.

[16] John A. Kasson, Minister to Vienna, for example, urged that in the event of an Anglo-Russian war, American privateers, licensed by Russia, be used to destroy the British merchant marine, thus leaving the admittedly poor American service supreme by default. The efforts of De Lesseps in Panama threw Kasson into a panic, and in 1880 he insisted that the United States establish control over any Pacific islands "which will be of importance to our national commerce and trade." The opposition to possessing outlying

territory he described as "simple imbecile." See Edward Younger, *John A. Kasson: Politics and Diplomacy from Lincoln to McKinley* (Iowa City, 1955), pp. 284–85, 293–95.

17 LaFeber, *New Empire*, p. 61.

18 *Ibid.*, p. 32.

19 Charles Beard, *The Idea of National Interest* (New York, 1934), p. 60.

20 Matthew Josephson, *The Politicos, 1865–1896* (New York, 1938), p. 103.

21 See Gabriel Kolko, *The Triumph of Conservatism, A Reinterpretation of American History, 1900–1916* (New York, 1963), p. 2.

22 Quoted in Josephson, *The Politicos*, p. 119.

23 David Pletcher, *The Awkward Years: American Foreign Relations under Garfield and Arthur* (Columbia, Mo., 1963), Chs. 7 and 14 in particular.

24 D. M. Dozer, "Benjamin Harrison and the Presidential Campaign of 1892," *American Historical Review*, LIV, 76.

25 Carl Degler, "The Nineteenth Century," in William H. Nelson, ed. *Theory and Practice in American Politics* (Chicago, 1964), pp. 38, 39.

26 Oscar Handlin, *The American People in the Twentieth Century* (Cambridge, Mass., 1954), p. 6. By 1900 almost 40 percent of the population lived in cities.

27 Henry Adams, rather dramatically, describes how, in the year of the depression, men "died like flies under the strain, and Boston grew suddenly old, haggard, and thin." *The Education of Henry Adams* (Modern Library ed.; New York, 1931), p. 338. A more prosaic description of the effects of the depression is Charles Hoffman, "The Depression of the Nineties," *Journal of Economic History*, XVI, 137–64.

28 Adams, *Education*, pp. 344–45.

29 John Higham, *Strangers in the Land* (New Brunswick, N.J., 1955), pp. 69–73.

30 *Ibid.*, p. 77.

31 LaFeber, *New Empire*, p. 54.

32 *Ibid.*, p. 56.

33 Denby to Bayard, August 13, 1887, *China: Dispatches*, Vol. 81. Wharton Barker's papers are deposited in the Library of Congress and constitute a fascinating repository of information on one man's obsession with the China market.

34 Olney to Denby, December 19, 1896, *Papers Relating to the Foreign Relations of the United States*, 1897, p. 56.

35 The most complete account is by William Braisted, "The United States and the American China Development Company," *Far Eastern Quarterly*, XI (February 1953), 147–65. The James Harrison Wilson papers, deposited in the Library of Congress, contain the story of another, even more unsuccessful American effort to secure railroad concessions in China.

36 Edward H. Zariskie, *American Russian Rivalry in the Far East, 1895–1914* (Philadelphia, 1946), pp. 34 ff.

37 Denby to Sherman, May 24, 1897, *China: Dispatches*, Vol. 102.

38 Pratt, in his *Expansionists of 1898*, underlines the effect of the concessions scramble on hitherto anti-imperialist businessmen who "saw the foundations" of their faith "crumbling as a result of the threatened partition of China." Pp. 258–62.

39 See correspondence between Denby and Sherman, January–April, 1898, *China: Dispatches*, Vols. 103, 104.

40 Charles Beresford, *The Break-Up of China* (London, 1899), pp. 443–44.

41 Olney to Denby, September 19, 1895, *For. Rel.*, 1895, Part I, p. 138.

42 See correspondence in *ibid.*, concerning antimissionary riots: also Sherman to Denby, May 15, 1897, *ibid.*, 1897, pp. 66 ff.; Rockhill to Denby Jr., July 28, 1896, *ibid.*, 1896, pp. 58, 59.

43 McKinley's speech is reproduced in *For. Rel.*, 1898, p. xxii.

44 Hay to Henry Adams, July 8, 1900, Hay Papers.

45 Hay to Paul Dana, March 16, 1899, Hay Papers.

46 Rockhill to Hay, August 28, 1899, Rockhill Papers.

47 In this same letter Rockhill wrote that " 'spheres of influence' *are an accomplished fact*, this cannot be too much insisted on." (Underlining in original.)

[48] Rockhill to Edwin Denby, January 13, 1900, Rockhill Papers.
[49] Hippisley to Rockhill, August 21, 1899, Rockhill Papers.
[50] Hay to Adams, July 8, 1900, Hay Papers.
[51] Davis to Reid, July 4, 1900, Reid Papers.
[52] Reid to Davis, July 20, 1900, Reid Papers.
[53] Circular Note of July 3, 1900, to the powers cooperating in China, *For. Rel.*, 1901, Appendix I, p. 18.
[54] Hay to A. A. Adee, September 14, 1900, Hay Papers.
[55] Rockhill, "The United States and the Chinese Question," Speech at Naval War College, Newport, August 5, 1904, Rockhill Papers.
[56] Hay to Theodore Roosevelt, May 1, 1902, Hay Papers.

The United States in Cuba, 1898–1902,
DAVID F. HEALY

[1] *Civil Report of General Leonard Wood for 1902,* Part 1, p. 271.
[2] See James P. Shenton, "Imperialism and Racism," in Donald Sheehan and Harold C. Syrett, editors, *Essays in American Historiography* (New York, 1960).
[3] Wilson, *An Address on Our Trade Relations with the Tropics,* p. 18.
[4] New York *Evening Post,* February 25, 1898.
[5] *Ibid.,* November 17, 1899.
[6] Wood to McKinley, April 12, 1900, copy in Leonard Wood Papers, Library of Congress.
[7] Root to Philip C. Jessup, November 19, 1924, printed in Jessup, *Elihu Root,* I, 289.
[8] Howard K. Beale, *Theodore Roosevelt and the Rise of America to World Power* (Baltimore, 1956), p. 72.
[9] Roosevelt to Hay, August 19, 1903, printed in Morison, *Letters of Theodore Roosevelt,* III, 567.
[10] The following discussion owes a debt to Dexter Perkins, *The Monroe Doctrine, 1867–1907* (Baltimore, 1937), pp. 398–405.
[11] *Congressional Record,* 56th Congress, 2nd Session, XXXIV, 3145–48.
[12] *Ibid.,* p. 3151.
[13] "Report of the Committee Appointed to confer with the Government of the United States," copy in Elihu Root Papers, Library of Congress.
[14] Claude Bowers, *Beveridge and the Progressive Era* (Cambridge, 1932), p. 144.
[15] Roosevelt to Hermann Speck von Sternberg, July 12, 1901, in Morison, *Letters of Theodore Roosevelt,* III, 116.
[16] Annual Message of the President, December 6, 1904, in *Works of Theodore Roosevelt* (New York, 1925), XVII, 299.
[17] Root to Wood, April 2, 1901, copy in Elihu Root Papers, Library of Congress.
[18] Jessup, *Elihu Root,* I, 325.

American Imperialism: Some Tentative Explanation,
ERNEST R. MAY

[1] *Literary Digest,* XVII (Aug. 27, 1898), 340; *Public Opinion,* XXIV (June 30, 1898), 807.
[2] *Catholic World,* LXVII (June 1898), 426.
[3] *Baptist Union,* VIII (May 14, 1898), 338.
[4] *Rand-McNally Banker's Monthly,* XVI (Aug. 1898), 143.
[5] M. Brewster Smith, Jerome S. Bruner, and Robert H. White, *Opinions and Personality* (New York, 1956).
[6] T. W. Adorno, Else Frankel Brunswick, D. J. Levinson, and R. N. Sanford, *The*

Authoritarian Personality (New York, 1950). The most devastating critiques are in Richard Christie and Marie Jahoda, eds., *Studies in the Scope and Method of "The Authoritarian Personality"* (Glencoe, Ill., 1954), and Gerhard E. Lenski and John C. Leggett, "Caste, Class and Deference in the Research Interview," *American Journal of Sociology,* LXV (March 1960), 463–467. Nevertheless the F. Scale developed by Adorno and his colleagues has been used with some effect in subsequent surveys. See the bibliographical note on pp. 103–104 of Ernest R. May, "An American Tradition in Foreign Policy: The Role of Public Opinion," in William H. Nelson and Francis L. Loewenheim, *Theory and Practice in American Politics* (Chicago, 1964), pp. 101–122.

7 Chicago *Times-Herald,* June 30, 1898; *Baptist Home Monthly,* XVIII (Aug. 1898), 253; Indianapolis *Journal,* July 5, 1898; Hamlin Garland, *Roadside Meetings* (New York, 1930), p. 410.

8 Barrows, in a commencement address at Amherst, New York *Tribune,* June 27, 1898; Louisville *Courier-Journal,* quoted in *Literary Digest,* XVII (July 2, 1898), 3–4.

9 *Congregationalist* and St. Louis *Observer,* quoted in *Literary Digest,* XVII (July 16, 1898), 79–80; Philadelphia *Public Ledger,* June 20, 1898.

10 Whitelaw Reid, "The Territory with Which We Are Threatened," *Century,* XVI (Sept. 1898), 788–794.

11 Philip Charles Newman, "Democracy and Imperialism in American Political Thought," *Philippine Social Sciences and Humanities Review,* XV (Dec. 1950), 351–367; James P. Shenton, "Imperialism and Racism," in Donald Sheehan and Harold C. Syrett, eds., *Essays in American Historiography* (New York, 1960), pp. 231–250; Robert M. O'Neil, "The Protest Against Expansion" (manuscript in possession of the author, Berkeley, Calif.). On characteristics of the anti-imperialists, see Fred Harvey Harrington, "The Anti-Imperialist Movement in the United States, 1898–1900," *Mississippi Valley Historical Review,* XXII (Sept. 1935), 211–230.

12 Brooks Adams, "The Commercial Future: The New Struggle for Life among Nations," *Fortnightly,* LXXI (Feb. 1899), 274–283; Alfred T. Mahan, "The Relation of the United States to Their New Dependencies," *Review of Reviews,* XIX (March 1899), 335–336; Charles A. Conant, "The Struggle for Commercial Empire," *Forum,* XXVII (June 1899), 427–440; Brooklyn *Eagle,* quoted in *Literary Digest,* XVIII (Feb. 18, 1899), 185; Grosscup, quoted in *Public Opinion,* XXV (Sept. 1, 1898), 260.

13 For Holls, see Alfred Vagts, *Deutschland und die Vereinigten Staaten in der Weltpolitik,* 2 vols. (New York, 1935), II, 589–590; also see Claude G. Bowers, *Beveridge and the Progressive Era* (Boston, 1932), p. 73; Morton Keller, *In Defense of Yesterday: James M. Beck and the Politics of Conservatism* (New York, 1958), 53–55; Teller, in 55 Cong., 3 sess., *Congressional Record,* p. 327; Frye, quoted in *Literary Digest,* XIX (Aug. 19, 1899), 213.

14 55 Cong., 3 sess., *Congressional Record,* pp. 96, 528–534, 562–563, 638–642, 733–739; Morrison I. Swift, *Imperialism and Liberty* (n.p., n.d.); Adams quoted in *Literary Digest,* XVIII (Jan. 7, 1899), 2.

15 55 Cong., 3 sess., *Congressional Record,* pp. 287–297, 438–439, 563–572.

16 Leech, *In the Days of McKinley,* pp. 354–358; Morgan, *McKinley and His America,* pp. 414–422; Paolo E. Coletta, "Bryan, McKinley, and the Treaty of Paris," *Pacific Historical Review,* XXVI (May 1957), 131–146.

17 *Speeches and Addresses of William McKinley from March 1, 1897, to May 30, 1900* (New York, 1900), pp. 185–192; Jacob G. Schurman, *Our Duty in the Philippines* (n.p., n.d.); speech by Reid, quoted in *Literary Digest,* XVIII (Feb. 25, 1899), 211–213; David J. Hill, "The War and the Extension of Civilization," *Forum,* XXVI (Feb. 1899), 650–655.

18 *Literary Digest,* XVIII (April 1, 1899), 363–364; *ibid.,* XIX (Nov. 18, 1899), 603.

19 *Literary Digest,* XIX (Aug. 26, 1899), 245–246; David F. Healy, *The United States in Cuba, 1898–1902: Generals, Politicians and the Search for Policy* (Madison, Wis., 1963), pp. 120–123.

20 *Literary Digest,* XX (Jan. 13, 1900), 389.

21 *Literary Digest,* XX (Jan. 13, 1900), 35–36 (April 7, 1900), 415–416; *ibid.,* XXI (July 7, 1900), 2–3; (July 21, 1900), 62; (Aug. 4, 1900), 123–124; *Public Opinion,* XXVIII (June 21, 1900), 772–774; Brooks Adams, *America's Economic Supremacy* (New York, 1900);

Charles A. Conant, *The United States in the Orient* (Boston and New York, 1900); Josiah Strong, *Expansion under New World Conditions* (New York, 1900).

22 *Literary Digest*, XX (March 31, 1900), 388–389; *ibid.*, XXI (July 21, 1900), 64; (Aug. 25, 1900), 215–217; (Sept. 15, 1900), 303–304; J. Rogers Hollingsworth, *The Whirligig of Politics: The Democracy of Cleveland and Bryan* (Chicago, 1963), pp. 173–175; William J. Bryan, *The Second Battle* (Chicago, 1900).

23 *Literary Digest*, XXI (July 21, 1900), 62; (Sept. 1, 1900), 241; *Public Opinion*, XXIX (July 5, 1900), 8–9; (July 19, 1900), 73; Marilyn B. Young, "American China Policy, 1895–1901," unpubl. diss. (Harvard, 1963). [Since published as *The Rhetoric of Empire: American China Policy, 1895–1901* (Cambridge, Mass., 1969).]

24 *Literary Digest*, XXI (Aug. 4, 1900), 126–127; *ibid.*, XXII (Feb. 16, 1901), 181–182; Thomas A. Bailey, "Was the Election of 1900 a Mandate on Imperialism?," *Mississippi Valley Historical Review*, XXIV (June 1937), 43–52.

25 *Literary Digest*, XXI (Oct. 20, 1900), 453.

26 Cortissoz, *Reid*, II, 265; Healy, *The United States in Cuba*, 142.

27 *Literary Digest*, XXV (Nov. 1, 1902), 543–544.

28 *Literary Digest*, XXIV (April 5, 1902), 456; (May 31, 1902), 733; *ibid.*, XXV (Sept. 20, 1902), 340; *ibid.*, XXVIII (March 5, 1904), 319. And even the *Globe-Democrat* had changed its tune by 1905, when it questioned the wisdom of assuming control over Dominican finances (*ibid.*, XXX [March 18, 1905], 387).

29 *Literary Digest*, XXX (Jan. 28, 1905), 120; (Feb. 4, 1905), 157; (March 25, 1905), 419–420; Morison, *Letters of Theodore Roosevelt*, IV, 734.

30 *Literary Digest*, XXIV (June 14, 1902), 791–792; *ibid.*, XXVIII (Feb. 13, 1904), 208.

31 John A. Garraty, *Henry Cabot Lodge, A Biography* (New York, 1953), p. 210.

32 *Literary Digest*, XXII (June 22, 1901), 751.

33 Leon Wolffe, *Little Brown Brother* (Garden City, N.Y., 1961), gives the best account of the early days of American occupation in the Philippines.

34 *Literary Digest*, XIX (July 8, 1899), 32; Leech, *In the Days of McKinley*, pp. 357–365, 397–409.

35 Gwynn, *Spring Rice*, I, 300.

36 Frederic Whyte, *The Life of W. T. Stead*, 2 vols. (London, 1925), I, 174.

37 See Koebner, *Imperialism*, pp. 221–236, 243–249; Elié Halévy, *History of the English People*, 2nd rev. ed. (London, 1951), V (*Imperialism and the Rise of Labour, 1895–1905*), pp. 93–110; and Semmel, *Imperialism and Social Reform*, pp. 59–64; E. Malcolm Carroll, *French Public Opinion and Foreign Affairs, 1870–1914* (New York, 1931), pp. 180–181; Brunschwig, *French Colonialism*, pp. 135–181.

38 John A. Hobson's *Imperialism* (London, 1902) is the best known, most systematic, and most important presentation of the case, but it was not immediately the most influential. Americans came to know Hobson's theory first through his *The War in South Africa: Its Causes and Effects* (New York, 1900), which sold well and was enthusiastically reviewed, as in, e.g., *Nation*, LXX (April 12, 1900), 285–286; *Outlook*, LXIV (April 7, 1900), 840; *Independent*, LII (April 5, 1900), 835; and *Atlantic*, LXXXVII (Jan. 1901), 55–56. *Imperialism*, which was published in an American edition late in 1902, was scarcely noticed at first. The only American journals in which I could locate reviews were the *Quarterly Journal of Economics*, XVII (Feb. 1903), 355, and the *Journal of Political Economy*, XI (March 1903), 311–315. Still, it is fair to say, because of the earlier book and the pirating of Hobson's theses by editors such as Stead, that the doctrines of *Imperialism* were in circulation.

39 Gwynn, *Spring Rice*, I, 301; Whyte, *Stead*, II, 167–168. See W. T. Stead, "The True Imperialism," *Review of Reviews*, XXI (May 15, 1900), 441–449.

40 Olney to S. B. Griffin, Feb. 5, 1900, Private Papers of Richard Olney, Library of Congress; Ira V. Brown, *Lyman Abbott, Christian Evolutionist: A Study in Religious Liberalism* (Cambridge, Mass., 1953), pp. 171–172; Bowers, *Beveridge*, pp. 176–177.

41 The following quotations are from Morison, *Letters of Theodore Roosevelt*, II, 1104, 1233, 1270, 1415.

42 W. D. Puleston, *Mahan* (New Haven, 1934), pp. 220–229; Vagts, *Deutschland und die Vereinigten Staaten*, II, 1509, 1575, 1971–1972; Bowers, *Beveridge*, pp. 176–177.

[43] Samuel A. Stouffer, *Communism, Conformity,* and *Civil Liberties* (New York, 1955). The assumption that establishment opinion is relatively wise is, of course, open to challenge. Sidney E. Verba, "Assumptions of Rationality and Non-Rationality in Models of the International System," *World Politics,* XIV (Oct. 1961), 92–114, suggests that the greater an individual's interest in a given issue, the more likely is his opinion to be a function of his personality and hence, perhaps, of his anxieties and neuroses. William A. Gamson and André Modigliani, "Knowledge and Foreign Policy Opinions: Some Models for Consideration," *Public Opinion Quarterly,* XXX (Summer 1966), 187–199, raise questions as to whether greater knowledge of or better understanding of an issue does more than fix an individual in beliefs toward which he is physically disposed. On the other hand, there is psychometric data supporting the more common-sense supposition that a relationship exists between, on the one hand, an individual's intelligence, education, and information on a given subject and, on the other hand, his sense of its complexities, his discrimination among the issues involved, and his capacity to change his mind. See Carl I. Hovland, Irving L. Janis, and Harold H. Kelley, *Communications and Persuasion* (New Haven, 1953), pp. 181–204; Hovland and Janis, *Personality and Persuasibility* (New Haven, 1951), *passim;* Milton J. Rosenberg *et al., Attitude Organization and Change: An Analysis of Consistency Among Components* (New Haven, 1960); Herbert C. Kelman, "Processes of Opinion Change," *Public Opinion Quarterly,* XXV (Spring 1961), 57–78; and Nathan Maccoby and Eleanor E. Maccoby, "Homeostatic Theory in Attitude Change," *Public Opinion Quarterly,* XXV (Winter 1961), 538–545.

[44] That this was not the case exclusively with the foreign policy establishment is demonstrated in Arthur Mann, "British Social Thought and American Reformers of the Progressive Era," *Mississippi Valley Historical Review,* XLII (March 1956), 672–692. The interplay of opinion movements in America, England, and Europe needs very much to be investigated, most obviously in relation to protectionism, economic nationalism, and social welfare legislation; and a factor to be taken into account, here as well as in connection with foreign policy, is the role of foreign reference groups and "reference idols." To what extent was American progressivism influenced by observation of Germany's experiments or by tendencies within the English Liberal party? To what extent in turn were Germans and Englishmen affected by what they saw of American progressivism and liberalism, as symbolized by Theodore Roosevelt and Woodrow Wilson? In what degree was cosmopolitanism or lack thereof, or differences in foreign reference groups, a cause of division within reform movements on both sides of the Atlantic?

SUGGESTIONS FOR FURTHER READING

All the articles reprinted in this collection are complete with footnotes, on the theory that any serious student will wish to know, in detail, on what evidence the historian has reached his conclusions. Moreover, the notes and bibliographies of past researchers are probably the best way to gain some idea of what is available, what sources might be fruitfully pursued, what areas look barren. In the text of my introduction and in the notes to the articles themselves, the student will find reference to most of the useful books and archives relevant to this period. In addition, students should look carefully at the excellent special issue on radical historiography prepared by *Radical America,* IV (Nov., 1970). The survey article on "New Left Historians of the 1960's" includes an annotated discussion of books on foreign policy (pp. 92–97) which can serve as a good core reading list on radical analysis.

Major studies of the period include: Ernest R. May, *Imperial Democracy: The Emergence of America as a Great Power* (New York: Harcourt, Brace and World, 1961); Julius Pratt, *Expansionists of 1898: The Acquisition of Hawaii and the Spanish Islands* * (Baltimore: Johns Hopkins Press, 1936); Walter LaFeber, *The New Empire: An Interpretation of American Expansion, 1860–1898* * (Ithaca: Cornell University Press, 1963); and two by William A. Williams, *The Tragedy of American Diplomacy,** (rev. & enlarged ed.; New York: Delta, 1962) and *The Roots of the Modern American Empire: A Study of the Growth and Shaping of Social Consciousness in a Marketplace Society* * (New York: Random House, 1969). H. Wayne Morgan, *America's Road to Empire: The War with Spain and Overseas Expansion* * (New York: Wiley, 1965), is a general survey that is critical of May and also challenges the emphasis on economic interpretations.

On the Spanish-American War itself, no student should be denied the pleasures of Walter Millis's *The Martial Spirit* (New York: Literary Guild, 1931). The book rewards both in its style and its social and historical insights. Margaret Leech's *In the Days of McKinley* (New York: Harper and Row, 1959) is an exhaustive study of the McKinley administration, valuable for its many details and the way in which it plunges the student into the daily routine of that government. Along with Leech's book, H. Wayne Morgan, *William McKinley and His America* * (Syracuse: Syracuse University Press, 1963), and Paul Holbo, "Presidential Leader-

* An asterisk following a title indicates that it is available in paperback.

ship and Foreign Affairs: William McKinley and the Turpie-Foraker Amendment," *American Historical Review,* LXXII (July, 1967), pp. 1321–1335, deny that McKinley was a weak president and contend that he had his own foreign policy.

On the link between Asia and the growth of an American empire, there are several new, and many older books of interest: Fred Harvey Harrington, *God, Mammon, and the Japanese: Dr. Horace N. Allen and Korean-American Relations, 1884–1905* (Madison: University of Wisconsin Press, 1944); Paul Varg, *The Making of a Myth: The United States and China, 1897–1912* (East Lansing: Michigan State University Press, 1968); Thomas McCormick, *China Market: America's Quest for Informal Empire, 1893–1901* * (Chicago: Quadrangle Books, 1967); Marilyn B. Young, *Rhetoric of Empire: American China Policy, 1895–1901* (Cambridge: Harvard University Press, 1969); William R. Braisted, *The United States Navy in the Pacific* * (New York: Atheneum, 1967). William L. Neumann offers a bemused look at the unchanging dedication of Americans to the China market in "Determinism, Destiny, and Myth in the American Image of China," George L. Anderson, ed., *Issues and Conflicts* (Lawrence: University of Kansas Press, 1959). Neumann's study of American-Japanese relations, an important though often neglected aspect of relations with East Asia, remains the best survey on this subject: *America Encounters Japan: From Perry to MacArthur* * (Baltimore: Johns Hopkins Press, 1963).

Three major books, differing greatly in interpretation though sharing the qualities of high scholarship and literary merit, are vital aids in placing the war and its aftermath in a longer time perspective: Albert K. Weinberg, *Manifest Destiny: A Study of Nationalist Expansionism in American History* * (Baltimore: Johns Hopkins Press, 1935); Frederick Merk, *Manifest Destiny and Mission in American History* * (New York: Alfred A. Knopf, 1963); and Richard Van Alstyne, *The Rising American Empire* * (New York: Oxford University Press, 1960). Among other studies providing a background for understanding expansion are Edward M. Burns, *The American Idea of Mission: Concepts of National Purpose and Identity* (New Brunswick: Rutgers University Press, 1957); Arthur Ekirch, *Ideas, Ideals, and American Diplomacy: A History of Their Growth and Interaction* * (New York, Appleton, 1966); Henry Nash Smith, *Virgin Land* * (Cambridge: Harvard University Press, 1950), a provocative and important volume in American studies; and Charles Vevier, "American Continentalism: An Idea of Expansion, 1845–1910," *American Historical Review,* LXV (Jan., 1960), pp. 323–335.

The role of public opinion and psychic anxieties in pushing the nation to war is advanced in Richard Hofstadter, "Cuba, the Philippines, and Manifest Destiny," in his *The Paranoid Style in American Politics* * (New York: Alfred A. Knopf, 1965), an essay that appeared originally in slightly different form in Daniel Aaron, ed., *America in Crisis* (New York: Alfred A. Knopf, 1952). The role of the press has been stressed in Joseph Wisan, *The Cuban Crisis as Reflected in the New York Press* (New York: Columbia University Press, 1934), and examined in George W. Auxier, "Middle Western Newspapers and the Spanish-American War, 1895–1898," *Mississippi Valley Historical Review,* XXVI (March, 1940), pp. 523–534.

An early important study of economic influences is Charles Campbell, *Special Business Interests and the Open Door Policy* (New Haven: Yale University Press, 1951). A recent study of expansion is Edward P. Crapol and Howard Schonberger, "The Shift to Global Expansion, 1865–1900," in William A. Williams, ed., *From Colony to Empire: Essays in the History of American Foreign Relations* (New York: Wiley, 1972). The importance of the quest for markets (especially the China market) remains an issue of contention among historians. Morton Rothstein, "The American West and Foreign Markets, 1850–1900," in D. M. Ellis, ed., *The Frontier in American Development: Essays in Honor of Paul Wallace Gates* (Ithaca: Cornell University Press, 1969), notes that farm leaders in the late eighties "argued that the basic solution to the problem confronting American farmers could be summed up in two words: Asian markets." In "The Myth of the China Market, 1890–1914," *American Historical Review,* LXXIII (Feb., 1968), pp. 742–758, Paul Varg has stressed that the market never developed and contends therefore that it was of little importance. Thomas McCormick, "American Expansionism in China," *ibid.,* LXXV (June, 1970), pp. 1393–1396, offers a partial rebuttal challenging Varg's framework of separating economic and security motives.

In view of the growing popularity of the work of William A. Williams and other members of the so-called Wisconsin school (LaFeber, McCormick, *et al.*), there has been surprisingly little focused, sustained criticism of their framework and conclusions. Robert Tucker, *The Radical Left and American Foreign Policy* * (Baltimore: Johns Hopkins Press, 1971), is critical and thoughtful. John Braeman, "The Wisconsin School of Diplomatic History: A Critique" (unpublished paper, 1967), is angry and abrasive. Irwin Unger, "The New Left and American History: Some Recent Trends in United States Historiography," *American Historical Review,* LXXII (July, 1967), pp. 1237–1263, is less harsh. Paul Holbo, "Economics, Expansion, and Emotion: An Emerging Foreign Policy," in H. Wayne Morgan, ed., *The Gilded Age* (rev. ed.; Syracuse: Syracuse University Press, 1970), focuses primarily on LaFeber's analysis and charges it with oversimplifying and neglecting important influences. Carl Degler, in reviewing Williams's *Roots,* in *American Historical Review,* LXXV (Oct., 1970), pp. 1780–1782, criticized it in terms of its evidence, its conclusions about politics, and its assumptions about history. Two sympathetic, but critical, reviews of *Roots* are Michael Meeropol, "W. A. Williams' Historiography," *Radical America,* IV (Aug., 1970), pp. 29–49, and James P. O'Brien, "Comment," ibid., pp. 50–53. In "Roots of Empire," *Progressive* (June, 1970) and in "Introduction," in Barton J. Bernstein and Allen J. Matusow, eds., *Twentieth-Century America,* (rev. ed.; New York: Harcourt Brace Jovanovich, 1972), pp. 319–323, 344–349, Bernstein, whose work has been influenced by Williams, raises questions about his analysis and that of other radicals (Harry Magdoff and Gabriel Kolko). Marilyn B. Young, "The Quest for Empire," in Ernest May and James Thomson, Jr., eds., *American East-Asian Relations* (Cambridge: Harvard University Press, 1972), poses similar questions.

On the issue of imperialism as such there is a long and tedious list of books bound to confuse even before they weary the reader. I have found the following to be both useful and readable, but the list does not pretend to be complete: V. I. Lenin, *Imperialism, the Highest Stage of Capitalism* * (New York: International Publishers, 1934); J. A. Hobson, *Imperialism* * (Ann Arbor: University of Michigan Press, 1965); James O'Connor, "The Meaning of Economic Imperialism" (Detroit: Radical Education Project, no date); Richard Koebner, "The Concept of Economic Imperialism," *Economic History Review,* 2nd series, II (1949); John Gallagher and Ronald Robinson, "The Imperialism of Free Trade," *EHR,* 2nd series, VI (1953); Oliver MacDonagh, "The Anti-Imperialism of Free Trade," *EHR,* 2nd series, XIV (1962); Robert Zevin, "An Interpretation of American Imperialism," *Journal of Economic History,* XXXII, no. 1 (March, 1972); Gabriel Kolko, *The Roots of American Foreign Policy* * (Boston: Beacon Press, 1969); George Lichtheim, *Imperialism* * (New York: Praeger, 1971); Bernard Semmel, *Imperialism and Social Reform* * (Cambridge: Harvard University Press, 1960); Bernard Semmel, *The Rise of Free Trade Imperialism: Classical Political Economy, the Empire of Free Trade and Imperialism, 1750–1850* (Cambridge: Cambridge University Press, 1970). There is also an interesting exchange in *Social Policy,* I, no. 3 (Sept.–Oct., 1970), "Does the U.S. Economy Require Imperialism?" by S. M. Miller, Roy Bennett, and Cyril Alapatt and a response by Harry Magdoff, "The Logic of Imperialism." Two anthologies have been very useful: K. T. Fann and Donald C. Hodges, eds., *Readings in U.S. Imperialism* (Boston: Porter Sargent, 1971) and, for comparative purposes, *Imperialism and Colonialism* (New York: Macmillan, 1964) edited by George H. Nadel and Perry Curtis. William Langer, *The Diplomacy of Imperialism* (2nd ed.; New York: Harper and Row, 1965), remains a useful introduction to foreign policy beyond the United States in this period.

A further study of the effects of imperialism on its not always acquiescent subjects is more difficult to pursue than it should be. A good start can be made in the following: Dana G. Munro, *Intervention and the Dollar Diplomacy in the Caribbean, 1900–1921* (Princeton: Princeton University Press, 1964), which is invaluable for the information it sets forth, though most unsatisfactory in its analysis; Leon Wolffe, *Little Brown Brother* (London: Longmans, 1961, or New York: Kraus Reprint, 1970), an account of American "pacification" of the Philippines; William J. Pomeroy, *American Neo-Colonialism: Its Emergence in the Philippines and Asia* (New York: International Publishers, 1970); Edward J. Berbusse, *The United States in Puerto Rico, 1898–1900* (Chapel Hill: University of North Carolina Press, 1966); and Earl S. Pomeroy, *Pacific Outpost: American Strategy in Guam and Micronesia* (Stanford: Stanford University Press, 1951). A recent study of the suppression of the Philippine insurgency raises all the hard and necessary questions about America's imperial progress and the opposition to it. See Daniel B. Schirmer, *Republic or Empire: American Resistance to the Philippine War* (Cambridge: Schenkman Publishing Co., 1972), The manner and meaning of Hawaiian annexation, an integral part of the history of expansion in this period, is best gained from William A. Russ, Jr., *The Hawaiian Republic 1894–1898: Its Struggle to Win Annexation* (Selingsgrove, Pa.: Susquehanna University Press, 1961), and Merze Tate, *The United States and the Hawaiian Kingdom* (New Haven: Yale University Press, 1965).

Differing assessments of 1898 as a turning point of American foreign policy are Thomas A. Bailey, "America's Emergence as a World Power: The Myth and the Verity," *Pacific Historical Review,* XXX (Feb., 1961), pp. 1–6, who concludes that America was a world power and so recognized before the war; and

Norman A. Graebner, "The Year of Transition — 1898," in Graebner, ed., *An Uncertain Tradition: American Secretaries of State in the Twentieth Century* * (New York: McGraw-Hill, 1961), who argues the contrary case — as does May, *Imperial Democracy*.

Two useful volumes on the years before 1898 are: David Pletcher, *The Awkward Years: American Foreign Relations under Garfield and Arthur* (Columbia: University of Missouri Press, 1962); and Milton Plesur, *America's Outward Thrust: Approaches to Foreign Affairs, 1865–1890* (DeKalb: Northern Illinois University Press, 1971), which also contains a very extensive bibliography for this period.

The anti-imperialism of the nineties has attracted considerable attention and a number of interpreters. An early, and still useful, introduction is Fred H. Harrington, "The Anti-Imperialist Movement in the United States, 1898–1900," *Mississippi Valley Historical Review*, XXII (Sept., 1935), pp. 211–230, which should be supplemented by his "Literary Aspects of American Anti-Imperialism," *New England Quarterly*, X (Dec., 1937), pp. 650–667. A recent well-written study is Robert Beisner, *Twelve Against Empire: The Anti-Imperialists* (New York: McGraw-Hill, 1968), which gracefully summarizes the literature and briefly and uneasily challenges the notions of Williams that the anti-imperialists were simply anti-colonialists who valued economic expansion overseas without the burdens of formal empire. Christopher Lasch, "The Anti-Imperialists, the Philippines, and the Inequality of Man," *Journal of Southern History*, XXIV (August, 1958), pp. 319–331, concludes that racism was a common component of the imperialist and anti-imperialist arguments. E. Berkley Tompkins, *Anti-Imperialism in the United States: The Great Debate* (Philadelphia: University of Pennsylvania Press, 1970), building on Harrington and largely agreeing with Beisner, is the most recent study of the Anti-Imperialist League and traces it briefly past the election of 1900 to its collapse two decades later.

Among the troubling problems of interpretation for historians has been the question of William Jennings Bryan's influence and the reasons for his support of the Treaty of Paris. W. Stull Holt, *Treaties Defeated: A Study of the Struggle between President and Senate over the Conduct of Foreign Relations* (Baltimore: Johns Hopkins Press, 1934), and Paolo Coletta, *William Jennings Bryan*, Vol. I (Lincoln: University of Nebraska Press, 1964) provide different interpretations. Richard E. Welch, Jr., *George F. Hoar and the Half-Breed Republicans* (Cambridge: Harvard University Press, 1971), is a useful study of a Republican opponent of annexation. Thomas A. Bailey, "Was the Election of 1900 a Mandate on Imperialism?" *Mississippi Valley Historical Review*, XXIV (June, 1937), pp. 43–52, concludes in the negative.

John W. Rollins, "The Anti-Imperialists and Twentieth Century American Foreign Policy," *Studies on the Left*, III, no. 1 (1962), pp. 9–24, stresses the expansionist impulses of the anti-imperialists of the nineties and concludes that their analysis and strategy triumphed in the twentieth century. In the same issue, Harold Baron and Thomas McCormick challenge portions of Rollins's argument. The relationship between reform at home and imperialism abroad is discussed by William Leuchtenburg, "Progressivism and Imperialism: The Progressive Movement and American Foreign Policy, 1898–1916," *Mississippi Valley Historical Review,* XXXIX (Dec., 1952), pp. 483–504, who finds an intimate linkage between the two impulses. Barton J. Bernstein and Franklin A. Leib, "Progressive Republican Senators and American Imperialism, 1898–1916: A Reappraisal," *Mid-America,* L (July, 1968), pp. 163–205, challenge Leuchtenburg's thesis, find that some of the leading Republican reformers opposed much of American adventurism, and conclude that the quest for economic expansion and the support of adventurism in these years may have been largely independent of positions taken on domestic policy. Jerry Israel, *Progressivism and the Open Door: America and China, 1905–1921* (Pittsburgh: University of Pittsburgh Press, 1971), following the notions of Williams and Wiebe, concludes that expansionism and efficiency-minded progressivism are intimately linked.

There are a number of general histories of the nineties. An exceptional volume is Robert Wiebe, *The Search for Order, 1877–1920* (New York: Hill and Wang, 1967), which analyzes the breakdown of "island communities" and the rise of extended interdependence. The book includes an extremely interesting analysis of foreign policy (pp. 224–255). Samuel Hays, *The Response to Industrialism, 1885–1914* (Chicago: University of Chicago Press, 1957), aims to avoid earlier molds of interpretation and thereby anticipates some of Wiebe's analysis. Ray Ginger, *Age of Excess: The United States from 1877 to 1914* (New York: Macmillan, 1965), interprets the period in terms of its exuberance, its frenzy, and its excess industrial capacity. Ginger also provides a sharply phrased bibliographical essay. A more conventional book is Harold Faulkner, *Politics, Reform, and Expansion, 1890–1900* (New York: Harper and Row, 1959). The economic history of the period is surveyed in Edward Kirkland, *Industry Comes of Age: Business, Labor and Public Policy, 1860–1897* (New York: Holt, Rinehart and Winston, 1961); and in Fred Shannon, *The Farmer's Last Frontier: Agriculture, 1860–1897* (New York: Holt, Rinehart and Winston, 1945). Party politics and structure in the period are examined in J. Rogers Hollingsworth, *The Whirligig of Politics: The Democracy of Cleveland and Bryan* (Chicago: University of Chicago Press, 1963); Robert Marcus, *Grand Old Party: Political Structure in the Gilded Age, 1880–1896* (New York: Oxford University Press, 1971); and H. Wayne Morgan, *From Hayes to McKinley: National Party Politics* (Syracuse: Syracuse University Press, 1969). Two earlier studies that stress the power of business in politics are: Matthew Josephson, *The Politicos, 1865–1896* (New York: Harcourt, Brace, 1938), and *The President Makers, 1896–1912* (New York: Harcourt, Brace, 1932). Arthur M. Schlesinger, *The Rise of the City, 1878–1898* (New York: Macmillan, 1933), is full of information. John Higham, *Strangers in the Land: Patterns of American Nativism, 1860–1925* (New Brunswick: Rutgers University Press, 1955), is a valuable study that tries to relate nativism to declines in confidence and downturns in the business cycle.